THREE MEN
AND A
BRADSHAW

THREE MEN
AND A
BRADSHAW

An
Original Victorian
Travel Journal

JOHN GEORGE FREEMAN
EDITED BY RONNIE SCOTT

BOOKS

1 3 5 7 9 10 8 6 4 2

Random House Books
20 Vauxhall Bridge Road
London SW1V 2SA

Random House Books is part of the Penguin Random House
group of companies whose addresses can be found at global.
penguinrandomhouse.com

Penguin
Random House
UK

First published by Random House Books in 2015.

www.randomhouse.co.uk

A CIP catalogue record for this book is available
from the British Library.

ISBN 9781847947444

Printed and bound in Great Britain by Clays Ltd, St Ives plc

Penguin Random House is committed to a sustainable future for our
business, our readers and our planet. This book is made from Forest
Stewardship Council® certified paper.

Mixed Sources
Product group from well-managed
forests and other controlled sources
www.fsc.org Cert no. TT-COC-2139
© 1996 Forest Stewardship Council

FSC

CONTENTS

FINDING
JOHN GEORGE FREEMAN

'Neatly written and illustrated with pen sketches,
a fine example of penmanship, very much in the
vein of *Three Men in a Boat*.'

These words were in the auction description for a Victorian
journal written by one John George Freeman, and they immediately caught my attention. Of course it pays to be cautious about
such things; it's hardly unusual for an auction house to allow
themselves a little poetic licence when describing a lot since
they are keen to sell it and secure their commission. However,
something made me linger over this particular entry.

Perhaps my optimism was in part due to the good fortune
I'd had in the past. In similar auctions I had managed to buy
the World War I diaries of Thomas Cairns Livingstone, and the
World War II diaries of Colonel Rodney Foster. They became,
respectively, the books *Tommy's War* and *The Real Dad's Army*,
and I was enormously pleased and proud to have helped bring
the stories of those remarkable men to a wider audience. Was
this a similar literary gem waiting to be discovered?

Well, faint heart never won fair lady (or journal), so trusting in my gut feeling, I bid on and eventually won John George
Freeman's journal. A few days later Royal Mail delivered it.
With great anticipation I tore away the bubble wrap and tissue
paper in which it was wrapped. As soon as I began to examine
the leather-bound volumes I realised that in fact the auction
house had greatly understated their magnificence. I skimmed
delightedly through page after page of John's exquisitely neat
handwriting, pausing now and then to admire the incredible
detail and character of the ink drawings.

It wasn't long before John's sharp wit and keen observations about Victorian society had captivated me completely. His journal seems to have an almost magical power to transport one back in time – it is so vivid, so saturated with the life and character of its author.

At the same time, the wealth of detail it contains about the locations John mentions fired my curiosity – I wanted to find out what those places were like today, and soon began to research in earnest. I was pleased to find that in spite of the fact that he was writing some 140 years ago, most of the buildings that he talks about are still standing, and most of the hotels he patronised are still in the hostelry trade. Perhaps there should be a Freeman trail where you can walk in his footsteps and relive his adventures. Certainly the brothers chose some incredibly beautiful locations for their holidays – visiting them in the name of research was no hardship!

It has taken three years to get John's work published. To use railway metaphors, the journey had a few visits to the sidings and the odd delay due to maintenance but overall the excursion was definitely first-class and the destination has turned out to be everything I could have hoped. My fellow travelling passengers have been great company (unlike many of John's carriage companions), especially Ronnie Scott, whose careful editing and footnote research has added to the wonderful scenery. I am also deeply indebted to John's descendants, who have been extremely generous in supplying additional material, namely the last two holidays in Scotland and South Wales.

It is extremely satisfying to have rescued another long-lost voice from the past. I feel both proud and privileged to have the chance to champion John's work. I also feel certain that he would love the fact that his work has now been published. I hope you enjoy reading about his adventures; perhaps you might at some stage travel the same paths yourself. I heartily recommend it – but don't forget your puggaree!

Shaun Sewell, Northumberland, 2015

INTRODUCTION

John George Freeman and the art of Victorian holiday travel

> To remain stationary in these times of change,
> when the whole world is on the move, would be a
> crime. Hurrah for the trip – the cheap, cheap trip.
>
> —THOMAS COOK, 1854

Tourism may now be one of the biggest industries in the world, but it was still in its infancy when John George Freeman and his brothers took to the railways and highways of Great Britain during the 1870s. We are fortunate that John recorded their travels in meticulous detail, illustrating his wry prose with sketches that might easily grace the pages of any Victorian periodical. *Three Men and a Bradshaw* brings together five of John's holiday journals, giving the modern reader a rare insight into the experiences of a Victorian holidaymaker.

We first meet our 'three men' at the start of their trip to Jersey in September 1873. They are John George Freeman, our diarist, aged 27, his older brother Joseph Henry Freeman (28) and his younger brother Charles James Freeman (23).

John was born in 1846 in Marylebone, London, one of the five children of Ann and Joseph Henry Freeman. The family had lived in Marylebone from the early 19th century, and by 1841 they were residing in Norfolk Street (now Cleveden Street), where Charles Dickens also spent several years of his early life.

The Freemans were in the tailoring trade, and at the time of the diaries Joseph was working as a tailor, while Charles ran a tailoring business at 134 Regent Street, Mayfair, very close to

the renowned Savile Row. George, another brother, who part-
nered John in his trek through South Wales, was also connected
with 134 Regent Street. In addition, John refers to his father,
'who keeps a shop for breeches'. John himself was a mercantile
clerk in a cotton warehouse, run by De Lannoy & Nash, Ware-
housemen, of 14 Friday Street, in the City of London close to the
Mansion House.

As the reader will discover, the brothers sometimes travelled with additional companions. Others who took part in their
trips are Lucy, who married Joseph Freeman in 1872 and lived
with him in Balham with their young son (born June 1873), and
Edward Falkner, a draper who lived in Camberwell.

His journals show that John was a respectable and God-
fearing member of the commercial lower-middle class. Like
others in his family, he was a committed member of the Baptist
Church, a singer in a leading Sol-fa choir and an adherent of
the Temperance cause. John and his brothers worshipped at
the popular Soho Chapel, 406 Oxford Street, but when on tour
were willing to sample the services of a variety of Protestant
churches, from an English Wesleyan chapel in North Wales to
Dunkeld Cathedral (Church of Scotland).

The Freemans may have been somewhat puritan in their
social and religious outlook, but they found great enjoyment in
the worldly pleasures that a holiday could deliver, and were early
adopters of the low-cost tourism that new forms of mass transit
– particularly the railways – made possible.

Tourism, as an activity for individuals, depends on the availability of two things – surplus money and surplus time. Real
income increased for most workers in the last quarter of the
19th century, and better employers offered a 56-hour working
week (which was enshrined in law in 1874). That said, there was
no compulsion for employers to provide paid holidays until the
Holidays with Pay Act of 1938.

The Railway Regulation Act 1844 obliged railway companies
to provide third-class accommodation on many services, which

helped working-class people to afford holidays at distant resorts. This legislation, which was intended to help people find work, included a luggage allowance of 56 pounds, which of course was very useful for the holidaymaker. Competition between train companies also helped to keep fares low.

John and his family were clearly making enough money to afford both time away from work and the expenses of holiday-making, but the diaries nonetheless contain many examples of prudence, if not parsimony. These holidays were still a luxury.

Each year John would ask his family and friends if they wanted to holiday with him, the party would consult their *Bradshaw's Descriptive Railway Hand-book* to help narrow their choices, and they would choose a destination. George Bradshaw's guide would reveal what opportunities the railways offered for combining trains with walking in their chosen area, and a local guide book would help in planning a route.

George Bradshaw, a mapmaker and engraver, published his first guide to railway travel in 1839, and his annual handbooks quickly became essential reading for travellers. They combined timetables for the various regional and national railway operators with descriptions of routes and destinations, helping travellers to plan journeys and choose holiday locations. Where appropriate we have included extracts from Bradshaw in this book to supplement John's own observations.

Victorian holidaymakers did not necessarily have to make their travel arrangements themselves, since this period also saw the birth of the travel agent. In 1875, the Freeman brothers bought their train tickets in advance from Thomas Cook & Son, which had opened its first London outlet a few years earlier at 98 Fleet Street, and had then established their headquarters in Ludgate Circus by 1873.

The Fleet Street shop was supervised by John Mason Cook, son of the founder, and sold travel tickets, guide books, maps, bags and cases, telescopes and stout footwear. John may have bought his first copy of Bradshaw from John Cook himself.

Patronising the Cooks' business would have appealed to the brothers, since Thomas Cook was a Baptist who began his business organising train trips for Temperance believers in Leicester to travel to public meetings in nearby towns.

John's writing reveals much about the typical Victorian tourist experience, with its focus on scenic walking routes, pleasure boats, gardens and other attractions to amuse and engage the traveller – not to mention a plethora of guides (in person and in print) waiting to help the tourist to enjoy their temporary surroundings.

But while Thomas Cook championed mass travel and large-scale resorts such as Blackpool, Morecambe, Brighton, Bournemouth and Scarborough, the Freemans used the infrastructure of mass travel to visit rural and coastal areas that had been made accessible by the railways and travel industry, but not commercialised to the same extent.

The brothers seem to have been drawn to scenery, romantic ruins, landscape and fresh air. They were certainly benefiting from the timetabled trains and affordable accommodation that the burgeoning tourist industry offered, but John and his brothers wanted time and space for contemplation, not the organised entertainment of the promenade and the bandstand.

In this sense, John, Joseph and Charles were also in the vanguard of a new way of looking at nature which came, perhaps surprisingly, from the way people viewed paintings. The language they adopted was derived from art galleries, not the open air: they adored the picturesque (views that looked like pictures), they admired the scenery (views that looked like the scenes in which people or events were portrayed) and appreciated landscapes (views like those paintings that were dramatic or sublime enough to fill a canvas without foreground figures).

Previous generations regarded wild seas as treacherous, mountains as dangerous and thick forests as hiding places for savage beasts. Romantic writers such as Wordsworth, Scott, Shelley, Byron and Coleridge hugely influenced how people saw 'untamed' and 'wild' nature, making it awe-inspiring rather than terrifying.

However, it would be misleading to suggest that the Freemans spent all of their time in silent contemplation whilst on holiday. For one thing, they adored singing; the brothers were active in the Tonic Sol-fa movement, which had been established in the 1840s by John Curwen, a Congregationalist minister.

Curwen and his followers assigned names to the seven tones of the major scale, a system that was far easier to read and remember than traditional musical notation. The names, familiar to many people from the film *The Sound of Music*, are: doh, ray, me, fah, soh, lah and te. The system allowed people without formal musical education to quickly become competent in learning new songs and in choral singing. Curwen first used Sol-fa to teach his Sunday School students to sing hymns, and went on to make such a success of the sight-reading technique that by 1891 around 2.5 million people in Britain were being taught in this way.

John was a member of Joseph Proudman's Sol-fa choir, which was made up of 70 male and female singers, and which had competed in the annual competition organised by the Tonic Sol-fa Association in the Crystal Palace, Sydenham, London, in 1873; he also played the cello.

On holiday, the brothers were keen to use the hymn books and tune books they were familiar with, not only because they were in Sol-fa notation, but also because they contained the hymns and psalms acceptable to Baptists and other Dissenters. The volumes included *A Collection of Hymns* (Methodist, 1870) and *The Bristol Tune Book: A Manual of Tunes and Chants* (first published 1863).

The journals also showcase John's wry observational humour and his wonderful sketches. In his account of his holiday in Jersey, he credits the magazines *Punch* and *Fun* with influencing his 'would-be humorous' drawings, and certainly the style of the former publication can also be seen in his writing, in which he blends observation and opinion, and uses a wide range of allusions to classical literature, the Bible and various Dissenter hymns and psalms, as well as secular choral favourites.

John's topics and style are also reminiscent of two bestselling Victorian authors of English comic novels. The first of these is George Grossmith, whose *Diary of a Nobody* was first published in serial form in *Punch*, beginning in 1888. It documents the life of Charles Pooter, a fictional City of London clerk struggling to negotiate the proprieties of life in a middle-class household in Holloway. Grossmith's book is a light comedy of manners, but delivered with sharp wit and much irony. Pooter undermines his rigid respectability with his dutiful recording of trivia and pretentious thoughts on everyday life. The accompanying illustrations, by George's brother Weedon Grossmith, also bear some resemblance to John's comic sketches.

By coincidence, George Grossmith grew up in Marylebone within a few hundred yards of John and their paths may have crossed when Grossmith was a reporter at Bow Street Magistrates Court and John worked in Regent Street. John may well have seen the Grossmith brothers' early contributions to *Punch* before the hugely popular Pooter diaries (which were published later than John was writing).

The other late-Victorian author with close similarities in style and content is Jerome K. Jerome, probably best known for *Three Men in a Boat*, to which of course this book owes its title. It was first published in 1889, and details a boating holiday on the Thames undertaken by three men and a dog. Jerome combines a travelogue delivered with observational humour and slapstick with a more subtle satire on the pretensions of Victorian society.

John was writing before these two English comic classics were published, but he was certainly living, reading and writing in the same circles. His diaries emerged from the same literary and social traditions, with strong but flawed narrators moving through unsettling times. John's journals can therefore be seen as prequels to these Victorian bestsellers, combining the comedy and pathos of the Grossmith brothers with the wit and relish of Jerome.

Sadly, John died at the age of 36, shortly after the brothers' last holiday in 1883. His diaries live on, however, as a fitting memorial to a keen observer of the early years of the travel industry, and of the changing times in which he and his brothers lived.

The journals clearly have great value as documents of social and cultural history. Just as importantly, though, they transport the reader irresistibly into John Freeman's world, a world of simple pleasures: feasting on fresh buttered rolls on a quayside, walking through the countryside on a sunny day, bursting into song on a scenic hillside. Everyday life for the modern reader may seem more exciting, faster and more frantic, but perhaps we can all learn something from the Freemans.

Ronnie Scott, 2015

JERSEY 1873.

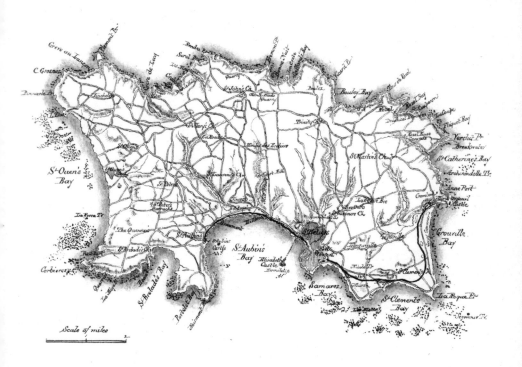

PROLOGUE

Charley and I had asked ourselves,
'Where shall we go this year?'
And Jersey was decided on,
Though 'twould be rather dear.

When Joseph said to me one day:
'I think we'll come with you,
'But much I fear that mal de mer
'Will visits make to Lu.'

'By all means,' I to him replied,
'So be it as you say,
'And let us hope old Nep won't wish
'For tribute on that day.'

Now just a few short days before
We had arranged to start,
A gent came o'er from Camberwell,
And opened thus his heart:

'O pity please to take on me,
'I am a friendless lad,
'Permettez-moi to go with you,
'And I shall then be glad.'

To him retorted Charles and I
In deprecating tone:
'We don't want to offend, but we
'Would rather go alone.'

But Joseph sent a little note,
With words dulcét and mild;
Said he: 'Why you can come with us,
'And be our little child.'

So off we on our travels went,
And if you're so inclined,
A full account of all our deeds
By reading on you'll find.*

---

* The travellers are John George Freeman (the author), his brother Charles James Freeman, their older brother Joseph H. Freeman and his wife Lucy, and their friend Edward Falkner from Camberwell. 'Nep' is Neptune, Roman god of the sea, who may demand 'tributes' from sufferers of mal de mer (seasickness).

THURSDAY 11 SEPTEMBER

Time: 8.35 p.m. The scene: the platform of Waterloo Station.* Principal persons thereon – as far as this diary is concerned – Edward Falkner Esq., the noted Camberwell draper, Charles Freeman of the 'Lane', and his fraternal relative John, all resolved to have a holiday and enjoy it, or know the reason why not. This trio was waiting for a married couple hailing from Balham, Joseph and Lucy Freeman by name, as the quintet had agreed to make an invasion of the island of Jersey, wind and weather permitting. These individuals at last arrived and after mutual congratulations Joseph purchased five little slips of paper – intrinsically worth about one farthing – for the enormous sum of nine pounds and ten shillings sterling, then we took possession of the compartment of a second-class railway carriage and at 9 o'clock precisely off we started on our expedition, for better or worse. Be it here recorded that though it was a 'mail' train ladies were allowed to travel therein, and notwithstanding the fact that Charles and myself are unmarried (and according to all appearances likely to remain so) we did not speculate in 'single' tickets. The conversation consisted of such pleasant subjects as railway accidents and sea-sickness: with regard to the former, we felt tolerably safe, as one had happened a day or two previously, which of course would make the officials more careful for the time being; as to the latter Charley and I had done our best to avoid the inconvenience arising therefrom by coming to a close acquaintance with some of Mr Morison's numerous family and having a capital meal at home before we started, while the Camberwellonian was in possession of Nux vomica to which as a specific charm he occasionally resorted.†

At Woking we stretched our legs for a few minutes on the platform and then rattled on again. There were but two other

* Waterloo Station was opened (as Waterloo Bridge Station) on 11 July 1848 by the London and South Western Railway.

† James Morison made his fortune selling Vegetable Pills, which claimed to cure all ills. They were exceptionally powerful purgatives, composed of aloes, jalap, gamboges, colocynth, cream of tartar, myrrh and rhubarb. Nux vomica was used to stimulate the digestion and as a general tonic. In large doses it is poisonous, since one of its active ingredients is strychnine.

THE TIMES, WEDNESDAY 3 SEPTEMBER 1873

FATAL RAILWAY ACCIDENT

(By Telegraph) Hartlepool, 2 September

Today, about half-past 12 o'clock, the passenger train from Sunderland was approaching Hartlepool Station at a speed of nearly 20 miles an hour, when, just after passing Trinity Junction, the engine left the rails, dragging after it three third-class carriages and one second-class. The engine struck the buttress of a massive timber footbridge which crosses the line at this point, hurling it to the ground, and with it two boys named Coward and Gill. One of them sustained a severe concussion of the brain, and the other a fractured skull. The bulk of the bridge fell upon the first carriage, smashing it completely to pieces, and burying its four inmates. A strong body of workmen was soon on the spot, and it was ascertained that Joseph Talbot, tailor, of Thornley, had been frightfully crushed and internally hurt. He was conveyed to the hospital, but expired on the road. Michael Watson, son of a blacksmith at Thornley, had his right leg fearfully injured. No hopes of his recovery are entertained. A woman named Webb, belonging to Wheatley Hill Colliery, was also injured on the head and the legs. She was conveyed to the Bridge Hotel, where she now lies. A fourth occupant of the carriage escaped unhurt, as also did the driver and fireman, George Short and Thomas Murrell. Had the accident happened at the dinner hour, when the bridge is usually crowded, the loss of life would have been appalling.

occupants of our compartment besides ourselves and they were very quiet, not to say morose; however, we were merry enough and certainly made sufficient noise for seven. At Basingstoke, ten minutes is allowed for refreshments etc., during which time we alighted and among other deeds inspected the postal carriage. This is specially fitted up and provided with a great number of pigeon holes, wherein to place the letters for various towns, and

by this means the sorting is being rapidly accomplished whilst the train is going at full speed.* Here also the two persons of the male persuasion before mentioned journeyed to the next compartment. Whether the two ladies there were of any attraction I know not, but am rather inclined to think we were too merry for their peace of mind. One could certainly say: 'And melancholy marked them for her own.'† Anyhow, we unanimously passed them a vote of thanks and appreciated their room more than their company.

It was nearly midnight before we reached Southampton, when the engine was taken off and horses proceeded to draw us down to the docks; meanwhile we wrote postcards and sent them to record our safe arrival. Immediately on boarding our steamer the 'Southampton', everyone rushed below to secure a berth by putting therein an overcoat, umbrella, bag etc.‡ There are but 21 of these in the second-class cabin (which we occupied), each of which is about six feet long, three wide and two high and is provided with a very necessary utensil resting on an iron ring in the corner so as to be ready for an emergency.§ It appears that in the high season the accommodation is quite insufficient to supply the wants of the numerous passengers; it is then a case of 'first come first served' and the unfortunate ones must do as best they can. However, on this occasion we had room to spare.

* The first purpose-built postal carriage, known as a Travelling Post Office, was introduced in 1838.
† The quotation alludes to *Elegy Written in a Country Church-Yard* (1751) by Thomas Gray.
‡ The PS *Southampton* was an iron-hulled paddle steamer built in 1872 by Barclay, Curle and Company in Glasgow for the Southampton, Isle of Wight and South of England Royal Mail Steam Packet Company Limited (known as the Red Funnel line).
§ The 'necessary utensil' is a chamber pot.

Went up for a short time on deck but, though a fine night, it was cold and very damp, so thinking we had better obtain a little rest while possible, we each retired to our respective berths, but it was some time before I fell to sleep owing to the strangeness of the place.

FRIDAY 12 SEPTEMBER

2.30 a.m. 'Hark I hear an angel calling', at least so it seemed, but on becoming thoroughly awake I found it was Lucy saying 'Joseph! Joseph!' However, that individual did not seem at all inclined to answer, so soundly was he sleeping. This being the case, I tumbled out and ascertained that the said lady wished for her shawl as she felt queer, and thought she would be better on deck. So I roused Joseph and he (though against Lucy's wish) accompanied her to the upper region. My sleep was rendered rather uneasy by the rattle of the aforementioned utensil against the iron ring by various performers who had by this time commenced in grim earnest. Some time after this, Joseph came from above to borrow the brandy flask for Lucy, who was very ill indeed. Charles, who had possession of this article, was half asleep and half awake, and whilst he was fumbling among his things, Joseph felt an inward movement and cried out: 'Make haste Charley, for goodness sake!' Truth compels me to state that the speed was not sufficient, and my eldest brother…but let us draw a veil over the scene. He rushed on deck and could not be prevailed upon to descend during the voyage.

About 5.30 a.m. I awoke and tried to persuade Charley to get up, but was unsuccessful. However, half an hour later he did so, and I followed his example, but unfortunately at this juncture a sudden qualm took possession of me. Knowing that 'he gives twice who gives quickly', I obeyed the generous impulses of my nature and gave Neptune his due to the amount of that coin which is supposed to be purposely made to enable Scotchmen to give to charitable objects, viz, one farthing. Having thus paid my footing, I was perfectly well during the remainder of the journey.

Arriving on deck, I found many persons engaged in the medical problem known as 'casting up their accounts', which they accomplished by adding to the washy deep, subtracting from

---

BLACK ON THE NIGHT MAIL

Via Southampton, daily direct service (Sundays excepted). The night mail (9 p.m. except Saturdays, when it is 5.15 p.m.), from London (Waterloo Station) carries a mail for the Channel Islands, leaving Southampton Docks for Guernsey and Jersey every Monday, Tuesday, Wednesday, Thursday, Friday and Saturday throughout the year at 11.45 p.m., Saturdays at 8.30 p.m. This service is performed by powerful steamers. In fine weather, the boat should reach Guernsey at 8 a.m. and Jersey at 10 a.m. Passengers may travel by any previous train. The railway carriages go alongside the steamer at Southampton, and luggage is placed on board without trouble or expense. Fares: Through from London, 31 shillings and 21 shillings. Return (one month), 45 shillings and 35 shillings. Southampton to the islands, 20 shillings and 14 shillings. Return, 33 shillings and 23 shillings. Steward's Fees included.

— BLACK'S GUIDE TO JERSEY
(EDINBURGH: ADAM AND CHARLES BLACK, 1870)

Pleasures of a sea voyage

their own persons, and multiplying the fishes' food. 7.30 a.m. Passed the isle of Alderney and the Casquets, these grim-looking rocks standing far out at sea, upon which are placed three towers with revolving lights which can be seen at a distance of 20 miles in fine weather to guard the mariner from venturing in that direction.* Edward now appeared on deck, wrapped in a railway rug that gave him the appearance of a 'spotted leopard', pretending to feel very ill. Soon after this, the sailors began hauling the cargo from the hold, which occupation continued and afforded us amusement till 9.30 a.m., when we arrived in Guernsey.

This seems a pleasant-looking place, but though the weather was dry it was not at all a bright morning. One of our fellow passengers, who had been in these regions before, gave us the information that refreshments were to be obtained here on shore at prices very much below those charged on the steamer, which are exorbitant, viz, sixpence for a cup of tea or coffee and other things in proportion. So Edward and Charley took his advice and rushed off whilst I stayed with Lucy, as Joseph had disappeared in the nether regions. As soon as he came on deck I followed suit, but hardly knew which direction to take till I saw Charley in a very excited state of mind, his mouth full and frantically waving aloft a piece of bread and butter. I followed, and indulged in a beautifully hot cup of coffee, roll and butter, all for the sum of two pence.

We would have repeated the dose but were afraid of missing the boat, which does not stop for any stated time but only sufficiently long to land the cargo. I cannot believe that this refreshment stall is opened for the gain of filthy lucre, but would rather think that it is supported by some charitable philanthropist who may, having been in the same position as ourselves, have resolved that henceforth the suffering and hungry of humanity should be benefited by having a cup of hot – not warm – coffee in place of the 'Chops of the Channel' which had been our sole nutriment since leaving England.* If such be the case, may blessings rest on him whoever he may be.

10 a.m. Steamer started off again, Lucy and Joseph not having been able to breakfast in the regions of bliss. Discovery made by Charley in the course of conversation that the before mentioned individual who had informed us of the coffee at Guernsey is a Sol-fa-ist and, more than that, belongs to Venables' choir.† Of course, we immediately commenced an animated discussion and very soon convinced him of the error of Mr V's ways.

Jersey at last. Passed the Corbiere rocks, on which a lighthouse is in course of construction; also St Brelade's Bay, which looks very pretty from this standpoint.‡

1 p.m. St Helier. This town is situated on St Aubin's Bay and has a very fine harbour built of granite or, more strictly speaking, three overlapping each other. On landing we handed our luggage over to a carrier for safe custody, and then proceeded towards the town. I had heard that lodging house touts abound here, and was just congratulating myself that the story was a gross exaggeration when I saw a flock of them waiting for their prey, who as they came from the steamer were at once surrounded. Having our greatcoats over our shoulders and an umbrella apiece, we were rather conspicuous personages and consequently the objects of their special attention.

* The Chops of the Channel are the short, broken waves felt when crossing the English Channel. The phrase can also mean the area where they are most severe, south of the Scilly Isles.
† The South London Choral Association was conducted by Leonard Charles Venables (1847–1928), who was a graduate and professor of the Tonic Sol-fa College.
‡ The Corbieres are, says Black's Guide to Jersey, 'a group of very grand and picturesque rocks jutting out into the sea, with extreme boldness, from the south-western extremity of the island'. They are the haunt of the cormorant or sea raven.

* Mr Parsonage is probably the Sol-fa-ist with the local knowledge of coffee prices.

This being the case, we formed a very imposing procession down the quay, having for escort a vehicle from the top of which the driver made orations while eight or ten persons, some of whom were certainly the reverse of respectable, card in hand dilated upon the advantages of being taken in and done for by their respective employers. At last we divided into two parties, but they did the same and before long we were in possession of a fine collection of cards. When some desisted, fresh faces returned to the charge like flies on a piece of raw meat. Some were catering for hotels, some boarding houses and some private apartments which, if they spoke the truth, were each and all little short of perfection. One old man was particularly attentive, but we were warned against him by one of his opponents who said with great vehemence: 'Don't listen to that old liar, Sir, his place won't do for you, Sir!'

1.30 p.m. Seeing that we could not do much in so large a body (Parsonage stuck to us like a leech) we deputed the two seniors to make an exploration for the company, whilst we others made our way to the Albert Pier and waited, promising to meet at the railway station in an hour.* Thinking to 'make hay while the sun shone', I did my best to make a sketch of Elizabeth Castle, which stands out in the bay about a mile from the mainland; it is quite . surrounded by water at high tide, but can be approached at low water over what is called a natural bridge consisting of stones thrown together by the action of the waves. It is said that once upon a time the whole of what is now St Aubin's Bay was fertile land, but the sea has changed all that.

Elizabeth Castle

2.30 p.m. Off to the railway station, but could see no Joseph or the 'spotted leopard'. I then explained to Parsonage that I hoped he would not allow us to keep him, as our friends did not seem successful in their search; he thought he would not and accordingly took up his quarters at Shaw's Hotel. Whilst speaking, I saw the two wanderers behind him but said nothing, as I did not care to have for a companion one of whom we knew absolutely nothing. I do not know that I should like to have a parson always with us, much less a Parsonage.

The result of their explorations was that they had not found anything at a reasonable figure which was suitable, and experienced some difficulty in obtaining three bedrooms. It was now past 3 p.m. so we all started on another tour and after several enquiries Edward and I knocked at the door of No. 16 Royal Parade, where the rooms seemed just what we wanted. On enquiring the terms of the interesting female in charge, she replied at first one shilling and sixpence per head a day which is, according to Cocker, £2.12.6, but which seemed to her equal to 25 shillings per week, and she even offered to make a reduction on this as we were going out to acquaint the others with our good fortune.* Having found them, they were of our opinion, so we took possession at once and were very glad to divest ourselves of all encumbrances and have a good wash.

Of one thing there could be no question, viz, that we were all in possession of remarkably good appetites but nothing wherewith to satiate them, so the question was: Shall it be the chops? (as they can be quickly cooked), to which the answer was soon given. 'Certainly, chops and tomato sauce, yours etc. Pickwick'.† While the necessary purchases were being made, I went to Ann Street to order our boxes to be sent up, but – owing to the motion of the boat and the want of food I suppose – was very giddy and had some difficulty in making progress. However, by the time I returned, dinner was ready and so was I. By the way of welcome a pianoforte downstairs struck up 'The King of the Cannibal Islands', but I hope his majesty does not reside here or

* The phrase 'according to Cocker' meant absolutely correct. It was derived from Edward Cocker, author of the authoritative and popular *Cocker's Arithmetick*, which was published in 1678 and ran to more than 100 editions.
† The allusion is to *The Pickwick Papers* (1837) by Charles Dickens. The words form the text of a letter from Samuel Pickwick to Tamora Bardell, his landlady.

* 'The King of the
Cannibal Islands' is a
traditional ballad; the
subsequent comment
seems to suggest that
Joseph is a former
superintendent,
the author a former
secretary and
Charley a librarian.
Edward and Lucy are
seemingly omitted.
† The surname Le
Sueur derives from
the French for a
shoemaker.
‡ 'Oh, for a thousand
tongues to sing' is a
hymn written in 1739
by Charles Wesley,
one of the founders
of the Methodist
movement.

our holiday may not be so pleasant as we have anticipated, especially if he takes a liking to cold ex-superintendent, ex-secretary
or librarian for dinner.*

This very necessary meal having finally disappeared, we of
the male persuasion strolled through the town to the College
Grounds. A fine view is obtained from this quarter as it is very
lofty, but the smoke from the houses spoilt the effect to a great
extent. The town consists mostly of narrow streets. King Street
is the great thoroughfare and contains some large and exceedingly long shops; the streets nearly in every case have English
titles, but the inhabitants' French names are the rule, 'Le Sueur'
being very common.† On reaching home we found Parsonage
had been enquiring after us, wishing to know where we intended
going tomorrow, so I suppose he will be under our window early
in the morning. Wrote home, but were all very sleepy and glad
to go to bed.

SATURDAY 13 SEPTEMBER

6.50 a.m. Rose and called my compatriots, but Joseph was so
overcome by his exertions of yesterday that he was not clothed
till nearly 8 o'clock when, as it had been raining, we of the male
persuasion, umbrellas in hand, strolled through the markets,
of which there is one each devoted to fruit, vegetables, meat
and fish. The contents of the first named are very plentiful and
magnificent in quality, causing us almost to exclaim: 'Oh for a
thousand tongues!'‡ Near here are several houses which are
great objects of curiosity in as much as they have lost any ideas
of the perpendicular they may have once possessed, and resemble their brother the leaning Tower of Pisa.

After breakfast, which by the aid of eggs and bacon we managed to put out of sight, the subject of discussion was 'How
should we spend the day?' While talking, the veritable Parsonage appeared and gave us the benefit of his advice, which was

to go out on a car; these are vehicles peculiar to the island holding about 25 persons, drawn by four horses and driven at a great pace in a rather reckless manner, turning sharp corners in a remarkably rapid style. Half a dozen different proprietors send out these cars every morning and as they are all provided with a guide to name the places of interest etc. it is a very good means of seeing the various points of interest.

10.20 a.m. Accordingly, Joseph, Parsonage and I rallied forth and had not gone far before we met the Royal Blue Car, upon which we mounted and were driven round the town in order to pick up any would-be excursionists, but as it looked as if it would rain every minute, people did not seem on pleasure bent. Calling at No. 16, we took in the other three numbers of our party, also our topcoats and umbrellas, and it was 11.20 a.m. before we fairly started, having two car-loads of tourists.

Our guide, who is known by the name of 'Joe the Royal Blue Guide', has a very ready fund of wit, though he sometimes 'draws the bow at a venture',* as may be inferred from the following fair specimen of his eloquence:

'Ladies and gentlemen, on the right is Gallows Hill, where until lately gentlemen not friendly with the government

* To 'draw the bow at a venture' is to utter a random remark that may hit the truth. The phrase occurs in 1 Kings, chapter 22, verse 34.

BLACK ON EXCURSION CARS

An excellent means of obtaining a general view of the whole island is afforded by the excursion cars which start every morning for different parts, returning in the afternoon. The cars remain at the most interesting places in the island a sufficient time to admit of their being leisurely inspected. A different route may be taken each day. The fare is 2s. Route 1 (Monday): Gallows Hill, Mount Cochon, St John's, 'Creux Terrible' or Devil's Hole, Mouriers Waterfalls, Sorel (lunch provided), La Lavoir des Dames, Mont-Mado Quarries, Frémont Point, Bonne-Nuit Bay, Proscrit's Obelisk, Sion Cemetery, Rouge Bouillon.

were often elevated in a pendent position so as to have plenty of fresh air.'

'Now gentlemen, no smoking abaft the funnel!'

'On the left is Martello Tower and you will please observe over the entrance the hole from which boiling lead was poured on any assailant.'

'Here is also the house where Mr and Mrs Manning were captured and at Rose Dale, King Charles the Second lived in 1845.' (expressions of surprise) 'Oh no! I mean 1645!'

'Perhaps, gentlemen, you are good at riddles. If so, you may be able to tell me what relation a loaf is to a railroad? …Give up? Why, mother of course; the first is a necessity, the second an invention, and necessity is the mother of invention.'

And so he from time to time kept us alive and had plenty to say for himself.

The scenery as we drove along was very pretty, though several smart showers fell and, as we were obliged to put up our umbrellas, this interfered both with the view and our comfort. The railroad runs down to St Aubin's Bay and in one part hangs over the beach so that when the sea is very rough, the traffic is suspended. Near St Aubins, as we were slowly ascending a hill, our guide said he would with our permission sing a song, and forthwith gave the nursery rhyme 'The death of Cock Robin'. We were all supposed to join in the chorus, which ended every verse and was as follows:

> All the birds in the air were sighing and sobbing
> When they heard of the death of poor Cock Robin

After this he favoured us with 'Hurrah for Jersey' with chorus, and then we arrived at St Brelade's Bay; here we all dismounted and preceded by the guide visited St Brelades Church; this edifice dates from 1111 but has little more to recommend it than its age. Close by is a low building called the Fisherman's Church which is supposed to have been erected in 785 and is the most ancient building in the island; on the walls are rude scriptural frescos, but as the place is now used as a lumber shed, the probabilities are they will soon be obliterated.

A sharp shower obliged us to wait some time, then the guide announced that according to the programme, the gentlemen would walk up the hill – which was a very steep one – leaving the ladies to follow in the cars; on the accomplishment of this feat Joe attached himself to the other vehicle and we drove across the Lueuvais, this is a sandy tract of land, once fertile but now little under cultivation owing to the quantity of sand blown over from St Owen Bay. When half way across it rained very hard, but this fortunately was the clearing shower for the day. Our driver took a short cut, omitting to view the Vineries, which are well worth a visit, missed our companions and arrived at Grève de Lecq about 2 o'clock.

This spot resembles Alum Bay very much; it consists of a hotel and a small barracks for soldiers lying between two lofty hills.* Lunch to satisfy the cravings of hunger was laid out in a pavilion on two tables, and the tariff was 'Bread, cheese and butter' sixpence, or 'Lobsters, cold meat, salad etc.', two shillings. Most of the party seemed to be of our opinion, viz, that the latter sum was too large an outlay when dinner would be waiting

* John and his companions visited Alum Bay during their visit to the Isle of Wight in August 1872.

Barracks & Hotel _ Greve de Lecq.

* St Mary and St
Lawrence are two
neighbouring parish
churches; by tradition,
Julius Caesar visited
Jersey after he
conquered Gaul in
56 BC. The guide
may be poking fun at
the legend, or at the
gullibility of tourists.
† 'The Hazel
Dell' (1853) is a
sentimental song
by George Friedrich
Wurzel in which the
singer laments his
darling Nelly, who has
just been buried in the
hazel dell of the title.
‡ Baksheesh can
mean tips for services
rendered, or bribes in
expectation of services
to be rendered.

our return at St Helier, so the majority of us attacked the other menu and did our worst in that direction.

Some of our companions indulged in a bath, but we walked on the sands and scrambled up the cliff, where two young soldiers were undergoing extra drill for having a 'drunk', as they termed it. It appears that each time a man is found worse for liquor he has to undergo four hours extra drill per day, and if this occurs four times in a year a fine of ten shillings is inflicted. One can hardly wonder at their misbehaving themselves, as the place must be extremely dull and they appear to have next to nothing to employ their time.

The order was now given: 'This way for the photographs, ladies and gentlemen!' Accordingly, Joe arranged us in a group in front of the car, some sitting, some standing, which he pronounced to be the most beautiful sight he had seen for many a day. He then took up a position at the side and taken we were, though as Lucy and one or two others began to giggle at the critical moment the *tout ensemble* may not be improved thereby.

We ought to have visited the caves but the tide was too high, so at 4 o'clock we remounted and turned our faces towards St Helier. The drive lay through beautiful shady lanes, the trees of which overhang and interlace at the top, forming a delightful shade during hot weather. In passing St Mary and St Lawrence churches the driver pointed out a stone on which he said Julius Caesar once dropped a tear when returning home from a ball, which accounted for the dirty mark to be seen thereon at the present day.* On the road we Sol-fa-ists sang 'The Hazel Dell' but the company did not seem to appreciate it, so I voted against any more, though Lucy wanted to go on *ad libitum*.† When persons are in public company I do not think it at all expedient to sing without being asked, as by so doing they make themselves as great a nuisance as the man who enters a railway carriage and commences to play a concertina, except that the latter adds insult to injury by applying for baksheesh at the close of his performance.‡

Joe did not re-join our car till near to St Aubins and, when accused of his want of attention to us, responded: 'Ah, but my heart has been with you gentlemen!' He then sang two songs of the comic species, which did not seem to be appreciated but caused much laughter by indicating three ladies as the graces Faith, Hope and Charity. Soon after this, he collected the fares and then round went his hat, as he said: 'To enable your humble servant and the driver to take a Turkish bath after our day's exertions.'

5.20 p.m. St Helier, when Joe announced that 'Passengers could change for the Red Sea, Alexandria and Egypt via the Suez Canal', and bade us good-day, recommending all to come again on Monday as 'It was the best thing to expand the chest, purify the lungs and make the hair grow'. He certainly is a very amusing fellow and, though he certainly says some very preposterous things, is civil and obliging without being rude.

Strolled through the market where Lucy made purchases for the morrow. I do not know that I have a foreign appearance but a native of La Belle France enquired of me in his native tongue the way to Hill Street. Of course, I was obliged to respond: 'Je ne sais pas, monsieur, je suis etranger ici.' Reached No. 16 by 6 o'clock and did full justice to a good dinner, after which, meeting the redoubtable Parsonage, we took a short stroll round the

Stout Gentleman — Ah! you are much too sharp for me!

* The Plymouth
Brethren is a
Nonconformist,
evangelical Christian
movement, with
autonomous
congregations and no
central structure. It
was formed in Dublin
in 1827.
† Morpheus was the
Greek god of dreams.

harbour. Jersey has the reputation of being rather a fast place, but it seems to me just the reverse; indeed hardly a soul is out of doors and there does not appear to be any promenade similar to Hastings or Brighton, not that I take a delight in that sort of thing, but I do not know of any other watering place minus this attraction.

9 p.m. Arrived again at our home and had a somewhat lengthy conversation with Miss Le Sueur as to the various chapels in the town. Their family attends the Plymouth Brethren, where a certain Mr Muloch preaches but, as she said he held forth for three of four hours at a time (though afterwards it appeared she meant the whole service lasted that time), thought we would not go there.*

10 p.m. Retired to make the acquaintance of Morpheus.†

SUNDAY 14 SEPTEMBER

6.50 a.m. Suddenly awoke from a somewhat troubled rest as I had been dreaming after this fashion: On our travels with Charles, we came to a very high and steep hill in Russell Square, which we ascended, and entered a house for the purpose of having a tune. For this we were taken before the magistrate but, just as he was about to pass sentence, I became aware that it was all a phantom of the brain. However, the daughter of the above named limb of the law – a most beautiful young lady of course – wished very much to accompany us, and doubtless would have made amends for all her father's cruelty, who I suppose would eventually have said: 'Bless ye my children.' All properly constituted tales end in this way.

My brother travellers were not ready till nearly 8 o'clock, when we directed our steps towards the inland portion of the town in order to inspect the various places of worship. These are very prolific, most shades of opinion being represented from the Established Church even to the Mormons, with Wesleyans being especially numerous. At last we found a Baptist Church in Grove Street, of which Mr Hider is the minister.* The town is very irregular so that one might easily lose oneself, which indeed we nearly did, but soon hit upon the right track again. A public notice states: 'Boys found playing at tip-cat or bowling hoops will be subject to the penalties of the law and parents will be held responsible for the conduct of their children.' I should not imagine the hoop trade is in a very prosperous condition.

9 a.m. Breakfast. Our appetites were not so good as if we had been for a long walk, so ham and eggs were required as an inducement to take just a little. 10.15 a.m. Strolled forth all together. The town was very quiet, Sunday closing being apparently quite the rule. A high wind was blowing from the south-east and the sun shining brightly at first. Soon after, it began to rain and we took refuge in the Baptist Chapel above mentioned. As a quarter of an hour was still wanting before the commencement of the service, we had plenty of time to look about us. It is a small place with whitewashed walls and a gallery at the back, holding about 200 at the utmost and has no superfluous ornamentation. The gentleman who showed us to our seats brought me a list of the tunes to be sung from the 'Bristol' (I suppose he must have seen my large 'Union') so I asked him if he could lend me a tune book.† He said he would see, but I heard no more about it and we were obliged to compose our various parts as best we could. Just before the service commenced a gentleman entered and walked right up the aisle with his hat on. Arriving at his pew, he doffed this article and put on a small skull cap, reminding us so irresistibly of Mr Jeffreys that we all began to laugh.‡

Mr Hider preached a very good sermon from Acts, chapter 2, verse 31, but the chapel was not half full. The singing accompanied by a harmonium was very fair, but as for the Sunday School, the scholars were only numerous enough to fill one square pew. After the service, Edward spoke to one of the deacons who said the building formerly belonged to the Independents but they had departed to more commodious premises so of course as it

* The Baptist movement, which began in 1609 in the Netherlands, is a Nonconformist Christian church that believes in adult baptism.

† *The Bristol Tune Book: A Manual of Tunes and Chants* (1863) was a hymn book mirroring the beliefs of the Bristol Baptist College and set out in Tonic Sol-fa notation, while *The Union Tune Book: A Selection of Tunes and Chants Suitable for Use in Congregations and Sunday Schools* (1854) represented the beliefs of the Baptist Union. At this time, hymn books contained only the words of the hymns and psalms, and perhaps the name of the tunes. Tune books contained music for the standard tunes and sometimes new hymns with both words and music.

‡ Mr Jeffreys, who is also mentioned on Tuesday, 16 September, in connection with singing, appears to be a member of the Freeman brothers' church in London.

is in a rather out-of-the-way spot the Strict Baptists took possession of it and equally of course there is a debt on the chapel.

After a short stroll, we made for No. 16 and such was the effect of the mid-day meal that three at least of my companions were very lethargic and declined to stir for some time. However at 2.45 p.m., by the joint endeavours of Edward and myself, we managed to call them to a sense of duty and started for a walk down the Grand Val. This is a most beautiful valley which runs due north from St Helier for four or five miles, hills covered with numerous trees and thick foliage being on either side, while down the centre winds a small stream which on its way turns several mills. Splendid views are to be obtained from every spot, especially looking towards the town with the sea, Fort Regent, church etc. in the background.

Having traversed about two miles, we seated ourselves on the bank and partook of some pears and grapes which we had brought, then sang 'Poland', which so alarmed an old lady in a house opposite that she came running out to see whatever was the matter, thinking perhaps some rioters were out for a holiday. However she saw we were quite harmless, so retired again into obscurity. We then essayed to return and, after trying to make a short cut but having to return again for our trouble, eventually came to a road which took us in the right direction.

5.30 p.m. Tea. Clouds which had been gathering for some time broke about half an hour later and it rained rather heavily. I had intended to pay a visit to the Chapelle Evangelique Française but, owing to the threatening appearance of the weather, thought I would bear my companions company; accordingly we visited the Congregational Chapel. It is quite a new building in the modern style of architecture and has an organ at either end. Charley suggested they would be played by electricity. I afterwards ascertained that the one used was only just opened, so suppose they will dispose of the other to some indigent church. The singing, led by a choir seated in front of the organ, was very good but why they should have a curtain in front of them I do not know, though certainly it was drawn back during the sermon. Mr Rutty (the minister) is an intellectual and fine-looking man, and preached from Luke, chapter 19, verses 41 and 42. During the sermon he compared St Helier in some measure to Jerusalem for sinfulness. I do not know to what particularly he alluded, but he spoke very strongly on the subject.

In crossing the parade on our way home, we saw an assortment of Jersey pairs on the seats. It seemed to me rather cold, but suppose the inward flame kept them warm. No backs are provided for these resting places, but of course every one brings his or her own.

9 p.m. Thought we would have supper, so asked for the pie left at dinner. Miss Le Sueur affirmed that her brother had mistaken it for theirs and eaten it, but she brought some of their own (which was made at the same time) as a substitute. This may have been so, but I strongly suspect they did not expect us to ask for it again so put an end to its existence.

10.45 p.m. Retired to Bedfordshire, but before so doing a sub-committee was appointed consisting of Charles and self to consider our plans for tomorrow.*

MONDAY 15 SEPTEMBER

Wind blew hard during the night, making such a noise at the windows that I was awakened several times.

6.30 a.m. As it was raining, said 'a little more slumber', but half an hour later it cleared off, so we dressed and walked down to Gregory's Carriage Repository, where there is a barometer.† It was evidently on the decline, and not even a shaking could induce it to put on a more cheerful aspect. The man in possession did not give us much encouragement, but said he thought the afternoon might turn out fine. Whilst out, several smart showers took place, between which the sun shone brightly. The season here has been a very bad one: The St Aubins railway has

* To 'retire to Bedfordshire' is to go to bed.
† The quotation 'a little more slumber' alludes to Proverbs, chapter 24, verse 33.

during the last week only carried 10,000 passengers and taken £123 against 18,000 and £233 during the same period last year.

8.45 a.m. Breakfast, when the sub-committee reported that if the present weather continued it would be wet, and moved a resolution that the company had better not go out for the whole day. This was strongly seconded by the rain, which came down in full force, and was unanimously carried, so dinner was accordingly ordered for 2 o'clock.

10.30 a.m. Parsonage appeared on the scene, and said he intended going with the Royal Blue to Bouley Bay, but we declined to accompany him. However, as it seemed inclined to hold up a little, we placed ourselves inside our topcoats, shouldered our umbrellas and sallied forth to the harbour. On our way there, it is no exaggeration to say, the wind blew down several streets, indeed so strong was it that at times we were almost brought to a standstill.

On our arrival at the harbour, a pilot boat was endeavouring to go out to sea but with the wind being right in her teeth she was obliged to tack and was driven back in the first attempt but succeeded at the second trial, all but grazing the side of the harbour. It was a fine sight to see her battling with the waves, and the crew had to look uncommonly sharp in handling the ropes. At the end of the pier the wind was perfectly furious, and one could hardly stand upright, much less make any progress. Obtained the information that this morning's mail has put back into the harbour, but afterwards ascertained that she took shelter in St Brelade's Bay. I should think the passengers had a lively time of it.

A new breakwater is building from Elizabeth Castle, to shelter the mouth of the harbour, and over this the waves were dashing and breakers seen on rocks far out to sea. After stopping here some time, we ascended the road to Fort Regent and turned to the right towards Samarez Bay. Very little is to be seen along the coast, it being flat and sandy, but there are plenty of rocks in the distance. As it was exceedingly windy and several smart

Squally

showers fell, did not proceed farther than Samarez railway station, whence we took the 25 train and reached our quarters half
an hour later. This line from St Helier to Gorey was only opened
last month, the stations are very small and I do not think it can
pay, as it has been more expensive in construction than the one
to St Aubins, and certainly does not run through so populous a
district.

Our appetites for dinner were in prime condition and the
demand rather exceeded the supply. But, finishing up with
Jersey Pears, we managed to obtain sufficient nutriment to keep
the wolf from the door, notwithstanding which the lazy portion
of our community could not be induced to face the wind again
till 3.45 p.m., when out we went intending to visit Elizabeth
Castle and Fort Regent. However, the tide was so high that the
former was inaccessible, so we turned our steps in the direction
of the latter. This strong fortification was built of granite in 1804
on the summit of a steep rock facing the sea, which is 350 feet
beneath. When we entered, a redcoat came forward, saluted
and proceeded to conduct us round. Fifty guns bristle upon
the ramparts, but not one carries more than a 100 pound shot.
'Woolwich Infants' are at present unknown in this locality but
our conductor said they measure five feet across the breach and

* 'Woolwich Infants'
were very large 35-
ton guns, made at
Woolwich Arsenal,
with 700-pound shells
that could pierce an
ironclad ship at three
miles.
† 'The cups that
cheer but not
inebriate' is a phrase
from the poem *The
Task* (1785) by
William Cowper.

BLACK ON ELIZABETH CASTLE AND FORT REGENT

Elizabeth Castle is an old and now useless fortress, built on the rocks to the west of the harbour. It is detached at high water, but connected by a causeway about a mile in length, laid bare at half-tide. The castle was constructed in the present state in the reign of Queen Elizabeth, on the ruins of an old abbey on the same spot, founded in the 12th century. It is much larger and more capacious than could be supposed from its external appearance, and during the Commonwealth held out against the Parliamentarians for more than six weeks. To the east of the harbour rises a steep and lofty ridge of granite on which is Fort Regent, an interesting modern fortress commenced in 1706, but completed only lately. It is accessible to visitors, and the views from it are very fine.

the shots are seven feet long.* Many of the cannon balls piled up here will be melted and recast as they would be perfectly harmless against the present race of ironclads. The fort is provisioned for seven years and the whole town undermined so that it could be blown up at any moment, which is a very pleasant reflection; communications also exist with Elizabeth Castle. Our guide, who was a bandsman, seemed well contented with his life, though apparently the garrison have not half enough occupation. A splendid view is obtained of the bay, town and adjacent parts, but the wind blew 'great guns'! In fact, had we been near the edge of the ramparts, I think we should have stood a chance of going down quicker than we came up.

Descended and found Elizabeth Castle still unapproachable. As heavy clouds were again gathering, made the best of our way to No. 16 and partook of the cup that is popularly supposed to 'cheer but not inebriate'.† One of Mr Le Sueur's daughters said we were quite welcome to go down at any time and play on their piano for an hour or so. Charley immediately availed himself of the opportunity and, notwithstanding the fact that said daughter was there, boldly entered and gave several impromptu performances, consisting mostly of commencements of anything that came to mind, but finishing nothing. What passed at the interview has not been revealed – perhaps Charley's diary may give the required information – but both Lucy and Edward were of opinion that the young lady played much better afterwards; notwithstanding all their persuasion, he could not be induced to pay another visit in that quarter. During the evening a heavy thunderstorm fell, accompanied by several flashes of vivid fork lightning; this will I hope wind up this showery weather. 9.30 p.m. Dustman.*

* The Dustman is a variation on the Sandman, a character in many northern European children's stories, who sprinkles magical sand or dust on the eyes of children to bring sleep and sweet dreams.

TUESDAY 16 SEPTEMBER

6.15 a.m. Emerged from between the sheets. We had intended to see the mail boat start but were too late, so wended our way over Gallows Hill which, as might be expected, is a barren-looking spot. Continuing our route we passed the cemetery and some nursery gardens, which were duly inspected, the latter containing many fine specimens of floriculture. The roads are so exceedingly numerous and winding that we almost lost our bearings, but by turning to the right found ourselves in the Val des Vaux, which runs parallel with the Grand Val, visited on Sunday. It is an exceedingly pretty spot, a stream rippling down the centre shaded by trees and foliage on either side in great profusion. After a good walk of nearly five miles, we arrived at home just after 8.30 a.m. quite ready for breakfast, and glad to find the

BLACK ON VAL DES VAUX AND GRAND VAL

To the north of St Helier are two beautiful valleys, the Val des Vaux and the Grand Val, which afford beautiful walks full of interest to the botanist. Many rare plants may be found both in the hills and in the valleys, and on the salt marshes adjacent.

same was quite ready for us; in the combat which ensued our larder was almost emptied, so good were our appetites.

After a little discussion, we determined again to patronise the cars, so though it was not very bright – wind a little more northerly – we sallied forth, armed as usual with our topcoats and umbrellas. Our first act was to look in at Shaves' to inspect the photographs taken on Saturday. They were not ready, but the shop man said the group was a very fine one, the finest indeed taken this season. This, of course, we took with a pinch of salt, as doubtless everyone is told the same to induce them to become purchasers. On arriving in front of the harbour, we were accosted by 'Harry Gordon the Paragon Guide par excellence' as he terms himself, and as he said his party would visit the caves first, decided to honour him with our company and mounted his car. We then drove through the town via the Paragon Stables, and ascended the hill taking the road by the cemetery. Another car – with which was Gordon – and a waggonette bore us company, but the company was not at all lively.

At St John's we paused for refreshments, of which some people seem to require a constant supply, especially of beer; here a thick Scotch mist began to descend and quite spoilt the

— *The Creux de Vis, or Devil's Hole.* —

view of Bonne Nuit and the quarries, which otherwise we might have enjoyed. Soon after this we put up at a house called the British Hotel, and alighting proceeded across an exceedingly wet hill to a famous place called the 'Creux de Vis' or 'Devil's Hole'. This is a very steep descent of about 150 feet consisting of jagged rocks. The bottom is rather difficult of access – especially on a wet day – but when there, one is amply repaid for the trouble. On attaining this desideratum, we found ourselves opposite a tunnel – surrounded by huge boulders of rock – penetrating the cliff to the sea which was clashing in with a deep hollow sound. Some of our party amused themselves by placing stones on projecting rocks, and trying to knock them with other stones, but were nearly overtaken by the waves while thus engaged. Only two other ladies besides Lucy ventured the descent, and really it required great caution to do so, as if one were to slip the consequences might be serious.

Arriving at the summit, I breathed again – in fact I often do so from force of habit – and we returned to the British to partake of milk which was very fine, almost like cream. The ladies and others rested in a room opposite the bar, which was I suppose called the 'drawing room', as the walls were covered with prints of all imaginable descriptions (except good ones), both French and English. Leaving this place, we proceeded on our journey and arrived at Grève de Lecq by 2 o'clock. Gordon immediately marched into the refreshment pavilion and, announcing that 'luncheon would now take place', put himself in position at the head of the table and commenced to carve a joint. I should think he received a commission from the hotel proprietor, as his example was contagious and certainly as many sat down to the two shilling collation as on Saturday partook of the sixpenny luncheon. We had provided for ourselves, so commenced to ascend the hill to the east, which overlooks a deep gorge called by everyone Crabbe, but not marked so on the map. Gazing from the summit, the view is exceedingly grand. The sides of the chasm are extremely precipitous, with huge masses of granite projecting in all directions, while the waves clashing at the bottom make the whole scene very fine.

One of the soldiers belonging to the troop stationed here conducted us over the hill, and among other things told us he had been 19 years in the army, had fought at Lucknow and other places, but was still a private. Enquiring how it was he had not received promotion, he said it was of no use trying as before long they were sure to have a 'drunk' and were then degraded to the ranks; so much for high moral tone in the army. While we were here, a sharp shower fell, but this was the last for the day. Returning to the pavilion, we found singing was the order of the day, but unfortunately it was of a description that has no attraction for us, viz comic music hall songs; the one that I heard had a chorus to this effect:

> Oh love scrumptious love,
> Love makes a man feel so awf'ly peculiar,
> Love, love, scrumptious love,
> A man's a fool when a man's in love.

It was not stated whether the persons singing were in that interesting state or not, but certainly all who joined in the chorus – both ladies and gentlemen – looked remarkably stupid. Neither am I in a position to vouch by experience for the truth of the last line, but couples would do well to remember that when they call one another 'duck', 'darling', 'deary' etc. and look so lovingly in public before other people they appear very foolish, though I am rather afraid they glory in it than otherwise. The burden of another song which I did not stay to hear was:

> For I'm so clevah, so awfully clevah,
> There ne'er was a fellah so awfully clevah.

The songster was not informed that he said what was not, but I feel pretty certain that he would have stood a splendid chance of heading the poll at an election as candidate for Hanwell Asylum.* The first named song was enough for me and I went into a more congenial atmosphere, viz, pure air. Several other car loads were there besides our own, making altogether about 100 persons; some of these were looking their worst preparatory to being photographed, so we being willing to add to the importance of the picture gave them the benefit of our figures. After this our own party were grouped in front and on the car and served in the same manner. The hotel proprietor pronounced it to be the noblest group he had seen this season, but he said much the same sort of thing last Saturday.

Gordon's promise to visit the caves was not fulfilled, nor do I think he intended to go there; neither did we see the Mourier Falls, which were in the programme.

4.15 p.m. Started for St Helier, and almost immediately the 'fellah' who was 'so awfully clevah' commenced singing a most ridiculous song to the tune of 'Auld Lang Syne', and in order that all might join in he gave out one line at a time (this was about the only proceeding which would have met with Mr Jeffreys' approval had he been with us) but when two verses were finished a sudden shock informed us that something had happened.† Upon investigation it was found that one of the traces was broken so we had to wait some time before we were again in motion.‡

From this point, the road was mostly the same as that travelled previously and calls for no comment, though force of habit constrained the vehicle to stay at a public house in St Aubins. Why people want or think they want to drink so much liquor passes my comprehension, unless it is that it makes one thirsty, instead of quenching one's thirst. Certainly I do not like this excursion so well as the 'Royal Blue'; most of the passengers were 'fastish' and as for Gordon he by no means approaches his rival Joe.§ He was with our ear but a very short time, but we apparently did not lose much, as even when we had the pleasure (or otherwise) of his company, the information he volunteered was absolutely nil.

* Hanwell Pauper and Lunatic Asylum opened in 1831, eight miles west of central London. It was the first purpose-built asylum in England and Wales, and grew to become the world's largest asylum.
† Mr Jeffreys: see Sunday 14 September.
‡ Traces are the straps that connect horses' harnesses to the carriage or wagon they are pulling.
§ Fastish here means 'somewhat dissipated'.

The hair apparent

Reached St Helier before 6 o'clock and inspected the photographs taken at Grève de Lecq. Of course, every one pronounced their own portraits very bad and their companion's equally good (Charley could say nothing too bad for his); the result was no purchases were made.

6.30 p.m. Dinner; this aristocratic time is instituted so that we may 'improve the shining hour' and not because we have suddenly become possessed of fashionable ideas.* We did not venture out again after this meal as there really seems nothing doing here in the evening. Fine night.

9.30 p.m. Retired to rest.

WEDNESDAY 17 SEPTEMBER

Awoke at 6 a.m. but were disgusted to find it had been raining again, and as it continued to do so did not rise till 7.30 a.m. As Lucy was going to market, Edward and I followed to act as light porters. It is the custom here for ladies – when they purchase the day's necessaries – to carry a basket on their arm or have an attendant to take charge of the same, as the shopkeepers refuse to send things home and do not even care to tie them up in paper. The stock which it was necessary for us to lay in was something extraordinary, and when I say that pears, bloaters, butter, plums, suet, bacon, eggs and sausages were deposited somewhere about our persons, it may be easily imagined we did not run very fast on our return journey.

After breakfast it was very cloudy and did not seem at all disposed to clear off. Nevertheless, after much discussion, we resolved to dare the elements to do their worst and, taking our overcoats and umbrellas, started out for the day, calling first at Shaves', where Joseph bought one of the photos previously mentioned; the *tout ensemble* except Charley think it very good. We turned to the left and passed the Imperial Hotel, which is a magnificent building, but I should not think there are half enough visitors to make it a financial success. About a mile from St Helier is St Saviour's Church, in the graveyard of which are two tombstones consisting of solid masses of granite weighing several tons. They form very imposing monuments, and certainly have the charm of novelty; a few of the inscriptions are in the French language but by far the majority are in English. A little past this, five roads meet together, where also the same number of oaks are planted, hence the name. They are not at all fine trees, which are extremely scarce throughout the island, though verdure is everywhere exceedingly luxuriant.

Hogue Bie, — or, The Prince's Tower

BLACK ON HOGUE BIE

Hogue Bie, or Prince's Tower, is one of the favourite points of view in Jersey. It is a tower on a low artificial hill, from which a large part of the island and some of its peculiar beauties may be seen. The tower is modern and not remarkable. It is built on a tumulus, probably of great antiquity. Up the hill, a path winds through gigantic hydrangeas, fuchsias and other flowering plants and shrubs. From the summit of the tower, the view is very pleasing.

1 p.m. Hogue Bie or Princes Tower. This was originally an old chapel but its use was discontinued at the end of the last century. It stands on a mound surrounded by tall trees thickly planted together, and the summit is 340 feet above the level of the sea, being the highest spot on the island. Having settled a certain cash transaction which is necessary before entering, we ascended and encountered a lad who called himself 'the guide'. From his statements I imagine he must have wandered far from the paths of truth, in fact quite lost his way; though certainly as he was cross examined after the manner of Mr Hawkins in the celebrated trial, I suppose he thought he must say something.* A small stuffed dog which has eight legs is on view. He informed us four were used on Mondays and Tuesdays and the others on two following days. As he had previously said the animal only lived three days, Joseph confounded him by enquiring how that could be, to which he had no reply. He also showed us a skin which he assured us originally belonged to a castaway that ate up a live missionary at the other side of the island.

On a clear day, a splendid panorama is to be seen from the summit of the tower, but unfortunately it was very misty, so that we had but a faint glimpse of what might have been our good fortune and even that was well worth seeing. Started off again, but we had not proceeded far when Lucy spied a man in an orchard and immediately expressed a desire to trade, so I was called in to act as interpreter as best I could. However, our notions of the French language did not correspond and it was with some difficulty that he made me understand that we were to enquire at the other side of the house. Here an ancient dame called one of the men, who acceded to our desire and gathered 26 fine apples, but said the master would make a price. This individual, who now made an appearance, was a sinister disreputable-looking fellow, not a bit like an English farmer; however, he showed us over his cider house and generally behaved very civilly. Lucy took a fancy to a beautiful tortoiseshell cat and kitten which were sitting on the grass and much wished to take away the latter, but though the woman wanted to sell it the man would not. Pocketed the fruit in exchange for sixpence, we said 'good morning' and went on our way rejoicing.

3.15 p.m. Gorey. This town consists of a few straggling houses and a harbour. Bills are to be seen in the windows with the inscription 'Apartments to Let', but I should think they are almost fixtures as I cannot conceive anyone coming here to spend a holiday. Overlooking the town is Mont Orgueil Castle, which is the principal object of interest to visitors. It is 220 feet above the level of the sea, built on solid rock and from its position was once no doubt almost impregnable to assault. It was built about 1,000 years ago, and one or two slight alterations

Mont Orgueil Castle & Gorey Harbour

in artillery have taken place in the meantime and rendered it now of little use as a military stronghold. On walking through the gateway, we were accosted by the warder, who armed with eight or nine large keys (to open the various rooms) volunteered to show us over the castle, which offer we accepted. On the walls are carved the coats of arms of several governors of the island, who have bravely defended the fortress; also there are one or two secret passages, while the cell in which condemned prisoners were once confined is a caution, being so frightfully damp that the inmates would be pretty certain to have for constant

BLACK ON GOREY, MONT ORGUEIL CASTLE AND THE CROMLECH

GOREY *is a fishing village and small harbour at the northern extremity of Grouville Bay, close to a fine headland, on which frowns the ivy-mantled castle of Mont Orgueil. The village consists of a well-built street, extending from the beach to Grouville. Gorey was at one time noted for its oyster fisheries.*

MONT ORGUEIL CASTLE *is the commanding object of the east coast of the island, and occupies the central point of that coast. Seen at a distance, it is a grand mass of buildings, but it hardly repays close examination. Parts of it are believed to be Roman, and to have been constructed by Julius Caesar, but this is doubtful. There is no charge for admission to see the interior of the castle, and the objects usually visited are the remains of the chapel; a deep well, said to be Roman; the ruins of the old prison for island culprits; the room where Bandinel and his son were confined in the time of Charles I; the cell in which Prynne was confined; and the apartments of Charles II.*

Behind Anne Port, at a short distance, is a DRUIDICAL MONUMENT, *one of the best now remaining in Jersey. It is composed of nine stones supporting a flat stone. All are of granite, and the flat stone measures 15 feet in length, ten in breadth and about three in thickness. This cromlech is in an enclosed field, but is easily found. It is well worthy of examination.*

companions rheumatism, neuralgia and other comforters of a like description.

A very necessary thing must have been the well, which is 160 feet deep and half full of extremely cold water, to which a stone takes four seconds to travel. The warder said a short time back a gentleman dropped his hat down this well and he (the warder) went down in a bucket after it, a rather dangerous experience which I should not care to imitate. Many years ago – it is said – during a siege four of the officers betrayed the garrison. When the fortress was retaken, they were captured and as a reward for their treachery suspended in iron cages from the walls and starved to death. The identical four chains used on this occasion have been hanging there till Monday last, when the violence of the wind blew one of them down. I can bear witness to the fact that one was on the ground, but for the strict truth of the other part of the story I am not responsible.

Here we were shown the cell where Prynne the Puritan writer was confined, but visitors are not allowed to go in on account of its unsecure state; also a statue of the Virgin Mary and Child which was found some time ago hidden in the walls, but visitors wishing to have a memento of the place so well employed their time in taking little pieces of it away, that now it is quite a matter of faith as to whom it represents, but to prevent further

Ancient Cromlech, Nr Mont Orgueil

* William Prynne, an
English lawyer and
Puritan campaigner,
was convicted in
1634 of seditious
libel and ordered to
be imprisoned for
life. He spent time in
the Tower of London,
Carnarvon Castle and
Mont Orgueil Castle
before being released
in 1640.
† A cromlech is a
prehistoric structure
built using very large
single stones, and
the term is usually
applied to the remains
of a chambered tomb.
The Druids were
the priestly class of
the Celtic peoples
of France, England,
Ireland, Scotland and
Wales, who flourished
from around 100 BC to
AD 100.
‡ 'Hail Smiling Morn'
(1810) is a song for
three voices written by
Reginald Spofforth.

mischief it is lodged in a cage.* The stone work of the castle is built in an extremely solid manner, and some of the flooring is of oak, four and a half inches in thickness, and very substantial. Until lately soldiers were quartered here, so some of the rooms are whitewashed and otherwise modernised, consequently the main interest lies in the associations of the place.

One would not have thought it an easy task to escape when in confinement here, but two prisoners once attempted to do so and both succeeded. One of them did not get any farther than the bottom – to speak plainly he fell and killed himself; while the other was soon afterwards recaptured. On making our exit we each signed our names in a book so that the world might know who had been there. Leaving the castle, we proceeded to a field near at hand, where is a capital specimen of an ancient Druidical Cromlech.† It consists of one very large slab of granite estimated to weigh 20 tons, resting on six others, and is a sample of our forefathers' handiwork, though how they elevated the first named mass of stone to its present position is more than I can say. Joseph, Charley and I climbed on the top and sang 'Hail Smiling Morn!'‡ Though a thick Scotch mist had begun to fall, and we each wore an overcoat, it seemed rather ironical.

5 p.m. Commenced our return to St Helier. Were at first in two minds as to which route we should take, but at last decided in favour of that via Grouville, for the sake of fresh scenery. From the latter place we intended to take the rail, but the station was so small that we did not see it, so we were obliged to walk the whole distance, not that there would have been anything to object in this if the elements had been propitious, but on nearing St Helier – though the rain had not fallen enough during the day to cause us to hoist our umbrellas – it descended with great vigour and, notwithstanding the fact that we stepped out well, we were pretty wet by 6.40 p.m. when dinner was sighted. Lucy was nearly done over, as she had certainly tested her marching powers rather severely, but it is only fair to add she came well out of the trial. Being averse to giving unnecessary trouble, we kept to

our usual custom of giving Miss Le Sueur as little as possible to carry down besides the plates and dishes, but as far as I know none of us were ever troubled with *the weights.*

— *The Weights* —

THURSDAY 18 SEPTEMBER

6.30 a.m. Made an inspection of the state of the weather, but damp seemed again to be the order of the day, so indulged in another snooze, then clothed ourselves and strolled through the town. Inspected the photographs at Barman's which were taken on Tuesday, but they were decidedly bad. While, owing to the want of good light yesterday, the other photographer (Badoux) had not printed any copies.

8.45 a.m. Breakfast. While indulging in this meal, rain began to descend in real earnest, owing to which a discussion arose as to whether we should venture out, or wait till it cleared up. However, as at 10 o'clock there seemed no chance of an abatement (though Edward avowed he could see blue sky), we resolved not to be idle. So, donning our overcoats, we march down to the 'Royal Blue' station to see if anything would turn up. On arriving we were considerably astonished to find the barometer had during the last few days risen from 'change' to 'set fair'. If this sort of weather is what is known as set fair in this part of the world, I think I would like some rain by way of a change. Unhappy thought – suppose the stable proprietors tamper with the weather glass in order to

BLACK ON TRINITY CHURCH
AND MANOR

The parish of the Holy Trinity is small, but includes much of the finest part of the north coast of the island, and is connected by omnibus with St Helier. From the second turning to the left after passing the church, a beautiful scene presents itself. In front is the winding road leading to Bouley harbour, beneath the blue sea, and in the distance the coast of Normandy.

tempt visitors to go out; this was denied.

After waiting some time in a blissful state of indecision, Joe the guide appeared on the scene and really made us feel quite cheerful by saying that he would 'guarantee a fine afternoon'. Being appealed to regarding the glass, he affirmed the 'clerk of the weather was married last week and of course was out of sorts just now; but he would provide hot water bottles and rugs for the company'.

As we wished to see Bouley Bay, Joe promised to drive there though it was out of the ordinary route, and as soon after a covered car appeared we mounted therein and were soon off, for better or worse. There were but 19 of us altogether, and some of these were outside so as better to enjoy the scenery. While the inside passengers – of whom, it is needless to say, we formed a portion – were protected from the rain by tarpaulin covers, which hung down the sides.

Our route lay along the high road to Trinity Church, the clock of which has apparently ceased to perform its functions. Joe fully explained this circumstance by stating that six years ago the parish clerk, being crossed in love by a young lady, ran away taking the key with him and neither clerk or key have ever been seen since. Consequently, the clock has never been wound up.

12.10 p.m. Bouley Bay. Here we descended and surveyed the scenery. That is to say, we should have done so, had there not been a thick rain falling, but we saw enough to be able to perceive that it must be a lovely place in fine weather. After some of the passengers had practised at 'pouring the spirits down to help keep the spirits up', in which I need hardly say the Freemans did not join, we mounted once more and proceeded on our journey. On the road, Joe did his best to enliven us by singing several songs; the chorus of one of them is as follows:

> I dote on the ground she walks on,
>> Her two bright eyes that shine;
> I would not take all the money in the bank,
>> For the girl that I calls mine.

Just as he was carolling these lines, a rather ancient female, dressed in the not very gorgeous costume peculiar to the island, appeared on the scene, of which he immediately took advantage by waving his hand in that direction, smiling and applying each line to her particular case. The peals of laughter which ensued must, I think, rather have astonished the good lady in question.

12.45 p.m. Rozel. The chief point of interest here is the Tropical Grounds, which we proceeded at once to inspect. The gardener escorting us repeated the scientific names of the various trees and plants, not one of which I now remember.

BLACK ON ROZEL AND LA CHAIRE

In the village of Rozel and near it are several houses and properties of interest, and the bay, though small, is at the foot of a fine bold valley running up the country and traversed by a carriageable road. It is a great place of resort for pic-nics during summer. The manor house is on high ground, and offers nothing remarkable; but there is an interesting residence called La Chaire, formerly the residence of Mr Samuel Curtis, whose great knowledge of botany enabled him to lay out his grounds so as to take advantage of the extremely mild and equable climate of the island.

Why persons botanically or otherwise inclined cannot talk in their mother tongue passes my comprehension; it is as absurd as interlarding one's ordinary conversation with sentences of French or German, which everyone would condemn as an exhibition of vanity. Nearly all the plants are exotic (as the name of the place implies), and some are certainly very fine specimens, but as it was raining very hard their beauties were considerably obscured. We derived one ray of comfort, as the gardener's man said the wind was getting round to the north and prophesied some fine weather. This, of course, we most readily believed, and blessed him for a true prophet. As one of our lady travellers was without an umbrella, Charley took compassion on her and offered the shelter of his; but what passed under that very convenient covering is more than I can state.

A short distance from Rozel are the Rozel Manor Grounds, where the 'Royal Blue' tourists have the sole right of entry. They are certainly very beautiful and well worth a visit. Geraniums flower here all the year, and some of the trees are the largest in the island, but the rain followed us in the most persistent manner and cast a damper on everything. The spirit of a Mark Tapley was required to enable one to feel at all cheerful, and it really seemed like the fulfilment of a certain Dartmoor proverb, which says:

> The west wind always brings wet weather,
> The east wind cold and wet together,
> The south wind surely brings us rain,
> The north wind blows it back again.*

Resuming our journey, our veracious guide pointed out the place where Mr Caesar popped the question to Mrs Caesar. This gentleman appears to be rather a favourite in the island for his wonderful doings, though it is questionable if he was ever here. We then had more songs, one of which has the following capital chorus:

Hurrah! hurrah! then sound the jubliee!
Hurrah! hurrah! the island of the free!
And so we sang the chorus from England o'er the sea,
As we went sailing on to Jersey.*

In this style we rattled by St Martin's Church and village, from whence some boys and girls ran along behind us in expectation of securing a few spare coppers. They certainly ran remarkably fast and, as the roads were exceedingly dirty, must have been splashed all over, notwithstanding which they followed us right into Gorey, which we reached by 2.30 p.m. Here, lunch was provided for those who were in want of it. Inside a butcher's shop is the following placard: 'Mind your own business.' It is a good motto and many would do well to adopt it, except when they are writing a diary, in which case absolution must be given.

3.15 p.m. Mounted to Mont Orgueil Castle under the guidance of Joe, who secured the keys from the warder. He has the history of the place well at his fingers' end; much of it was the same as we heard yesterday, but according to his story, the head of the statue of the Virgin Mary was stolen and £20 reward offered for the recovery of the same. He also drew on his imagination a little in some instances. On arriving at the summit the rain happily ceased, and the clouds partially cleared off so that the coast of France was quite visible. Seated on the parapet, Joe gave amongst other items, a capital account of the last invasion of the island by the French in 1781, when the invaders were defeated – though the commanders of either side, Major Peirson and Baron Rullecourt were killed – after a sanguinary encounter in the Royal Square, St Helier. Thirteen of the prisoners were confined to a cell at Mont Orgueil, of whom ten were shot and the remainder starved to death. For some time they were fed on conger eel soup flavoured with marigolds, but at last all the former disappeared and they succumbed, being no longer able to exist on marigolds. The latter part of this story was, of course, subject to discount.† Soldiers were quartered in the various rooms till

* This song appears to share the traditional roots of the American Civil War song 'When Johnny Comes Marching Home' (1863).

† The attempted French invasion of Jersey, in January 1781, saw 1,000 French troops easily defeated by around 9,000 locals in a skirmish that lasted 30 minutes.

recently, and boards are still hanging with an inventory of the fixtures, at the bottom of which is a note stating: 'Whoever loses his board will be charged two pence for a new one and one penny for the screw.'

4.45 p.m. Bade adieu to Mont Orgueil and started off with faces towards St Helier. Rain began to fall about the same time and continued to do so during the remainder of our journey. We had not gone far before Joe proposed to have a game at roadside whist, to which we gladly assented. The rules are as follows: the individuals on each side of the car keep a sharp look on their side of the road, and if they see any of these objects they count as here specified; windmill, [water] pumps, wheelbarrow, ladder or grindstone all one point, goat or well for two points, a pig in a sty for three points, a grey house for five points and a cat in a window asleep wins the game! These numbers are added together until 31 is obtained, when victory is declared to belong to the fortunate possessors of that score. It is a more exciting game than one would imagine, as each person calls out and points to the object scored. We rather startled some of the natives by our energy, one man especially who was wheeling a barrow turned round as if he had been shot on hearing 'Wheelbarrow! One!' My side won two games and our opponents one, but the fourth was I believe a tie, both sides claiming the victory. After this, both parties drew largely upon their imaginations, they for instance counting the steps of about twenty bathing machines as ladders, while we on one occasion began to score at fifteen, and soon became totally disorganised. However, we all arrived safely at St Helier a little before 6 p.m. having – considering the weather – spent a very pleasant day. This was mainly owing to the vivacity of our guide and the company, which was rather more select than usual. Indeed we quite forgot to remind Joe that his prophecy of fine weather had failed most signally.

6.15 p.m. Dinner. When I say that it consisted of two ducks, beans, potatoes and apple pudding and that only a few bones were left, one may judge of our feelings afterwards. During the

Finale furioso

evening we descended to the parlour and joined in some singing with the Misses Le Sueur, using mostly the 'Services of Song'.* But as there was generally only one copy or at the most two for pianist and singers, it may be readily imagined there was much room for improvement.

10 p.m. Separated for the night.

* *Services of Song* was a Nonconformist songbook, with words and music, including songs for groups, duets and solo singers.

FRIDAY 19 SEPTEMBER

6 a.m. I tumbled out of bed with the joyful exclamation: 'I say Charley, it's a beautiful morning!' This so startled him that he jumped out as if an explosion had occurred underneath the bed. Edward, mistaking the time by exactly one hour, did not rise so early (though I called him) so we three brothers went down to the harbour in order to see the London boat start, but found she had gone away some little time.

Three natives were engaged in fishing from the pier, but they did not appear to have caught anything, except perhaps a cold. They reminded me of the following conversation which is reported to have taken place between two gentlemen:

First married piscator: 'Ah my friend, how our lives resemble this fish!'

* Cheapside is a
street in the City of
London, well known to
the Freeman brothers.
They are obviously
surprised to find a
location of the same
name on their holiday
island.

† Vraic is a local
dialect word for
seaweed.

‡ The married couple
are Joseph and Lucy;
a commissariat is a
military department
responsible for
supplies of food and
equipment.

Second married piscator: 'Indeed! How so?'

First married piscator: 'Why, don't you see? Man is the fish, woman is the line, her smile is the bait, love is the hook and marriage is the frying pan!'

As the morning was very fine (the wind had changed to north-west), and we were armed with towels, we walked along St Aubin's Bay, and had a capital bathe near Cheapside – fact, really!* The water was quite warm and almost as smooth as glass, the bottom nice and sandy but a good deal of vraic was floating about, and we were obliged to wade out a long distance before reaching any depth of water.† I had a very fair attempt at a swim, making as many as 12 strokes at once, but as the tide was receding I took good care not to venture out of my depth.

9 a.m. Breakfast, when no doubts were expressed as to the advisability of going out for the day, and at my suggestion we adopted the route as hereafter related. In the first place, leaving the married couple to provide for the commissariat, we others proceeded to Government House and obtained an order to visit Elizabeth Castle, after which met altogether at the railway station, where I left my note book, but fortunately for this diary – or unfortunately as the reader may think – found out the loss in time to recover the same.‡ Elizabeth Castle was the first of our explorations, and as the tide was low we were able to reach it by the natural bridge which is about a mile in length.

On presenting our order we were admitted to the fortress and, seeing that the artillerymen were about to practise at the guns, seated ourselves on the turf to view the spectacle; and a fine one it certainly was. The youngest (for they were mostly under 20) were tossing the shots about for amusement, but on the officer appearing and calling out 'Eyes front!' they immediately fell into position, proceeded to clean out and load the guns, and at the word of command fired with a report that was deafening and seemed to make the very ground tremble. The target was a small white flag about 2,000 yards out at sea, at which was discharged both shell and 32lb solid shot. Some of the former especially were beautifully directed, exploding just above the flag and falling into the water in all directions.

An officer who was watching the proceedings told us the report from these guns is a mere nothing, as when firing with large ones in casemates, the effect is so stunning that blood trickles from the men's ears and they are often deaf for some little time afterwards; that some of the shells contain nearly 400 small shot – the effect of such a missile exploding among a body of men may better be imagined than described – and finally that at Shoeburyness, where the practising range is eight miles in length, a cannon ball will make a leap of two clear miles after first touching the ground.*

Proceeded to the top of the castle, whence we saw the last three rounds fired, then – after due interview with the warder – visited the armoury. Here there is a good selection of firearms, ranging from the Brown Bess to the Snider, also old English armour and pikes.† Amongst other relics there are several of the Russian war such as a soldier's cap, eagles etc.; also specimen fuses of the Gatling, Mitrailleur and other guns.‡ Edward was inspecting one of these when the warder said in a matter of fact way that if knocked hard it would explode and tear his hand to pieces, upon which he dropped it rather sharply. Perhaps the chief object of interest is a large pair of boots which originally encased the feet of Charles the Second. They are certainly very remarkable-looking fellows, being square at the toes and four inches in breadth with a heel fully as wide and three inches high; the leather of which they are made is exceedingly thick but rather tender and has several holes; it has not undergone any repairs.

1.15 p.m. Having duly inspected the castle, we came out of it and found there was not time to visit the Hermitage – as we were afraid of being overtaken by the tide – but do not think we lost much, as it is only a rock where Saint Helier is reputed to have dwelt as a hermit.

* A casemate is a fortified gun emplacement from which guns are fired.
† Brown Bess was the standard British Army flintlock musket; Snider (named after its inventor, Jacob Snider) was a breech-loading rifle used by the British Army from the 1860s.
‡ The Russian 'eagle' was a badge featuring the Imperial Eagle crest, worn on soldiers' hats or caps; the Gatling Gun was an early machine gun, invented by Richard Gatling in 1861; the Mitrailleur Gun was a rapid-fire musket or rifle.

St Aubin's

Arriving at Cheapside, it was suggested that we should dine at Lake's or call in at No. 14 Friday Street and see if business was in a prosperous condition, but on second thoughts we decided not to do so.* Whilst waiting for the train we were greatly surprised to see that the means of communication with the castle was already cut off. Indeed so quickly does the water rise that many persons have at different times been drowned, being overtaken by the tide.

2 p.m. Took train for St Aubins. The carriages on this line are of a very novel character, being constructed with projecting

BLACK ON ST AUBINS

St Aubin's Bay occupies the central part of the south coast of Jersey, being enclosed by the Noirmont promontory on the west, and the low land and marsh of Samarez on the east. It is one of the largest, and is usually regarded as the most picturesque, of the Jersey bays. The town of St Aubins is small, but clean, and has two or three decent inns and a market place. Lodgings may be had. There are no remarkable public buildings.

BLACK ON ST BRELADE'S BAY, THE FAIRY CAVES AND ST BRELADES CHURCH

St Brelade's, this most beautiful bay and interesting locality, extends from the Fret Point to Les Juteurs. On the western side of the bay there is a delicious little cove, with fantastic rocks and recesses, known as the Creux Fantômes, or fairy caves. It is well worthy of a visit, though seldom explored. Close to the little headland that forms the cove in question is seen the church of St Brelades, one of the oldest buildings, and certainly the earliest Christian church, in the Channel Islands. The church is small and plain, and without tower or spire, but is singularly picturesque.

platforms on either side, so that passengers can walk along the same and enjoy the fresh air and beautiful scenery (instead of being cooped up inside) which, when the weather is fine, is very pleasant.

A quarter of an hour brought us to St Aubins, which is a pretty neat little town, and the place deserving of that name in the island besides St Helier. Ascended the cliffs and enjoyed a view of the beautiful prospect beneath. The front of the cliff here is covered with vegetation, and below – surrounded by water – is St Aubins Castle. The tide being high and the sky a deep blue, that colour is reflected over the whole bay, presenting a most magnificent sight. Here we enjoyed our lunch.

Continuing our travels, we encountered a pig which had just met with a violent death by running his neck against a knife, with which the butcher – after having scalded it – was now busily engaged in a shaving operation. He offered to act as barber for us should we require it, but this we declined with thanks. Having duly arrived at St Brelades and refreshed ourselves with milk – for which we appeared to be always ready, and which I strongly recommend as being far preferable to beer or spirits – we crossed over the hill to a small cove called Le Creux Fantômes, or Fairy Caves but, the tide being high, were not able

— *Beau Port* —

to descend to them. After passing a small battery erected here, we came at last to the end of our explorations, viz, Beau Port. This is – as the name implies – an exquisitely pretty little bay, being nearly surrounded by granite rocks which project in all manners of fantastic shapes, one of them standing out alone in the middle. We were much struck by the spectacle, but luckily it did not hurt us. I have tried to make a sketch of this charming spot, but am bound to say it is not a successful effort as the beautiful blue sea glistering in the rays of the sun gave quite a different effect to that of sombre ink.

4.40 p.m. Quitted Beau Port and, as we wished to catch the 5.30 train from St Aubins, Lucy had rather a sharp walk, especially as a portion of the route lay uphill; she responded nobly to the call and we arrived with seven minutes to spare. During our journey to St Helier, just as the train was about to start from Millbrook Station, the guard, spying someone in the distance, cried out to the engine driver: 'Hi! Stop! Here's a mon a-coming!' And, much to our amazement, the train was delayed. The 'mon' however was a woman, but hardly was she seated than another native was seen and waited for. No other individual being in sight, we resumed our journey. Of course, as it is only a single line, it did not much matter, but just fancy this happening in London! Reached home in good time for dinner, after which I wrote to Zeph and did not retire till 10.30 p.m. Parsonage left Jersey by this morning's boat and Edward intended to do the same tomorrow, but owing to the fine weather has changed his mind and wired home to that effect.

* Jupiter Pluvius is the rain-bringing aspect of the god Jupiter, head of the Roman pantheon.

SATURDAY 20 SEPTEMBER

6.45 a.m. Became alive to the fact that we ought to be up and doing, but were sorry to see Jupiter Pluvius had again been up to his little games.* Having arranged our toilettes after our various manners, Joseph and self took a short constitutional while the other three went to market for the general good. 9 a.m. Breakfast, about which time it began to rain. As the sky was looking very overcast and the wind was in the ominous south-west quarter, there appeared to be probability of a wet day. Therefore we were rather undecided in our movements. Remembering the motto 'Nothing venture, nothing have', we proceeded to Green Street, taking our umbrellas by way of precaution but (fortunately as it afterwards turned out) not our overcoats. Never before during my holiday have I spent nearly so much time under the shelter of these two necessary, but by no means at all

St Martin's Church

times pleasant, coverings. Yesterday was the beginning of the better things respecting the weather, though had our trip taken place just one week later, we should hardly have had a drop of rain. Booking for Gorey, we took seats in a railway carriage and amused ourselves during the journey by roadside whist. Such was our energy in specifying the various objects along the route that I think the single native who was in our compartment must have imagined we had taken leave of our senses.

11.25 a.m. Gorey. Our object being to visit Bouley Bay and the intervening country, we marched along the high road to St Martins and arrived there an hour later. The church here is an old one but has recently been restored. The inscriptions on the tombstones in this and other country churchyards are nearly all written in French, while in St Helier the majority are in English. One in particular struck me as telling a sad tale, viz, the deaths of six brothers and sisters during a period of little more than four years. Underneath are the following lines. To say this from the heart under such circumstances must require more than ordinary faith and resignation.

> L'Eternel les avait donnés, l'Eternel les a otez,
> que le nom de l'Eternel soit beau.*

As the church seemed to me worthy of being transferred to paper, I stayed behind in order to make a sketch of it; and here it may be as well to observe that most of the Jersey scenery in this diary is taken from photographs, but some is from rough outlines made on the spot, though the weather was not very suitable for outdoor artistic efforts. For the would-be humorous figures I am mainly indebted to 'Punch' and 'Fun'.† Resuming my journey, I imagined my confreres would be a long way ahead, so stepped out accordingly, but had not proceeded far before I came upon Joseph in the middle of the road with the information that the others were to be found in an orchard close by. Thither we went and found they were laying in a stock of pears.

Two of these three fruit trees, the farmer said, yielded him £8 last year: this would be nearly 2,000 to each tree reckoning one halfpenny for each pear. The fruit certainly was splendid, and the branches were propped up to prevent them breaking down by the weight. Lucy here saw another kitten and again wished to become a purchaser, but it was not for sale.

Continuing our journey we certainly presented a most extraordinary appearance. It being warm, Lucy had entrusted her jacket to Joseph's keeping who (for greater convenience) had pocketed his cap; Charles's hat was bent down like an inverted saucer; Edward's was at the very back of his head; while the pears together with our lunch caused all our pockets to protrude in the most alarming manner. Lucy was rather tired and more than once was it necessary to say, 'Haste thee, nymph!' but with little effect.* Blackberries on the hedges were very plentiful and many of them were consumed as our as forces progressed.

2 p.m. Rozel. This is a small place with a harbour, but the latter has not the appearance of being much used. Turning to the left we had not proceeded far before a rumour arose that one of our party was missing – viz – Joseph, and as he was not visible to the naked eye, we all – at a given signal – sang out at the top of our voices: 'Joe!' This was repeated several times waking the echoes all around, still the last one was not to be seen. However before we had time to concoct an advertisement of 'Lost, stolen or strayed, a young man who answers to the name of Joseph, rather tall, having in fact nearly grown through his hair, sings bass and is very fond of bagatelle. Any person bringing information to No. 16 Royal Parade will be liberally rewarded', the individual himself was seen looming in the distance and soon began to blame us for going on without him. He said he had been down three different roads and had not heard our united calls. Happy thought: 'All's well that ends well.'

By the roadside here are apple trees, whose fruit falls in the road. We helped ourselves thereto *ad libitum*. Though not very large, they were sweet and certainly not dear at the price. Perhaps

* 'Haste thee, nymph' is a phrase from the poem 'L'Allegro' (1645) by John Milton; it also appears in *L'Allegro, Il Penseroso ed Il Moderato* (1740) by George Frederick Handel.

Lane &c near Trinity.

this is the species known as the 'Rhodum sidus'.* Finding a nice spot, we seated ourselves and lunched from the variety of things contained in our pockets, then proceeded to Bouley Bay, where we arrived about 3.20 p.m. This is a picturesque spot, surrounded by steep hills on either side, but has not more than half a dozen houses, including a hotel. Edward, Charles and I scrambled down to the bottom, while Joseph and Lucy sauntered along the top, but we did not gain much by this operation – except a good warming – as the best view is to be obtained from the summit. Near the hotel were some sheep grazing, and among them a very fine ram tethered by a chain, which a man warned us was a very fierce fellow. Lucy however (doubtless thinking her smile could subdue the ferocious animal) said she was not afraid. She ventured near and fed him with apple. Certainly he seemed quite quiet but immediately she turned to go away, he saw his opportunity and charged, butting her twice rather fiercely. Lucy screamed a little but was soon out of the way and unhurt as her dress no doubt took off much of the force. According to the man above mentioned, he is in such a bad temper – the ram not the man – that he is to be killed, having only this week knocked down a lady and gentleman – before this occurrence – just by way of diversion.

4.15 p.m. Trinity Church. A postal notice here intimates to the natives that letters are only collected three times a week; just fancy! This and other public communications are all written in French; indeed we were told that many of the country folk had never visited St Helier, or 'town' as they call it, and certainly they cannot understand English at all. Sketched a very pretty lane near here. After which we amused ourselves with roadside whist; though the required objects were not very numerous, Joseph startled several persons by shouting at the top of his voice if a pump or well were visible. On one occasion he was asked what he required by a man who happened to see him, and on another he tried to climb a wall about nine feet high but was obliged to give up the attempt in despair.

Arrived at No. 16 in good time for dinner, after which meal we strolled through the town. The inhabitants really do seem to liven up a little on Saturdays as they then take to marketing, but on other days the place is very quiet and looks as if nothing short of an explosion would waken it up. Returning home, I essayed to write up these notes, but was so very sleepy that I was obliged to give it up as a bad job and retire to private life, which important event happened at 9.30 p.m. As we did not indulge in suppers we were not troubled with…

— *The Nightmare* —

* The Bible Christian Church was a Methodist movement founded in 1815 in north Cornwall. By 1820 it had established a presence in the Channel Islands. It appointed men and women equally to the ministry.

7.15 a.m. Up again; sorry to see rain had been falling during the night, but glad that the wind had veered round more to the north. After a little while our hearts were rejoiced to see the sun burst forth as if he meant business; accordingly Joseph and self resolved to take advantage of the phenomenon, so walked down to the sea and had a good bathe. I exercised my slight swimming powers to the best of my ability. Returned, donned our go-to-meeting clothes and then partook of the morning meal generally known as breakfast.

After a short walk I determined to be a Frenchman for the day. So, separating from my companions, I entered the Chapelle Wesleyenne Française. A gentleman immediately informed me that it was a French chapel (thinking probably that I had made a mistake) and asked if I would like a seat, to which of course I replied in the affirmative. I had a good mind to request a place near to the pulpit so that I might hear the service more distinctly, but the minister preached from Romans, chapter 8, verse 28 very clearly, more so indeed than any foreigner I have ever heard. This beautiful chapel was erected in 1847 and has lately been repainted and adorned. I estimated it will seat 1,800 persons, and it is the largest building in the island with the exception of a chapel lately erected by the Bible Christians.* The singing was rather tame, though there was a capital organ and choir, but then the building was not more than one third full. Of course, the usual half-quarterly collection took place, the donations for which were put into a queer sort of box with half of one side taken out so as to admit the hand. The service was concluded by 12.15 and as the congregation streamed down Grove Street they quite filled the thoroughfare. As dinner was not yet due, I strolled on the pier and met my companions. The weather was beautiful, the sun shining brightly and no wind. If it is only like this on Tuesday, Neptune will not receive much in way of toll.

1.30 p.m. Dinner, which consisted of rabbit pie and tapioca pudding. The former revived memories of a certain meal at Freshwater Gate when Charley and I were on our tour last year.* On this occasion also we did our best, and the residuum would not have yielded much if put up to auction. 3.30 p.m. We of the male persuasion went for a walk to Victoria College and its sur- roundings, leaving Lucy at home as she was very sleepy. On our return, we found she had not enjoyed much rest as the younger Miss Le Sueur had been with her all the time. She had done all she could – short of telling her so – to let the intruder know she was not wanted. This young lady is certainly in possession of a most remarkable tongue.

5 p.m. Tea: but really so soon after dinner it seemed quite a work of supererogation; nevertheless, we did our best under the circumstances.

6.15 p.m. I made my way to the Chapelle Indépendante in Halkett Street, which is pretty and compact.† The whole of the service was conducted by Pastor Hocquard – a perfect French- man in manner and gesture – in a very energetic style, the text being Luke, chapter 19, verses 37 to 41: the service of praise was well led by a choir and harmonium but the congregation – which was very fair – did not join with their voices if they did with their hearts. After the service I strolled round to Salem Chapel where my compatriots had gone to hear Dr Muloch. The chapel is plain, even to meanness, having no more furniture than is absolutely necessary. The congregation numbered 58; I had the curiosity to count them as they came out. On the chapel wall was this notice:

> The Lord cometh with 10,000 of his saints.
> Prophetic addresses every Thursday.

In my opinion, the Doctor makes a great mistake by trying to reveal the prophecies. Those who do so are certain to make great blunders, only bring ridicule on themselves and their cause, and can do no possible good.

* John and Charles visited the Isle of Wight in August 1872.
† The chapel housed a Congregationalist group.

* 'Canaan's Happy
Shore' is a campfire
spiritual from early
19th-century America.
Its tune was borrowed
for 'John Brown's
Body' (1861) and 'The
Battle Hymn of the
Republic' (1861).

On arriving once more at No. 16, the people below played a
variety of tunes including 'On Canaan's happy shore', but did not
entice us down and we soon after bade each other 'Goodnight'.*

MONDAY 22 SEPTEMBER

After waking and seeing the now quite familiar sight of wet
window panes, we performed our toilettes and at 6.45 a.m. as we
had all (save Charles of course) agreed to bathe before breakfast
– weather permitting – proceeded to the seashore, but the more
we advanced the lower fell the spirits of a portion of our contin-
gent. Edward declared it was too cold to venture in and Lucy,
following his bad example, was of the same opinion. Joseph
tried to raise her drooping courage and persuade her it would
never do to return home without having a single dip, but she
did not seem to see it in that light. Nevertheless, by dint of great
exertions we at last arrived at the bathing machines, or rather
where they ought to have been. On enquiry – which the above
named lady did not at all wish to make – we found they were
put under cover for the winter season. Great were the rejoicings
manifested at this announcement by the young lady in question,
who went away with Edward to do a little necessary marketing
for breakfast. Joseph and I, not being at all dependant on such
things as bathing machines, soon appeared in the elegant cheap

BLACK ON THE COST OF LIVING

*The expense of a visit to the Channel Islands is moder-
ate, even to tourists, compared with an English, Welsh or
Scots trip. Except a small amount payable on all imports, the islands are
untaxed, as far as strangers are concerned. The prices of tea, sugar, wine,
spirits and tobacco are thus greatly below the price of those articles in
England. In Jersey, British coins are chiefly current, and British currency
is demanded in the hotels throughout the island.*

and most fashionable costume of our ancient forefathers and much enjoyed our dip.

9 a.m. Breakfast. Since this was the last day of our sojourn here, a poll was taken of the free and independent electors present as to what should be the *pièce de résistance* for dinner. The election was by ballot and, though by no means advocates of women's rights, we allowed Lucy to have a vote. The result was: Fowl three votes, Sausages one vote and Fish one vote. We all proceeded to the market, also to purchase several other dainties, among which were three baskets full of grapes, apples and pears for our brothers, sisters etc. in London town. Monetary transactions here are rather complicated, as prices are quoted in Jersey coin which has 13 pence to an English shilling, and the pound weight is two ounces heavier than ours, but in some of the shops things are priced at so much 'British'.

Having completed our purchases and resisted the insinuations of two carriage drivers who wished to have the pleasure of our company for the day, we visited Badoux's to inspect the photos taken last Tuesday. Perhaps it was owing to the weather, but they certainly were very bad portraits. Opposite the parish church is a hotel called the 'Grasshopper', which has hanging

* A 'fly' was a horse-
drawn public coach,
similar to the modern
taxi.

out by way of a sign a most ferocious-looking beast – it cannot
be an insect as it is almost four feet long. This was a source of
much merriment to us when passing in that direction and – by
particular desire – I have endeavoured to give some idea of the
same. It is hardly so savage in appearance as the original which,
when one is beneath, seems as if it would pounce upon the
unwary traveller and put an end to his existence.

12.30 p.m. Having executed our little et ceteras we proceeded
by Val Haisaut to the Val des Vaux. The day, which had been
improving ever since early morn, was now gloriously fine and
made the picturesque views of the valley look exquisitely beautiful. Oh, if it had been thus all the time! Nevertheless, we were
thankful it was not worse. Edward like a dirty boy took to grub-
bing up ferns and carrying them – earth and all – in his arms.
There evidently is no accounting for taste. Lucy also evinced a
predilection to enter the various orchards which we passed and
speculate in apples and pears, but only once was she allowed to
satisfy her desire. Owing to the want of signposts, we became very
foggy as to our position, but after due enquiries found ourselves
in the Grand Val and soon recognised the identical spot where
we sang 'Poland' on Sunday week. After this, however, we again
lost our bearings, the result of which was that towards 5 o'clock
we were near St Saviour's Church. By putting on the steam, 5.15
saw us safely housed once more and ready for dinner. If all elec-
tions by ballot terminate like this one, I certainly should have no
objections to have at least one every week. It is only right here
to give due praise to the Misses Le Sueur as cooks; their pastry
was very good and everything gave general satisfaction, the best
proof of which is that very little was ever left.

Made our last tour through the town to order the fly and purchase various eatables for tomorrow, among other things some
sausages which I hope will not go to feed the fishes.* Having
packed up and made all things straight for tomorrow, retired to
rest at 10.45 p.m., taking care to have a lamp burning all night so
that I might be able to see my watch at any time.

TUESDAY 23 SEPTEMBER

Woke up several times between 3.30 and 4.30 a.m., but did not finally rise until the latter when I roused my compatriots and we soon finished dressing and packing. 5.30 a.m. Breakfast: to which I must confess we did not do justice, but allowances must be made under such trying circumstances, and really it is the first time we have sinned after this fashion. 6 a.m. Jersey time: fly drove up and departed with the married people and luggage but Charley and I walked down to the boat in double quick time, mindful of the various rumours we had heard of her going off before the specified hour; we arrived with plenty of time to spare.

All is bustle on board the 'Havre' (which is the boat for the day), and as the moment for departure draws near, the mail cart appears in the distance and sets us cogitating whether there will be any unlucky ones come just too late, when lo! Behind the said cart is a gentleman accompanying a truck full of luggage, which he does his best to hasten along. It is all in vain and, though another two minutes would have seen him on deck, the fates are inexorable and almost immediately the mails are on board we sheer off. Great excitement prevails among the sightseers, especially when the said individual calls out: 'Hi! Stop, captain! My wife and children are on board!' No reply is vouchsafed, but on his again calling out the captain gruffly replies: 'Well, you can't jump that distance can you?' alluding to the space between the pier and boat, but afterwards says he will leave his family at Guernsey. The gentleman immediately makes an offer of £2 to the crew of a four-oared boat if they can row him to the steamer, which they attempt to do, but it is absurd, though if the captain would only ease our engines they might easily overtake us. The wife – who by the way has six or seven splendid rings on her fingers – looks very much inclined to open the floodgates, but on second thoughts alters her mind and under the circumstances bears up very well.

The morning is beautiful, but no sooner are we in St Aubin's Bay than the sea begins to heave a little and some of the passengers commence to do the same. The stewardess brings an assortment of basins so that no one should be kept waiting, and we are now fairly on our voyage home. Lucy, who is determined not to be ill if she can help it, seats herself on the paddle box, while we take possession of three camp stools on the middle deck. A fourth is wanted for Joseph who, however, vows he will not descend into the lower regions for any consideration. Charley and self now take a stroll towards the stern to see how things are progressing in that direction, but while there we spy two of the officers issuing tickets, so make tracks for the front, as they might be under the impression that two such respectable gentlemen were first-class passengers and insist upon classing us under that category notwithstanding all our assertions to the contrary. After a little time these two gentlemen come to the fore part of the vessel and in the course of conversation ask me if I belong to the lady on the paddle box (or vice versa), but of course I most indignantly repudiate the insinuation. Then he says 'Oh! She said the gentleman in a blue cap was her husband. Perhaps it's you, Sir!' speaking to Joseph, who smilingly acknowledges the soft impeachment, but is considerably astonished by a gentle demand for five shillings as extra fare for Lucy's elevated situation, which is for first-class passengers only. In vain he says she is coming down almost directly. The officer is inexorable and the money is reluctantly paid, with the reflection that if it will keep her from being ill it will have been well spent. Charley and self congratulate ourselves on not being caught napping and think: 'Five shillings saved is five shillings earned.'

7.45 a.m. Pass the Weymouth boat on its way to Jersey. During promiscuous conversation with our fellow passengers, we ascertain that one couple had been very comfortable in their private apartments, but things had been stolen right and left (or rather, things left were taken without any right), and only last night a pound of sausages which they had saved to bring with them this morning had been 'eaten by the lodging house cat'. On another occasion nearly an entire cake disappeared, vanishing at the rate of a slice per day till the whole was no more. Upon enquiring, we find this abode of bliss is situated at No. 1 Royal Crescent, kept by a Mr Vaudin. This was the place recommended by the 'old liar' on our arrival, and which our two explorers inspected and thought of taking, but went farther and most certainly did not fare worse; as may well be imagined, mutual congratulations ensue at our narrow escape.

A fierce dog chained up under the bulkhead of the boat spends much of his time barking and affords us much amusement, though we take care not to get too near. One of the sailors this morning, when going to stroke him and say 'poor dog', left a piece of his jersey in his mouth.

8.55 a.m. Guernsey. With a lively remembrance of our former arrival here Edward, Charles and I at once rush off and each indulge in a cup of coffee, and roll and butter. There is nothing to complain of, but it really does not seem so good as on the last occasion. I suppose this is accountable to the fact that we are not so hungry. Lucy and Joseph do not seem to care for refreshments, or rather I think are afraid of the results; anyhow they do not follow our example. 9.30 a.m. Farewell to Guernsey: a portion of our cargo consists of pigs' carcasses; not the nicest thing to look at for those who are inclined to be unwell. Lucy still continues on the paddle box and there seems every prospect now of her making the voyage in triumph. 10.30 a.m. Make a survey of the vessel: many at the stern are in 'doleful dumps', if one may judge by their facial expression; the dog also is fed but no one cares to venture near him.* Proposal made that we have a game at 'Daniel in the lion's den'. Edward to act the part of Daniel, but with characteristic modesty he declines the honour.

11 a.m. Pass the Casquets. As hunger begins to make an appearance a portion of the sausages etc. are demolished; even Lucy partakes of our comestibles, though I think she is half afraid. Joseph will neither eat anything nor venture down in the

* The phrase 'doleful dumps' appears in *Romeo and Juliet* (1597) by William Shakespeare.

BLACK ON THE CASQUETS

Approaching the islands from England, the Casquets Rocks are first seen. They are part of a numerous group about 1½ miles in length from east to west, and half a mile across. They occupy a prominent position, and are extremely dangerous to ships coming up channel. They rise abruptly out of deep water in the direct track of vessels. There are three lights on them, all revolving and placed on towers. A bell is sounded in foggy weather.

cabin, so as to make doubly sure against any misadventure. The sea is now very rough, the boat pitches, and some who have held up hitherto, now give way to force of circumstances, so that fully three fourths of the passengers are hors de combat. Even the aforesaid dog formerly so fierce is affected by the common failing and is quite quiet. 1.20 p.m. Hearing that the steward and others are dining in our cabin, descend to see that no one is putting their feet on our fruit, which is under the table, but find it is all right. The dinner consists of boiled bacon and cabbage, the odour of which under the circumstances is not very inviting, especially to those who are lying in their berths under the impression that it is preferable to being on deck. It seems to me they make a great mistake, as certainly nothing is so good as plenty of fresh air.

2.45. To the shores of Old England once more. We are off Poole, which is the first point visible; the weather, which has hitherto been bright but with a strong wind, now becomes

The Casquets

cooler; consequently we don our overcoats. 3.30. Catch the first glimpse of the Needles (off the Isle of Wight) for which we have been watching for some time. It seems now that we have some chance of catching the 7.20 train from Southampton, which we hope will be the case, as the next one is at 1.20 a.m. Two large steamers cross our bows, and several ships with all sails set are in sight which, as there is a capital breeze, is a very fine spectacle. The passengers begin to look more cheerful, and the dog gives a bark to show he is still alive.

5 p.m. Make enquiries of one of the officers as to how far he thinks we are from the Needles, and he says that we shall not be there for three quarters of an hour. They really seem close by; when we first saw them the distance must have been quite 26 miles. The captain and mate make a tour among the passengers to solicit for the widows and children of two of their sailors who have lately been killed by accident while discharging their duty. If they do this on every voyage, I should think they would realise a pretty good amount, as no one can well refuse to give, even if they feel so inclined.

5.45. The Needles, behind which on the cliff is a striking resemblance to a woman's head caused by the green grass thereon. The coloured cliffs at Alum Bay look very pretty, but the sun was rapidly disappearing over the horizon, presenting a beautiful spectacle such as is never to be seen when on shore. In passing Hurst Castle, signals are exchanged stating we have on board 71 passengers, 43 of whom are for London; this intelligence is telegraphed to Southampton, where a special train will be put on to convey us to the metropolis. 'The shades of night are falling fast' and it is rather chilly, so some of us take refuge in the cabin and have a chat with the steward.* Lucy, however, is not to be moved from her paddle box till we actually reach Southampton Docks, which event transpires at 7.45. It is now 'every one for himself', and each individual seizes his luggage and makes his or her way to the Custom House. One poor Irishman is quite at a loss as to what he ought to do, so I, on being appealed to, set

* 'The shades of night were falling fast' is the first line of the poem 'Excelsior' (1841) by Henry Wadsworth Longfellow.

him right. He says he has had nothing to eat since yesterday and has been *très malade*. His looks certainly give additional proof to his speech, and may be imagined by anyone who has suffered in like manner.

At the Custom House we are compelled to open our packages to show if there is anything contraband therein. Whilst doing so, a very strong odour of Eau de Cologne impregnates the air, and Charley chuckles at the idea that someone has met with an accident. He is much distressed at finding that it proceeds from the contents of one of his bottles, and the scent has completely saturated some of our linen. It is fortunate it is no worse. This ordeal over, the train is reached and at 8.20 p.m. we are off for London in a very sleepy state. No event worthy of note occurs during the journey until Lucy and Joseph leave us at Clapham Junction, when an affecting farewell takes place. At Waterloo Station another agonising separation is seen, after which Edward procures a cab and rushes home to his wife and the bosom of his family.

It being now within half an hour of the time when ghosts and goblins are supposed to make their appearances – viz, midnight – porters are few and far between. Anxious to be off, and having – to all appearance – secured our portmanteau, we shoulder the same and make the best of our way out of the station. A sudden bright thought all at once electrifies my brother's mind. Says he: 'Just let's have a look if the other bottle of Eau de Cologne is still intact?' No sooner said than done. Down goes the portmanteau and – oh! horrors of horrors! – how shall I describe the sight which meets our gaze: there right before our eyes is 'somebody else's luggage'! In such a momentous moment, what shall be our course of action? The crisis has evidently arrived: shall we strike an attitude and place our right hands where our hearts are supposed to be and exclaim: 'Let us dissemble?' No! Perish the thought! 'Honesty is the best policy': up goes the portmanteau, back we march with hasty strides and soon meet a porter with our property and set matters right. The two articles in question are like twins – label and all – until examined closely, hence the mistake. 'A shilling saved is a shilling earned', so Charley and I act as our own porters and walk the rest of the journey. Crossing Waterloo Bridge, the toll collector refuses to take a Guernsey penny, which proves he is wide awake, especially as I put it head upwards.

12.15 a.m. Ha! Ha! What is the vision which is now slowly revealed to my enraptured sight? Do my eyes deceive me? Am I in the land of dream? Is it the house of bondage? No, rather let me say the home of Freeman. I hesitate a single instant. I agitate the communicator, a brief interval of suspense ensues and then – methinks I see my father? It is without doubt that illustrious individual the great weather oracle. Immediately, we are locked out from the street and in each other's arms, and so ends our trip to Jersey.

What we did not see at Jersey

NORTH DEVON 1874

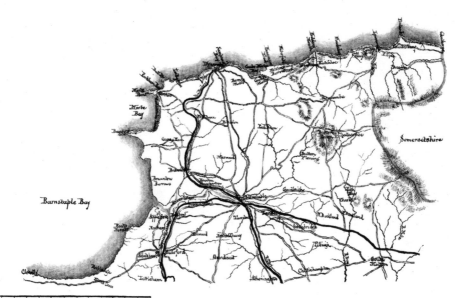

Scale of miles

PROLOGUE

The holidays will soon be here!
Hurrah! Hurrah! 'Tis worth a cheer
From business to be free;
But first of all I must decide
With whom to go (then buy a guide),
Now let's think who it shall be.*

At Balham now the married pair†
Instead of breathing seaside air,
Have other cause for joy;
A great event in June occurred,
Of which perhaps you have not heard,
They had a baby boy!

Who does not yet know A from B
So therefore you will plainly see,
They cannot come away;
Whilst Edward of the Falkner race,
This year must not desert his place
But with his children stay.

Yet stay, there yet doth one remain
Who willing is to go again
To seaside spots with me;
Says he in taking thus his stand:
'I will abide at thy right hand,
'And take a tour with thee.'

'Charley, well said, now for the place
'Which we shall with our presence
   grace,
'Say you the sea?' 'Of course.'
'How shall we go, do you prefer
'To run the risk of mal de mer,
'Or ride the iron horse?'

'Twas thus we held a council long,
Argued the matter pro and con
In quite a learned style,
Till Ilfracombe at last was thought
To be a quiet new resort,
Though distant many a mile.

But just a few short days 'ere we
Had fixed for starting to the sea,
Came Joseph into view;
Said he, my wife don't care to go
Away this year with baby, so
I think I'll come with you.

---

* The 'guide' was a local guide, to be used alongside Bradshaw's handbook for the appropriate part of the country.
† Joseph Freeman and his wife Lucy.

SATURDAY 11 JULY

3.55 a.m. Rose up with the worm. Of course, every intelligent person knows that the lark is a tolerably early riser, but the insect above named – always excepting the slow-worm – must turn out of bed even sooner, or it would not be caught, as we are constantly told it is. I had some difficulty in arousing Joseph as, owing to his very proper desire to leave everything connected with the shop (pardon me, I should have said the 'Regent Street fashionable emporium') in correct order, he had not retired between the sheets more than an hour.* After doing as much justice as possible to an early breakfast provided by Annie we bade 'au revoir' to those who were fated to stay in London town, then Charles and I started off leaving to Joseph the honourable position of rear guard.

5.45 a.m. Great Western railway station; ticket clerk late, general public clamorous. In due time the former arrived, but when I asked to be booked for Ilfracombe to my surprise the answer was: 'You must wait till the 6.45 train'.† Several other persons were caught in the same trap: the timetables were very complicated, so we thought it better to be in time for the first train. Joseph did not see the joke, and thought it hard to have been cheated out of his sleep; however, he retired into a first-class waiting room and indulged in '40 winks'.

6.30 a.m. Purchased the necessary tickets and inspected the conveyance that was to carry us to 'fields fresh and pastures new'.‡ The third-class carriage excited our utmost disgust, being low in height, dirty, badly ventilated and generally fitter for cattle than human beings.§ However, being economically inclined, we supposed we must endure it and took seats accordingly but just as the train was about to start Joseph – who had previously gone on the platform – appeared at the door gesticulating wildly.

* Joseph's 'shop' was at 134 Regent Street, Mayfair, London.
† The Great Western Railway linked London with the south-west and west of England, and much of Wales, from its terminus at Paddington.
‡ 'Fresh fields and pastures new' is a popular misquotation from Milton's elegy *Lycidas* (1638), which closes with the line 'Tomorrow to fresh woods, and pastures new'.
§ From 1844, railway companies were obliged by law to carry third-class passengers at a cost of no more than a penny a mile.

By his directions we immediately made our exit, and the guard put us in a second-class carriage just as the engine began to puff. Four other gentlemen were our companions. Very soon, one of them asked if we had any objection to smoking, to which request of course he received an affirmative reply. Soon after this, three of them went to sleep, so we were tolerably quiet.

7.45 a.m. Reading. Here of course we studied a newspaper and lent the same to our fellow prisoners, so that they might do likewise. 8.50 a.m. Swindon. In consequence of a contract entered into with the refreshment contractor when this line was first made, all trains are compelled to wait here ten minutes. This applies even to expresses, and is felt to be a great inconvenience by many. Promenaded the platform, stretched our legs, surveyed the despised third-class carriages and faintly imagined what it was to be there. Congratulated ourselves accordingly, also administered some palm oil to the guard to cure a slight irritation of the hand, with which he was afflicted.* 9.55 a.m. Bath. Though often requested to go to this city I have never yet had that pleasure. Still, it is well worth seeing, being hilly with many fine churches and trees; altogether a very picturesque place.

10.30 a.m. Bristol. As we had two hours to spare, we strolled through the city to see what was to be seen. The River Avon,

BRADSHAW ON BRISTOL

Bristol is a cathedral city, seaport and parliamentary borough in Gloucestershire, 118 miles from London, on the Great Western Railway and on the Via Julia, or Roman road, made by Julius Agricola, which crossed into Wales at Aust Ferry. The chief manufactures are engines, glass, hats, pottery, soap and brushes; there is a trade in sugar, rum etc. The oldest part of the town is in Temple, Peter and other streets, where picturesque timber houses are seen. There are many buildings worth notice. Population, 154,093.

A TELEGRAPH STATION. HOTELS: THE QUEEN'S HOTEL, CLIFTON HOTEL.

upon which it is built, is crossed by a drawbridge which permits vessels of large size to pass; the streets are not at all imposing, but churches seem to be very numerous and some of them very old, the Temple to wit, which has such an oblique tendency that the bells are not rung for fear of shaking the structure down (this is what we were told). The surrounding houses also appear to suffer from the same malady. In one of the streets is a statue of Neptune erected in 1588 to commemorate the defeat of the Spanish Armada. Past Colston Hall the houses visibly improve and, ascending a hill, we came upon what is called The Park.* Here we surmounted some railings and partook of an 'al fresco' meal on the grass, which was very acceptable. A gentleman took the trouble to inform us that we were trespassing, but it being explained that we were strangers he did not disturb us, upon a promise not to repeat the offence. This is not at all likely, as we may never be in Bristol again.

Returned to the railway station, but half an hour elapsed before we started again on our journey. Clifton, of which a very good sight is obtained from the rail, is a very pretty place with fine houses and trees. Each side of the river being very hilly, it is spanned by a suspension bridge about 240 feet in height, which is partly made of the materials of old Hungerford bridge.† Had we known the train passed here, we should certainly have walked on and inspected it more closely. The breadth of the river at this time was about 30 feet, but at high water it would be quite five times as wide.

1.30 p.m. Portishead. Walked at once to the steamboat which was waiting at the pier and took seats in the front. The decks on these vessels are raised about seven feet above the ordinary ones, affording a capital promenade in fine weather and shelter beneath should it happen to rain. Left Portishead at 2 o'clock with the water as smooth as a mill pond, but afterwards the breeze freshened a little. The scenery along the coast was not very striking, but Clevedon is a nice, neat, cleanly-looking watering place, and here we partook of some provisions which we had

* The Park is likely to have been Tyndall's Park, to the west of the city centre.

† The 'old' Hungerford Bridge was a suspension bridge for pedestrians crossing the River Thames. When it was pulled down in 1860 to make way for the Hungerford Rail Bridge, the chains were reused in the Clifton Suspension Bridge, which opened in 1864.

the forethought to bring, and which someone had impudently labelled 'Thorley's food for cattle'.* Some distance past this – near two islands which stand out in the channel – a steamer appeared, and the helmsman guided the other paddle box onto ours. This did not seem to me a particularly safe operation.

Hereabouts the wind blew rather strongly, the result being that many of the passengers grew meditative and gazed into the water, but as they did not appear to enjoy the sight very much we did not follow their example. Began to be cold, consequently descended to the lower deck. The scenery as we neared our destination was very grand, consisting of lofty hills covered with what seemed to be furze, but which we afterwards discovered to be trees densely studded with foliage.

6.40 p.m. Lynmouth at last: where a boat was awaiting us. As no pier has yet been built here, this mode of landing is necessary but not very popular, especially with ladies. Being modest, we did not expect a public reception, and were consequently rather surprised at seeing many of the inhabitants come out to meet us. There was also a small triumphal arch bearing the words 'Welcome home', and cannon fire. It was said that all this was in honour of one of the neighbouring gentry, but this may be taken for what it is worth.

LYNMOUTH & LYNTON.

BRADSHAW ON LYNTON
AND LYNMOUTH

☞ *The scenery in the neighbourhood of these two places is 'wild and beautiful, magnificent and lovely', to use the words of a handbook of Devon, the writer of which observes that it is quite beyond his powers to attempt a description of the scenery abounding in this fascinating neighbourhood. The accommodations for visitors are pretty nearly equal in each.*

There are in both places lodging houses innumerable. The tourist should proceed to the far-famed Valley of the Rocks on foot, along the Cliff Walk, where the scenery is very fine. The view in the valley is exceedingly grand. The East and West Lyn valleys are very beautiful also, but the tourist should employ a guide to accompany him on his first visit to these and other principal points of attraction in this picturesque neighbourhood.

LYNTON HOTELS: VALLEY OF THE ROCKS HOTEL, CASTLE HOTEL, CROWN INN.

LYNMOUTH: AN EXCELLENT INN CALLED THE LYNDALE HOTEL.

* Charles James Collins was the schoolmaster of the British School in Lynton, according to the *History, Gazetteer and Directory of the County of Devon* (1879).
† William Peake's entry in the same directory reads: 'fishing tackle manufacturer, landscape photographer, and lodgings, 2 Lyncliff Terrace'.

At first we had thought of staying at Lynton, as a certain Mr Collins (the schoolmaster and a Sol-fa-ist) might have been able to accommodate us, but finding he had departed for his holiday Joseph made enquires at the Lyndale Hotel.* Perhaps the proprietors thought we were noblemen or gentlemen with plenty of loose cash; the result of a recapitulation of his tariff was that we beat a hasty retreat, went farther and certainly did not fare worse. After two fruitless enquiries, very comfortable private apartments were secured at No. 2 Lyncliff Terrace (proprietor Mr Peake), where we at once deposited our extensive wardrobes, performed our ablutions, ordered tea to be ready at 8.30 and then strolled to Lynton.† This village is situated midway up a very steep hill – about 900 feet high – and although the walk was rather fatiguing the view made ample amends for the trouble. Opposite were hills equally lofty; below Lynmouth; to the left the sea bathed in the rays of the setting sun, while the sweet scented odours from the luxuriant foliage which here abound on every side perfumed the air. This was doubly enjoyable to us as we had but so lately left smoky London.

Returned to our new abode and, as tea appeared to be all ready, rang in order that the eggs might be boiled. Instead of this, Mrs Peake asked if she should clear away, which idea we most unanimously rejected. Explanation then ensued, and it appeared that she thought we wished for tea at 7.30. Consequently, it had been waiting for us while we had been roving on the Lynton Hills. This was certainly a bad beginning but, being hungry, we soon made short work of that which was before us; butter, milk and eggs were all of the best quality and duly appreciated. Though now past 9 o'clock it was quite light but, feeling tired, we soon retired to rest, being previously informed – regarding tomorrow's dinner – that the famed Lynmouth butcher had disposed of all his joints. Our hostess thought she could procure a 'chick' from the Lyndale Hotel as they were always ready to oblige her; perhaps had they known who it was for they would not have been quite so willing!

SUNDAY 12 JULY

After a delightful and refreshing sleep I awoke at 5.45 but knowing it would be of little use to ask my companions to turn out so early, also feeling rather sleepy myself dozed off again for another hour, when we all dressed and sallied forth to enjoy the pure air.

Lynmouth (pronounced Linmurth) is situated at the junction of the East and West Lyn rivers which here discharge themselves into the sea, and whose waters rushing over the many stones that lie in their beds make a murmuring sound, which can be heard some distance off and which seems at first very like rain falling among trees. On either side are lofty hills; in fact, as far as the eye can reach, there is nothing but hills, not

ENTRANCE TO LYNMOUTH.

bleak and bare or merely grassy, but crowded with vegetation forming beautiful views in every direction. Crossing the bridge by the hotel, we proceeded by a series of winding paths up the opposite hill, which is known as The Torrs; the scenery was very beautiful but not a soul did we meet.

9.15 a.m. Attack on breakfast began and persisted in with much vigour; while this was going on a face appeared at the window, which we eventually ascertained was owned by Mr Peake, who said he had arranged to show a Bristol gentleman over the surrounding country and invited us to come also. Now, we had fully intended to go to the Wesleyan Chapel at Barbrick Mill in the morning, but as our landlord assured us that the afternoon service was generally the better of the two, we decided to reverse our proceedings and accept his offer, as to have a guide is generally much preferable to wandering about by oneself. He descanted on the excellence of the Free Church which he evidently attends; it is mainly supported by a lady of property as the parish church is very ritualistic.* However, we thought we should hardly appreciate the services.

10.20 a.m. The Bristol gentleman – Brightman by name – having appeared on the scene of action, we all proceeded down

* The Free Church of England was founded in 1844 by a number of Low Church clergy and congregations who objected to what they saw as attempts to introduce Roman Catholic dogmas and practice into the Church of England.

VIEW ON THE LYNN NEAR WATERSMEET.

to the Lyn valley following the course of the river. The view is
simply lovely, and on either side is an immense hill, between
which the stream – about 30 feet wide and clear as crystal –
rapidly rushes. Its course is constantly intercepted by huge
boulders of stone forming numberless delightful little cascades,
whirlpools and eddies, and is crossed by several rustic bridges,
the few stretches of level water appearing all the cooler and
cleaner by contrast. Fish also are plainly discernible darting
to and fro, ferns and trees are in rare abundance and the views
at every bend of the river are certainly most enchanting. Several artists were sketching and really they could not well have
chosen a prettier spot. Through this valley we all wended our
way till we reached Watersmeet, which is the name given to a
spot where another river joins the Lyn. Here we overtook two
individuals who seemed to be known by our guide – in fact he

appeared to have formed the acquaintance of nearly every one we met – and they immediately attached themselves to our party, receiving from us the highly appropriate names of Mr and Mrs McShabby!

After this we commenced to ascend the hill, and the higher we went the finer was the view until the whole valley was visible, hill rising behind hill in grand succession, the many tints of green giving a charming effect, while the river was at such a distance beneath that it appeared like a ditch and did not seem to move at all. When we first started from Lynmouth, our guide carried his coat on his arm and, it now being very hot, Joseph and Charles followed his example. A large number of flies pestered us in a very irritating manner, seeming to select the two above named individuals as their special object of torture.

Then we turned our faces homewards across fields and farms, till we were near to Lynmouth, when Mr Peake conducted us down a slope which was exceedingly slippery on account of the dry weather, to a ledge of rock from whence we enjoyed a view up the valley of the West Lyn, which was perfection itself and formed a fitting climax to our morning's ramble. Even Charley said 'he had never seen such beautiful scenery, and that was saying something for he had seen a good deal'. From this point, we rapidly descended and though caught in a shower soon managed to reach Lyncliff Terrace without any damage.

Dinner had been ordered for 1 o'clock but it was quite an hour later before operations were commenced on the aforesaid chick, bacon etc. To this succeeded raspberry and cherry pie accompanied by clotted cream, the sudden and total disappearance of which was – to say the least – remarkable and spoke volumes for the invigorating qualities of the Devonshire air. After one or two smart showers during dinner time, Jupiter Pluvius began to send forth his blessings in the shape of a small thick penetrating rain, which continued all the afternoon and quite prevented us from visiting Barbrick Mill Chapel. However, we employed ourselves by letter writing, after which – having had such a late

* National Schools in England and Wales were established and funded by the National Society for Promoting Religious Education, to provide free schooling for the children of the poor, in accordance with the teachings of the Church of England. British Schools were similar, but funded by the British and Foreign School Society.

† A wide-awake hat was a hat with a low crown and very wide brim, while a billycock was a hard felt hat with a rounded crown, also known as a bowler hat. The latter was devised by London hat-makers William and Thomas Bowler for the politician and soldier William Coke.

‡ Here and elsewhere in the diaries, the brothers are witnessing – and taking part in – the early days of the tourist industry in the United Kingdom.

dinner – we did not feel much inclined for tea. Therefore, as it was not raining quite so heavily we ordered that meal to be ready at 8.30 and then started for Lynton. As may be imagined, the road up the hill was very muddy and not in a favourable state for walking, but we eventually reached the Congregational Chapel, which is a nice, clean-looking edifice, built in the modern style and accommodating about 160 persons. A gentleman standing at the door informed us that the congregation was more numerous in the winter as they were often kept at home by visitors during the season. Joseph asked him if he could oblige us with a tune book, and he kindly volunteered to send a lad for one, requesting to know if we preferred Sol-fa or Old Notation. Of course, we stuck to our colours and chose the former, which when it arrived proved to be a 'Bristol'. According to this individual, Mr Collins is very successful in teaching Sol-fa at the National School; they never had such singing there before.* Mr Clarke – the minister – preached a good practical sermon from the chapter containing the account of the raising of Lazarus; he spoke to us afterwards enquiring if we were engaged in Sunday School or other work for the Great Master. The singing also – led by a harmonium – was very fair for so small a congregation.

Returning, we saw the one active and intelligent policeman who keeps the country in peace and quietness, and who Mrs Peake is quite confident would catch any thief should an anomaly ever appear. This functionary, and in fact all the Devon Constabulary, do not glory in the regulation helmet but wear a low kind of hat something between a 'wide awake' and a 'billy cock', and do not seem to be overburdened with work.† Took a short stroll towards the sea, where perhaps some day will be built a parade. Indeed, we were told that a limited company is about to be started – and what is it people will not subscribe to now-a-days? – in order to make a pier and other fashionable improvements, for at present there is really no promenade where ladies can show their fine dresses and false hair to much advantage.‡

Modern fashions

9 o'clock: Tea, very refreshing. Beautiful sunset and rainbow, hoped all the rain necessary would come down during the night. 10 p.m. Charles and I retired to bed, but Joseph sat up till 12 o'clock writing to his beloved Lucy.

MONDAY 13 JULY

6.15 a.m. Turned out of bed. Heavy showers had fallen during the night but, as it was not actually raining, I walked down to the hotel and endeavoured to make a sketch. Charles soon afterwards favoured me with his company, but Joseph did not put in an appearance till 7.45. Having inspected the barometer – which had risen a trifle – we ascended the Lynton hill, following the course of the West Lyn till near Barbrick Mill, which we did not reach. The roads were exceedingly muddy and, as the journey there was all uphill and returning quite the reverse, it was very tiring. The sun tried to come out and encourage us, but was not at all successful.

After breakfast, I paid Peake a visit at his shop, as he knows the country well and had promised to send us for a long walk. His directions were extremely numerous and to his mind no

LYNDALE HOTEL.

doubt perfectly explicit, but I must confess they were hardly so to mine. I pretended to understand, thinking we should certainly meet someone to direct us, which idea, as will be seen, was hardly borne out by the facts. Met Mr Brightman, who was in great glee on account of the rain, which would he said be very good for the anglers. I did not sympathise with him on this score.

Having laid in a store of provisions to keep the wolf from the door – houses for the refreshment of the inner man are few and far between in this part of the country – we crossed the bridge by the Lyndale Hotel and proceeded up the Countisbury hill. The first thing that attracted our attention was an adder; not a lad working out a sum in simple addition, oh dear no, but a snake! It had shuffled off its mortal coil, so there was no occasion for fears on our part. A man soon after met us and, as he seemed to be inclined to be chatty, we tested his knowledge upon the snake question by asking him the species. To our surprise, he said he was blind and had been so since 1811. Upon Joseph intimating that one would not have thought such was the case from his appearance and general movements, the old man seemed quite offended. Adder bites, he said, were poisonous, but he knew how to cure them merely by saying a few words and applying a certain oil to the wound. Of course, we were anxious to obtain so valuable a secret, but this could only be disclosed to ladies. If

Ladies "keeping" a secret.

bitten, we could ask for Blind Bale, whom everyone knew. This we promised to do, and went on our way rejoicing.

Countisbury is a small village with an ugly church, past which we encountered the McShabby tribe with whom, out of common politeness, we had a short gossip. On reaching the Foreland a rest was enjoyed on the edge of the cliff, which here rises almost precipitously from the sea and commands a splendid view. Small boats below look like insects and even the Ilfracombe steamer, which was coming along, appeared quite insignificant. Notwithstanding the distance, we could hear the paddle wheels quite plainly, and whilst passing we greeted those on board with 'The March of the Men of Harlech', but it met with no response. It must have been audible to them, as Mr McShabby afterwards said he heard us singing 'Hail Smiling Morn' at what must have been a very long way off. As Mr Peake had told me there was no occasion to go all round the Foreland, we crossed a couple of fields with the intention of making a short cut, but had not gone far before a deep ravine covered with furze etc. – at the bottom of which ran a stream – intercepted our path. A council of war was held, and rations issued to the troops, who were provided with a number of boiled eggs and other stores. This finished, we decided to advance or perish in the attempt. After several trials, Charles was successful, but we had by this time nearly lost our way. However an angel in human form, or rather I should say a lady leading a horse, appeared on the scene and kindly put us in the right direction. By this short cut we had wasted nearly an hour, so we resolved for the future to keep to the beaten track as much as possible.

Our route lay along a zigzag park half way up the face of the cliff, which sometimes was covered with trees and formed a most refreshing shade, at others with short grass on which were browsing hundreds of rams. Rabbits were often seen darting from place to place with a celerity and sureness of foot which we much envied. A series of gorges or clines, to which those of the Isle of Wight are pigmies, considerably lengthened the journey, as it was necessary to go two or three hundred yards inland to round each one. Still, the view all along was exceedingly magnificent, the only drawback to which was the flies. These insects stuck to Joseph and Charles in preference to me, which of course showed their wisdom. The latter observed that if in business they would be sure to succeed owing to their perseverance, and scandalously wished for my violoncello with which he thought I could certainly frighten them away.*

4.45 p.m. Glenthorne. This is the residence of the Rev. W. Halliday; it is beautifully surrounded by trees, but far from any other human habitation and I do not think I should care to live in such solitude, especially in winter.† The grounds are open to public inspection, but we had arrived much later than we had anticipated. Enquiring of a man how long it would take us to return to Lynmouth, we were considerably astonished when he answered: 'Well, I think you may get there tonight.' This being the case, we did not visit the garden but commenced to ascend the hill, halting midway to rest ourselves before the return journey and to consume the remainder of the provisions. My two comrades took off their boots so as to obtain as much comfort as possible, and while waiting here a chaise approached containing a clerical-looking gentleman and a very pleasant young lady, so Charles and I made enquiries of the former as to the route. He seemed to think the journey rather a long one, but kindly stopped and gave us full directions in writing, adding as he bade us goodbye: 'And if you have a spare three penny piece, you can put it in the box at Brendon Church, as we are much in want of funds.' This I promised not to forget, and we afterwards ascertained he was the Rev. Wise, the rector of that parish.

5.25 p.m. Turned our backs upon Glenthorne, but had not gone far before we came to the Lodge, opposite which was a white gate. Our director had told me to turn through a gate of this description, but we had our doubts as to this particular one, which were confirmed by the woman of the house. She professed to know a much shorter route, and almost intimated that it was necessary to buy some of her ginger beer in order to unlock the secret. This we did, but her directions were rather foggy, so we determined to keep to our written ones, which in the end proved correct. Going up this carriage road was very tedious, as it is a continual uphill zigzag from Glenthorne to the top of the hill, and is said to be three and a half miles in length.

6.30 p.m. Came to a signpost pointing the traveller to Lynmouth and Brendon respectively. We had meant to take the latter route, but our hearts failed us as we could not tell how long the distance might be, and no one was visible to give the required information. Consequently, we went the shorter way and had not gone far before we saw a man who was trying to lift a barrel of ale into his cart from the side of the road, where another individual had deposited it 'to be left till called for'. We gave him a help up, or I think he would have toppled it over and he might have waited a very long time before any assistance came. The view from here of Brendon valley was surpassingly lovely, consisting of beautiful wooded hills and dales as far as the eye could reach, over which the sun's descending rays cast a glowing golden tint. We could do no less than stop and admire such charming scenery.

After a little more walking, we found ourselves again at Countisbury, where we refreshed our inner man with milk. Not wishing to return by the same road as traversed in the morning, we descended to the valley beneath and followed the course of the Lyn river, travelling over the same ground as yesterday, and arrived at Peake's soon after 8 o'clock.

We had ordered lamb for dinner and, just as there are overgrown boys, so I suppose young sheep are sometimes as big as their fathers. The one that contributed our joint must have been tending that way, or perhaps the sea air makes everything grow extra fast here; it certainly appeared rather large, even for hungry mortals like ourselves. It went away considerably diminished, and eventually proved very useful for sandwiches. Joseph and Charles retired rather early into oblivion, after which Mr Peake came in and chatted upon our day's proceedings. He said – notwithstanding our faux pas – we had had a capital walk and done very well, to which sentiment I heartily agreed and then went to bed at 10.45 p.m.

TUESDAY 14 JULY

6.30 a.m. Emerged from the land of dreams all rather sleepy after yesterday's exertions, and having reclothed ourselves we proceeded to inspect Glenlyn. These beautiful grounds (close to the Lyndale Hotel) are the private property of W. K. Riddell Esq., but are open to the public twice a week. Through them runs the West Lyn river, by the banks of which we walked for nearly a mile when it abruptly ended (as far as these grounds are concerned) by huge rocks, from behind which the water rushed, forming a small cataract. The descent is all along very steep and, as the stream is always pouring towards the sea, one might think it would soon be exhausted, but it is supplied by many rivulets from the hills and is no doubt in winter quite a torrent. The scenery is exceedingly beautiful and well worth a visit.

8.45 a.m. Breakfast. After which we laid in a stock of sandwiches but, just as the time for starting was at hand, it came over very dull and misty and a thick mizzle began to fall.* This state of things continued for some time, much to our discouragement, but not to be idle we sent a letter to the loved ones at home. For want of something better to do, Charley put this piece of intelligence on the envelope. I do not however vouch for its accuracy.

Elderly female (putting her head out of the railway carriage window): Oh! Mr Guard! Mr Guard! What is the matter? Is the train stopping because of an accident?
Guard: Oh it's nothing, old lady; the engine driver was eating winkles and has dropped his pin. He's a-looking after it, and we should go on again as soon as he's found it!

12.15 p.m. As it nearly ceased raining, we sauntered down to the harbour to see if there were any crumbs of comfort regarding the weather. To our great joy the barometer had risen a little and, better still, the coastguardsman said it was sure to be fine before long. The thermometer stood at 82 degrees and a thick white mist overhung all the hills towards the sea, having a very singular appearance. Chatted with Mr Peake and McShabby, who had been for a walk together; the latter was in a tremendous heat and vowed he had had quite enough walking with such a rapid companion. We obtained directions from the former as to the best part of the country to visit, and took care to put everything down on paper so that there might be no mistake this time.

1.40 p.m. Procured a supply of small change, of which people in the country seem to be very destitute. Perhaps they are under the impression that the unlucky tourist – when making a purchase – will say: 'Oh, never mind that trifling amount, it is really of no consequence.' But our financial affairs were managed according to Cocker and not in that fashion. This feat accomplished, we proceeded up by the East Lyn river, shortly after which the sun burst through the clouds and it was gloriously fine during the remainder of the day. Joseph's and Charley's great enjoyment was to throw large stones into the water and watch the splash resulting therefrom; some were so heavy that their

WOODSIDE HOUSE & BRIDGE.

combined efforts could hardly move them. I looked on, as 'there is no accounting for taste'.

At Woodside Bridge, we rested and dined, meeting a party who evidently meant business, as they all – even the ladies – were provided with alpenstocks.* On the bridge Charley left the following memento of our visit: 'Freeman Bros.; Solfaists; Dum spiro cano; While I breathe, I sing.'

3.35 p.m. Started off again, climbing up the bank onto the high road, 'And a very long way, too'. Just past this, we were about to take the wrong path but fortunately saw a board right up in a tree directing us to Brendon. To the left we accordingly turned and mounted a very steep hill, which might truly be called 'Hill Difficulty'.† There was no shade and the sun was blazing in tropical style, so my comrades, thinking that 'desperate diseases require desperate cures', took off their coats, turned up their trousers and generally looked rather disorganised, while every now and then one of us would exclaim: 'Oh! What a day we are having!'

After passing Ashdown, we reached Brendon Church, which had lately been renovated and an account of the expense incurred, with a list of the subscribers thereto, was posted in

BRENDON CHURCH.

the porch, showing a deficit of £88. Mindful of our yesterday's promise, we dropped a small donation into the box wrapped up in the paper of direction written by the rector, after which Charley searched among the tombstones for curious epitaphs while I endeavoured to sketch the church.

5.15 p.m. Started off for Brendon Village, which is a long way from the church, in fact there are hardly any houses near the latter. On the road a lad in a cart asked Joseph if he would like to have a ride, to which he assented, and with me mounted the said vehicle. Charley preferred to keep on terra firma, and I must say I wished I had done the same, as the jolting was really terrible and there being no seat it was necessary either to stand or sit on the side of the cart, both of which were equally unpleasant. The view here down a long stretch of the river was very fine, but a little later we crossed it and bearing away to the left ascended a very high hill, half way up which we rested ourselves and sang 'The Comrades' Song of Hope' and 'Poland'.* At the top were two boys who had evidently been at mischief, as when I pretended to follow them they scampered off as fast as they could. Also an ancient native who opened his mind to us on the subject of rheumatics, which were a great source of trouble to him.

* 'The Comrades' Song of Hope' was written around 1850 by Adolphe-Charles Adam as a chorus for four male voices. It has been arranged for choirs, and remains popular.

† The comet was
'Coggia's Comet',
identified in April
1874 by Jérôme
Eugène Coggia at the
Marseille Observatory.
It could be seen easily
by the naked eye
during June and July,
and its brightness
earned it the name
'the Great Comet of
1874'.

Charley recommended carrying a potato in his trousers pocket; he did not promise to try this remedy, but I should not say a large one would be conducive to rapid walking. Crossed the Countisbury Down, which is 1,100 feet high, and arrived in Lynmouth by 7.50 in time to see the passengers land from the Portishead boat.

As Mr Peake, among his various occupations, sells photographs of the surrounding country, we purchased a few from him as a souvenir of this lovely spot; after which that most necessary dinner rapidly disappeared before our combined attack, and the feat of making a large raspberry pie and cream vanish from human sight was performed with a celerity and completeness worthy of Dr Lynn or Professor Hall.* 10.15 p.m. Retired into private life; very fine night, the comet and stars shining most brilliantly.†

WEDNESDAY 15 JULY

7.10 a.m. Rose up and packed our knapsack and bag together; this done, Charles and I climbed up to Lynton, where we left them to be forwarded per coach to Ilfracombe. The sun began shining very brightly even this early, so we had pleasant anticipations of a good baking later in the day. After a capital breakfast we settled our little 'William'; it was certainly very reasonable, more so than we had expected, and I can confidently recommend anyone coming to Lynmouth to go to No. 2 Lyncliff Terrace.‡ Everything is very comfortable – raspberry pie especially – and as Peake (though he is rather conceited) knows the country well, he can and will give advice as to the best walks, which is a great consideration. Before starting we went down to this individual's shop to obtain full instructions regarding the route to Ilfracombe, but immediately he saw us he exclaimed 'Ah! Run after that man and woman, I have just sent them on and they know all about it!' Now as it was piping hot we were not at all in a running humour, nor did we feel any ardent craving to be with the McShabby tribe (for it was to them he alluded) so declined his offer and he forthwith made a map on a piece of paper for our guidance; after which we took leave of Lynmouth. I can heartily advise any of my friends to visit this charming little spot, which as it is pierless evidently cannot be surpassed.*

* Another pun. The village has no pier (and so is pierless) and, Freeman implies, no competition (and so is peerless).

† Three glee songs for choir singing, from the first part of the 19th century.

10.20 a.m. Instead of going through Lynton to the 'Valley of Rocks', when half way up the hill we turned to the right where a good path leads all along the face of the cliff. Huge masses of rock project overhead, and if they were to roll down what a crash there would be; doubtless someday this will occur. One large clump appeared to us higher than its fellows, so we determined to mount to the top, but almost immediately saw the McShabbys a little way ahead, so concealed ourselves until that danger was past – at any rate for the present – then by careful climbing we reached the summit of our ambition, seated ourselves and viewed the magnificent scenery. On one side many hundred feet below was the sea, and on the other the 'Valley of Rocks'; from the name one would expect to see stones projecting from the earth in all directions, this is only the case at the sides, and the valley itself contains nothing much larger than pebbles.

Being musically inclined, we favoured an audience consisting of three individuals some distance down below with 'Escape from the City', 'Hail Smiling Morn', and 'See our Oars', but, as no signs of approval were shown, descended and continued our journey, passing two rocks known as 'Ragged Jack' and 'Castle Rock'.† The reasons for such names are not very apparent; perhaps it is because they bear no resemblance to either.

BRADSHAW ON THE COUNTRYSIDE AROUND ILFRACOMBE

 The walks in this neighbourhood are very beautiful, and afford delightful excursions and views.

* Imperfectly quoted
from 'The Burial of Sir
Charles Moore after
Corunna' (1817) by
Charles Wolfe.
† Now known as
Woody Bay.
‡ The Battle of
Inkerman was fought
in November 1854,
during the Crimean
War. The allied
armies of the United
Kingdom, France and
the Ottoman Empire
repelled the Imperial
Russian Army.

Several ladies were here amusing themselves by sketching; this seems rather a favourite pastime among the visitors, and certainly there is no lack of subjects. Leaving the sea on our right, we turned a little inland passing Lee Abbey at 12.15 and, soon after, again hove in sight of the redoubtable couple whose room we preferred to their company. McShabby had evidently been gathering ferns, of which he had a basket full on his arm. It would however have shown more wisdom on his part had he collected them on the return journey instead of carrying such a load the whole time:

'Few and short were the words we said,
'And we spoke not at all of sorrow' *

We bade the worthy pair farewell and proceeded in company with a coastguardsman and his dog; this individual seemed rather surprised that we were going via the cliff as it was a distance of quite 20 miles but was nevertheless the best route for scenery. He appeared very proud of his four legged friend, which we were informed was given to him by an Oxford gentleman and his father was head-master there. I have heard of learned dogs but never one to equal this.

1 p.m. Woodabay.† Parted from our companions, who were bound for Martinhoe. The cliff here commences to be well wooded, like the walk to Glenthorne, many thousands of trees being both above and below, in some places so thickly planted that it was quite dark underneath. Passed a bridge named in honour of the Battle of Inkerman, and shortly after a waterfall: what water there was fell from a height of about 20 feet, but in the rainy season it is no doubt quite a little cataract.‡ Ever since we started, the sun had been shining in full power, clouds of mist overhung the hills – in consequence of the heat – and sometimes we were actually above them, this being our first journey in cloudland. The scenery now changed, stones and slag taking the place of verdure. Two things are almost ubiquitous on these

Devonshire hills, viz, stone walls and rams. The first are doubt-less erected instead of hedges to divide property, but it must have been a labour of toil to carry the materials up to such a height. The latter, some of which have splendid horns, find here a first rate pasture and are wonderfully surefooted, standing out on seem-ingly inaccessible crags and running about with no fear of danger.

The path was a very fair one, but the many small stones which had rolled down from above rendered walking rather fatiguing, though doubtless good for boot makers – Mr Pocock to wit. Whilst strolling along and swinging my umbrella a little carelessly, it slipped from my hand and rolled over the edge of the path; most fortunately, as it did not travel far, I was able to reach it. A few more feet and it would hardly have been safe to try as the small loose stones form but a very bad foothold. Of course I could have applied at one of those shops where a bill is always kept in the window to this effect: 'Umbrellas recovered at the shortest notice', but I hardly think the result would have been satisfactory.*

Since parting with the coastguardsman, we had not met a single individual; but one now came in sight appearing to us most unnecessarily laden with an umbrella, stick, two coats and a bag, all of which were on his back. This, he said, steadied him. He did not mind ascending, but in coming downhill the jolting was dreadful. He had just come from Hunter's Inn and showed us the size of a loaf which was there set before him (18 by 10 inches); he also was of the opinion that the sight round the next corner was so magnificent that he felt ready to cry. After a little chat we bade this traveller farewell, and in half an hour were at Heddon's Mouth (2.45 p.m.). Here, finding a crystal stream, we sat down to lunch. Seldom have I more enjoyed my mid-day meal: opposite was a tremendous hill slanting at an angle of about 40 degrees while the sun was shining so brilliantly that the rippling waters at our feet sparkled like diamonds, the whole forming a dining room not to be surpassed, and we felt much more inclined to sing a Te Deum than to cry.

3.30 p.m. Off again past the Hunter's Inn. In answer to our enquiries, a lad gave us the welcome intelligence that there was only one more hill to ascend, after which the road would be pretty straight. When I say that this was Holstone Burrows (1,187 feet high) and that it was a long time before we gained the summit, it certainly does make a difference. Passed through Trentishoe and, as our motto was continually 'Excelsior', I – for the first time – followed my companions' example and amid a general chorus of 'what a day we're having!' doffed my coat and unbuttoned my waistcoat.* Shade there was none, and it was very hot, nevertheless being at such an elevation there was a nice breeze, and the view of the surrounding country was splendid.

5.45 p.m. Combmartin.† Before entering which, we succeeded in obtaining some milk, but only one glass, however we added water *ad libitum* which quenched our thirst equally as well. This village is composed mainly of one street quite a mile and half in length; it has a very fair harbour and church, but the latter we did not have time to inspect. The houses are nearly all whitewashed outside, but good ones appeared scarce. Trade also seemed very flat and, though I offered to make it a little brisker by purchasing for Joseph a splendid red cotton handkerchief with Freemasons' emblematical signs thereon, he declined the same without thanks. The chief production of the place appeared to be children, and not shy ones either, as many of them called out as we passed: 'Please Sir, give me a penny?' When asked, they were totally unable to give any reason why we should be so liberal. The language of the inhabitants is forcible, as may be gathered from the following oratorical effort: 'Be quiet, do! You worrit me out of my life, you dirty little thing: you're like I don't know what!' This we heard addressed by one child to another a few years younger than herself. Joseph seemed half inclined to stay the night, but we decided to adopt the pawnbroker's motto and 'Always keep advancing'. So, after resting a little again, we pushed forward. It was now 7 o'clock and the atmosphere being nice and cool we steamed along in fine style passing Watermouth Castle and

Pleasure for all?

Bay, where a sailor offered to row and a man with three donkeys offered to ride us to our destination, but we said nay to both.

7.40 p.m. Sighted Ilfracombe, and we then had some idea of the Crusaders' joy in beholding Jerusalem.* However, the end was not yet, and it was past 8 o'clock before we fairly entered the town at the 'quick march', creating I think rather a sensation with our puggarees flying and all looking rather fiery about the nasal organ from the sun's burning rays.† Before leaving Lynton, we had asked Mr Peake if he could recommend us to comfortable apartments, and were referred to a certain Mr Catford, a photographer. However on enquiry we found he had no room for visitors, but kindly took us a few doors off where was the very thing we required, here therefore at No. 23 Portland Street we at once took up our abode. The first necessity was to secure our luggage which had been forwarded per coach in the morning, so I went to the booking office and was of course much gratified to find it was closed for the day. So we had to do as others have done under similar circumstances: go without it.

9 o'clock. Tea, which we much enjoyed after our long journey, and two hours after we all went to bed, having written letters etc.

THURSDAY 16 JULY

6.45 a.m. Opened our eyes; all rather sleepy after yesterday's exertions. Having dressed, we proceeded for a short stroll, also to procure our luggage and enquire regarding trains from Bideford

* Christian knights from Europe captured Jerusalem in 1099 during the First Crusade.

† A puggaree is a thin muslin scarf tied round a sun hat or helmet to shield the wearer's neck from the sun.

to Barnstaple, as we intended to visit Clovelly there being an excursion by steamer on the morrow to that place which would suit us capitally. The town of Ilfracombe (pronounced coomb) rather disappointed me; none of the streets are worthy of much mention – the best is the High Street – nor is there an esplanade or houses fronting the sea like unto other favourite marine resorts. However, the inhabitants rejoice in a pier, not a long one but rather belonging to the dumpy species, which forms one side of a capital harbour. Here, the old familiar cry greeted us: 'Boat, Sir! Boat, Sir!' Notwithstanding that it was a splendid morning, we thought 'Breakfast, Sir!' to be more in accordance with our feelings, so acted upon that idea without further delay.

This important matter settled, we paid Mr Catford a visit and asked his advice upon the day's journey, which he gave us gratis. While traversing the High Street we met many specimens of the human race, both male and female, the former endeavouring to shield themselves from the sun's rays by the aid of puggarees, the latter by Dolly Varden hats, which seemed to be much in vogue.* These individuals were doubtlessly going to lounge up and down the Capstone Parade, but this not being in accordance with our ideas of enjoyment, we progressed in an opposite direction and having purchased sundry articles calculated to keep

ILFRACOMBE.

BRADSHAW ON ILFRACOMBE

☞ *Ilfracombe is a considerable seaport town, and now a fashionable watering place, on the north coast of Devon, near the mouth of the Bristol Channel. The harbour is considered the safest and most convenient along the whole coast. It is formed like a natural basin, and is almost surrounded by craggy heights that are overspread with foliage. The town is built partly at the bottom of a steep declivity, and partly up the side of it. New buildings and streets have been built to afford accommodation to visitors. The terraces and public rooms, forming the centre of Coronation Terrace, have been constructed, the hot and cold baths at Crewkhorne have been formed, and a number of new houses erected on the eastern side, commanding an extensive prospect over the town and Bristol Channel to the Welsh coast.*

HOTELS: THE CLARENCE HOTEL, SITUATED AT THE HIGHER END, AND THE BRITANNIA AND PACKET HOTELS, AT THE LOWER END OF THE TOWN. THERE IS A BOARDING HOUSE ON THE QUAY, AND EXCELLENT PRIVATE LODGINGS IN EVERY PART OF THE TOWN.

us from starving, arrived at Trinity Church by 11.20 a.m. This is the parish church, and in the graveyard are two slabs of slate bearing an inscription concerning the names and ages of six natives who have lived more than 100 years which, I suppose, is intended to impress the reader with favourable ideas regarding the healthiness of the locality.

Leaving Trinity, we had the pleasure of toiling up a very steep hill under the rays of a burning sun, which were however tempered by a beautiful breeze; after walking some distance we met two tourists coming from Lee. Of course, we all said: 'Isn't it hot?' This led to a conversation regarding each other's doings. Happening to mention Clovelly, they expressed a wish to go there in a yacht, if a few companions – ourselves for instance – could be found to share the expense, as that was a much pleasanter mode of transit than the steamer, which was a rickety, slow sailing boat. This we promised to think over, and to let them know the result of our mediations.

1.20 p.m. Lee Bay. This is a small sandy cove surrounded by rocks. Those whom we had just left informed us that better bathing was to be had the other side of the bay; we asked a yokel if such were the case and, receiving an affirmative reply, ascended a hill in search of this desideratum. The sun was hereabouts excessively hot, so much so that sheep were to be seen extended in layers side by side under the shade of the hedge, presenting a curious spectacle, whilst pigs did not seem able to move.

2.30 p.m. After having transferred some of our provisions from the outside to the inside of our waistcoats and rested awhile, we proceeded farther and certainly fared much worse. Perceiving a road which apparently led to the sea, we followed it till – much to our delight – it came to an abrupt termination in a field. Nothing daunted, we went straight ahead surmounting hedges and like obstacles till the point of our ambition was reached. Here certainly was the sea, but its bottom was so rocky that bathing was quite out of the question, so we proceeded to scramble over the rocks in the hope of something better. A singular phenomenon is here to be seen, viz – thousands of thin slatey stones a few inches in length wedged together sideways by the sea, as closely and evenly as if they had been deposited there by hand. The farther we went, the more difficult was it to advance, till at last we not only came to a standstill but – as the tide was advancing – were compelled ingloriously to retreat; the only point gained by this procedure was that Charley slipped into a pool of water and probably cooled himself, though he hardly seemed to appreciate it.

Our scattered forces having reassembled, we refreshed ourselves at a running stream, in which Joseph – like a wise man – laid the flask in order to cool it. The only visible result was that the top came off. I do not think any of us were ever so thirsty as during this holiday; we really resembled three walking sponges, and though it is said 'One swallow does not make a summer', I am sure a hot summer makes one swallow. The question now was how to get back again. Road there was none, so up we went over hedges, ditches and cornfields till a certain signpost in the high road was reached, which we had passed two hours and a half before. During this time I can hardly say we had made much real progress.

As it was now 4 o'clock, we held a consultation and determined that our intended trip to Woolacombe Sands could not be performed, especially as we much wished to have a bathe. We therefore cried 'peccavi' and were soon back again at Lee Bay.* Here, in a very short space of time, off came our coats and into the sea went our bodies. The bottom was sandy, the water smooth and we enjoyed it all the better because of our previous exertions. In saying we, exception must of course be taken to Charles: I had thought that under the circumstances even he would try a plunge, but no, he was not to be persuaded even though I offered him the first wipe of the towel. Joseph averred he had never had such a lovely dip in his life, and I think I may say the same.

5 p.m. Turned our backs towards the sea and our faces in the direction of Lee village, which is a little distance inland. The principal and indeed only object of attention here is the church, which is famous for its ritualistic services.† It will only seat about 90 persons, but makes a grand show of stained glass, flags

* 'Peccavi' is an admission of guilt or sin, from the Latin word meaning 'I have sinned'.

† St Matthew's Parish Church, built in 1833 in the Early English style of Gothic architecture. The organ, by Dicker of Essex, was added in 1867.

LEE CHURCH & SCHOOL.

* 'Forgive, blest
shade' is a hymn
composed in 1795 by
John Wall Callcott.

† 'O Father whose
almighty power'
is a chorus from
the oratorio *Judas
Maccabaeus* (1746)
by George Frederick
Handel. It was
dedicated to the
Duke of Cumberland
and his victory at the
Battle of Culloden in
April 1746. 'Cuius
Animam' is the
second movement of
the devotional work
Stabat Mater (1841)
by Gioacchino Rossini.

‡ Those who
buy shares in the
expectation of a price
rise were (and are)
called bulls. John was
evidently concerned
that the cow was,
in a similar manner,
considering giving him
a 'rise' high off the
ground.

§ William Gammon
ran the 'hairdresser
and fancy repository'
at 6 High Street,
Ilfracombe. One
meaning of the
word gammon (now
outmoded) is flattering
talk intended to
persuade someone
to act in a way that
benefits the talker.

and a crucifix, also some of the old wood carving is well worth an
inspection. Hearing strains from within of 'Forgive, blest shade'
– the very mention of the last word was inviting – and finding
the door open, we entered and saw a young girl practising at
the organ, while the servant was blowing the bellows.* Charley,
of course, was quite in his element and, though not generally
considered a ladies man, he made friends with the performer,
who played several more pieces under his superintendence
among which were: 'O Father whose almighty power' and 'Cuius
Animam'.† Meanwhile I endeavoured to transfer the church to
paper, and if it is not considered good, please attribute it to the
following fact: a cow was behind me dining off the grass and the
more she ate the nearer she approached until I began to fear she
might be 'speculating for a rise'.‡ However she eventually turned
tail and thus relieved my mind.

On the return journey nothing worth noting happened and
Ilfracombe was safely reached by 8.15. It is not often that a man's
name is appropriate to his trade, but one individual of this town
– a hairdresser – rejoices in the cognomen of Gammon.§ What
could be more suitable? Of course, he attends principally on
ladies. On arriving at No. 23 we were glad to find dinner ready.
The bill of fare was as follows: Lamb, peas and potatoes, followed
by raspberry pie and clotted cream. Whether our landlady (Mrs
Haynes) thought we were Irish or not I cannot say, but she put
no less than 20 specimens of the last named vegetable before us.

10 p.m. Retired to our bed chamber and were soon fast asleep.

FRIDAY 17 JULY

6.45 a.m. Turned out of bed and after the usual daily performance with the soap and flannel, I visited the Post Office in search
of letters, whilst Joseph and Charles went to make arrangements
with the visitors whom we met yesterday as we had decided –
wind and weather permitting – to venture to Clovelly in a yacht.

After breakfast we put a few necessary things in our knapsack, purchased some provisions for the voyage and then marched down to the pier. Here we had appointed to meet at 9 o'clock, but neither our fellow travellers nor the yacht were in sight; the latter however soon appeared and we were taken to her in a row boat. As there was nothing else to do, I proceeded to cook our accounts for, be it understood, we shared our riches in common, Charles being treasurer, I cashier and Joseph supervisor or grumbler in general, though I must say he did not avail himself much of his privilege and – though 'too many cooks' is said to be a bad thing – our cash was always correct to the penny.

9.30 a.m. The two truants at last appeared, and we set sail without further delay. The yacht was about 25 feet long by six wide; not very large, but easily managed by one sailor – a sun-burnt fellow named Ben – who was well up to his business. Of our companions (we did not ascertain their names) one was dark and the other fair, and the latter immediately informed us that he had never been sea-sick but wished to feel the sensation, therefore had partaken of a very hearty breakfast consisting of mushrooms, eggs, boiled fish, melted butter and other slight et ceteras, so as to be generous if Father Neptune should call for his dues. I doubt the sincerity of this device, but still I only judge by my own feelings, which were quite the other way.

It was a beautiful morning, and though the sun was hot as usual, there was a fair breeze which sent us along capitally. Ben complained of the badness of the season (all sailors do this) but thought the new railroad would be an improvement, because when visitors come by water from Lynmouth and are ill during the passage, they are afraid to venture on the sea again, while if the journey were all by land they would feel bound to have at least one row or sail. He also said he once saved one of his mates who had fallen into the seas during a gale by catching hold of his hair, and had himself tumbled or been washed overboard on eight different occasions, yet could not swim a single stroke.

At Lee we noted the flagstaff, and plainly saw that it was as well that we turned back when we did, as there was no way round the rocks. Near Morte Point, Ben threw out a line to see if there were any flat fish about. As they did not appear, our fair friend said perhaps it would be better if he put his breakfast overboard, and in the most business-like manner put his fingers down his throat, with the wished-for result. He seemed rather to enjoy it than otherwise, and recapitulated the various articles as they appeared. Opposite Baggy Point a large number of gulls surrounded us, swimming and making a chattering noise; and shortly afterwards a gurnet was hauled on board.* It was 10 inches long, jumped about in a very lively manner and took 20 minutes to die, gasping for breath in a manner very painful to see.

12.30 p.m. The wind freshened a little, and we speculated among ourselves as to whether we should arrive at our journey's end before the steamer; Ben said that unless 20 persons appeared she would not start, so were glad we had not waited for her. After catching a herring, which made much less fuss about dying than the gurnet, a good wind took us along at a fine pace and after a capital voyage we arrived at our destination about 2 o'clock, having all enjoyed ourselves amazingly. The yacht could not run aground as the coast is extremely rocky, so we landed by means of a small boat at a charge of sixpence each;

CLOVELLY — FROM THE SEA.

this is not so bad for the boatmen, as half an hour afterwards the 'Prince of Wales' came in with about 50 passengers, who each had to pay the same fee.

Until lately, the New Inn was the only place of accommodation in Clovelly, but Ben recommended us to visit the Red Lion, which is managed by an old sea-captain on a more reasonable tariff; this we accordingly did and at once secured beds, in (which proved to be) the only spare room. After a little rest, we proceeded to see this remarkable little spot, said to have formerly been a resort for smugglers. The houses are very clean, and surrounded by trees, but the great curiosity is the extraordinary angle at which they are built: the single street is formed of 236 steps a yard in length and 80 ordinary ones. The incline is about one in four or five, and as the roadway is paved with round stones from the seashore, one may judge what it is to take a stroll to the top of the village. Here we parted from our fellow voyagers, as they intended to return in the yacht and therefore had not much time to spare.

All the adjoining country belongs to the executors of a certain Colonel Fane, who in return for a view of the grounds exact tribute from visitors – I suppose the natives pass free.* On the entrance gate, it is stated that all profits are given to charitable objects, but this seemed to be discredited by the excursionists, many of whom paid their sixpence and passed on. Their time was extremely limited, and we were highly amused at seeing them toil along in a state of profuse perspiration, fearing lest the steamer might start without them.

The scenery here is well wooded and very pretty, but the main object of our search was the Gallantry Bower, which is a species of summer house erected on the verge of a precipice 387 feet high, commanding a grand view of the cliffs for some distance. Joseph and I having discovered this, we called to Charles in order that he might come and share the prospect, but received a reply that he had found the true bower, and notwithstanding all our assertions he was not to be moved, imagining that it was

* Lieutenant-Colonel Henry Edward Hamlyn-Fane, a soldier and Conservative MP, became the owner of Clovelly Court when he married Susan Hester in 1850, and died in 1868.

a hoax. However he was too sharp for once, so, as he would not come to us, we went to him and there found another little rustic house overlooking a spot known as The Wilderness. This is an ironical name, as it is a valley luxuriant with verdure which, as the sun was shining brightly upon the various tints of green, formed an exceedingly pretty sight. Visitors appear to have felt compelled to inscribe their thoughts on the wall of the bower after this fashion: 'Do not visit The Falcon at Bude or your blood will be sucked', 'The landlord's language at The Taunton in Bideford is forcible but very unparliamentary'. Here we demolished our provisions, after which my younger brother neatly tied a block of wood in the paper which had contained them, and put a memorandum inside with these words written thereon: 'Please tie this up for the next stupid.' It looked exactly as if someone had left their dinner behind, and we only wished we could have been present to witness the finder's pleasure at its contents. Turning a little inland, we obtained some milk at a farm house and soon after came to Clovelly Church, which is rather remarkable for one thing: nearly all the tombstones are made of black slate, which has a very sombre appearance. The following inscriptions which I copied down do not speak very well for the native poet, whoever he may have been. The first seems rather extraordinary, as people do not generally compose verse at the early age of two years; nevertheless, here it is:

'Think not that youth will keep you free
For death at 21 months called off we.'

The next is rather quaint but contains some good thoughts:

'Yee mortal friends that here on Earth abide
'Grieve not for us who here in Dust are laid
'Our Glasses were run we could no longer stay
'Our Saviour call'd and we made haste away
'The Graves which next may open may be yours

'Therefore ye standers-by that look here on this
'Repent amend you sinfull lives what is amiss.'

Meeting one of the inhabitants, we fell into conversation with him. He expressed his opinion that it was an imposition to charge so much to go in the late Colonel Fane's grounds and told us we could easily enter The Hobby from the top of the village without paying.

8 p.m. Back again at the Red Lion, quite ready for our tea-dinner, which returned the compliment. I can recommend the Clovelly fish – judging from the specimens submitted for our approval – as excellent, and the tea was so strong that eight lumps of sugar were requisite to sweeten a single cup; altogether I am inclined to think we had a capital meal. Now a word about our inn, which certainly has abundance of sea breezes as the waves almost wash its walls. The present proprietor being an ex-captain, some of the furniture is rather curious, consisting of various articles which doubtless he brought from foreign lands; also, the pictures are more celebrated for their elaborate colour than artistic effect. Everything is very clean, in fact so much so that we had our meals off the floor; that is to say we did not have them on it. While last and not least the charges are extremely moderate, though at the New Inn – according to all we heard – the tariff is (to speak mildly) rather exorbitant. Wrote home with the Clovelly penholder, in which is a piece of glass about the size of a small pea, on looking through which a miniature view of the village is seen. I am not aware however that this improved the letter.

10.45 p.m. Retired to a state of somnolence.

SATURDAY | 8 JULY

6.30 a.m. Turned out of bed after a rather restless sleep, caused by an energetic cockerel who began practising voice exercises before it was light, and after, too. 7.15 a.m. Strolled up to the

CLOVELLY.

top of the village, of which I tried to make a sketch; Joseph and Charles soon after joined me but we did not venture far. While returning we were startled by cries of 'Papa! Papa! Oh! Oh!' and then a voice replied 'I'm a-coming.' This was repeated several times till we began to think: 'Well, here is a model father who is determined not to spoil his child by neglecting the rod, and his tender feelings for his offspring seem to have made the latter feel very tender!' Great was our surprise at finding that all this commotion was made by a parrot; on seeing us, it was with difficulty he could be induced to repeat the cry, but favoured us by imitating the bark of a dog.

8.40 a.m. Breakfast. Fish again, very good; which, having settled together with the bill, we took our departure at 10.15 after a good discussion as to who should have the honour of carrying the knapsack up the 'tremendous steep'. It must be very difficult to walk here during the winter when it is slippery and, however pleasant it may be as a holiday resort, a continual residence might modify that opinion as the nearest good doctor lives seven miles off; there is a medical man at about half that distance, but perhaps he would be as likely to kill as cure his patient. On reaching the top of Clovelly, instead of turning to the right we proceeded over the brow of the hill, and thus reached what is termed 'The Hobby'; through these grounds winds a carriage road, both sides of which are thickly studded with trees. The foliage affords a most refreshing shade, whilst deep ravines every now and then break up the sight; altogether it is a most delightful spot.

We had not gone far before Charley, hearing the flask shake in the knapsack, asked me to see if it were all right. In doing so, I unfortunately held it by the top which, being loose, remained in my hand, while the flask itself fell to the ground cracked in many places and quite useless. But it was not of much use after all, as we passed running streams almost as often as we wished to slake our thirst. After a pleasant walk of about three miles along The Hobby we came to the high road (11.40), and another mile further is Horns Cross, where we rested. As there was very little shade it was exceedingly hot, so much so that the tar on the telegraph posts was quite soft. We didn't meet many persons, but the occupants of a brake which we passed must have thought we took our pleasures in rather a remarkable manner.* Notwithstanding the heat, Joseph was great at carrying the knapsack, and in fact seemed to walk rather better with than without it. Made enquiries for a farm house where milk could be obtained, but the yokels stared at us stupidly – as if we were monsters they had never seen the like of before – and said 'Dunno, Zur!' Eventually success crowned our efforts, when we lunched.

* A brake was a large wagonette, which is a four-wheeled carriage for six or eight people.

Devonshire lad (when asked for information) "Dunno 'Zur!'"

BRADSHAW ON BIDEFORD

This is a small municipal borough, containing a population of 5,742, chiefly employed in shipbuilding, the manufacture of sail-cloth, cordage, pottery and bone lace. It has a free grammar school, of which Z. Mudge, a native, was the master.

A TELEGRAPH STATION. HOTEL: THE COMMERCIAL HOTEL.

3.30 p.m. Bideford. On our entry into this town it seemed almost deserted, and we began speculating as to whether the inhabitants were baked up by the intense heat. Meeting one or two boys, we asked them what made it so hot but they only stared at us with open mouths. However, on reaching the High Street things did seem a little livelier. The town may be praised for its general cleanliness and can boast of a capital river – the Torridge – crossed by a bridge with 23 arches, the foundation of which is said to have been laid by angels. The *tout ensemble* here is very pretty and would make a capital landscape. The church is certainly the finest we saw in Devonshire; the original one was erected in the 14th century, but has lately been pulled down and rebuilt as near as possible in the old style, and will seat about 2,000 persons. In the churchyard adjoining, the ancient tombstones are placed side by side against the wall, which gives it rather a singular appearance.

4.40 p.m. Started from Bideford by rail, passing Instow and Appledore on the road. The heat was certainly a thing to be remembered, and everyone on entering the carriage made some remark about the weather. After a pleasant ride, we arrived at Barnstaple by 5 o'clock. There was nearly an hour to spare, so we left the knapsack at the station and strolled through the town, which is large and clean with many good shops, especially in the High Street. Our principal object was to search for a dairy, as we were very thirsty. After finding one which had not a drop of milk, we were more successful in a second attempt, and rather astonished the woman in charge by emptying two glasses apiece in very quick time. Then, having bought some refreshments to keep away hunger, made the best of our way back to the railway station, where we looked for three seats on the coach. I forgot to say that one of the shops in the town was closed on account of the annual 'wayzgoose'.* No explanation was offered as to whether this bird was of a ferocious species or not, but we did not meet it, which was a cause for congratulation.

The train from London was due at 5.50, but was very much behind time, and fully an hour elapsed before we started. As the new rail was to be opened on the following Tuesday, this was the last coach that would run from Barnstaple to Ilfracombe, and therefore was looked upon with some interest by the inhabitants.† We had a full complement of passengers, and the luggage was piled on the top at a dangerous height, while the rapid manner in which we were driven along did not add at all to its safety. After our morning's walk, the drive in the cool evening was very pleasant. The scenery was rather confined as the route lay in a valley nearly all the way. Halted midway at Fry's Hotel

* A wayzgoose was an annual social outing organised by a club or organisation (originally by a master printer for his apprentices and workmen).
† The Ilfracombe branch of the London and South Western Railway was officially opened on Monday, 20 July 1874, and extended the line from Barnstaple to Ilfracombe.

BRADSHAW ON BARNSTAPLE

This seaport town is situated on the River Taw, which is crossed by a bridge of 16 arches. It first became a chartered town in the reign of Edward I, and was formerly surrounded by walls and defended by a castle. It had also the privilege of a city and a harbour. The streets are well paved, and the houses built of stone. The principal manufactures are baise [a thin woollen cloth] and woollens, chiefly for the Plymouth market. It has also a trade in bobbin net [machine-made cotton netting], paper, pottery, tanning, malt and shipbuilding. Its population is 10,743.

A TELEGRAPH STATION. HOTELS: THE FORTESCUE ARMS, THE GOLDEN LION.

where the horses were scraped down very unceremoniously, and some of the passengers felt compelled to descend for beer.

On reaching Ilfracombe, as we were going at a rattling pace, a donkey walked from the side of the road in between our four horses, and for the moment it seemed as if he would at least be severely injured, but somehow he extricated himself and did not seem to be at all agitated or any the worse for the adventure. Our driver was in a great rage with the poor animal, and used the language the reverse of parliamentary, which he repeated on our leaving the coach because I did not 'tip' him sufficiently; declaring with an oath that we should not have had such good seats had he known it. I suppose as it was his last drive on this route he thought everyone ought to remember him handsomely. What for I cannot say; we certainly had no reason to be thankful to him. This system of giving gratuities is a very bad one; if necessary it should be included in the fares and then one would know what there really was to pay. It was 9 o'clock before we gained our apartments and dinner, after which we did not go out. Mr Catford informed us that swarms of visitors had arrived during the day and many had difficulty in securing shelter.

SUNDAY 19 JULY

As we intended to go some little distance to chapel in the morning were lazy and did not rise till late. After breakfast – 9.30 – we started off for Berrynarbor, where Mr Catford said was a chapel, and we thought we should like to see a rural service in all its simplicity. Near to the Hele turnpike turned right and plodded along an exceedingly dusty road, which was not improved by the fact that the sun was blazing in truly tropical style, so we adopted the coat-off, waistcoat-unbuttoned, trousers-turned-up costume, which did not look very much as if we were going to a place of worship. Just fancy walking to Soho in this style, would not the good people – Mr Jeffreys to wit – open their eyes in astonishment?* Under the circumstances it seemed to me that the most suitable tunes for the morning's service would be Blaizemoor, Cookham or Burnham.†

After an hour's travel we came in sight of the village of Berrynarbor. It is on a hill and looks very picturesque in the distance, with the church, which has the highest and finest steeple hereabouts, standing out in bold relief. As we had not been able to obtain any definite information whether a service was actually held at the chapel during the morning or not, we enquired of the natives respecting the same but without any good resulting, as they gave contrary replies. Had we asked where was the public house and at what time it opened, I rather think there would have been no difficulty in obtaining a reply. In due time we arrived in the village and, being shown the Dissenting Conventicle, opened the door and walked in.‡ It was quite deserted and, even if service had been held there, I think I should have felt inclined to beat a retreat, for a more disreputable place – for God's house – it has never been my lot to see. Beyond the bare walls, a few plain pews and half a dozen hymn books and bibles, there was nothing else in the place; added to this, it was damp and smelt quite unpleasantly, so we were glad once again to get into pure air.

The bells were now calling the Berrynarborites to church, so – it was 'Hobson's choice' – into that edifice we went and there seated ourselves.§ The service was by no means lengthy, the minister's discourse – from Romans, chapter 6, verse 23: 'The gift of God through Jesus Christ our Lord' – only lasting 15 minutes. What he said was very good, but that earnestness which goes so far in impressing a congregation was lacking. I strongly suspect it was a bought sermon, but perhaps I may be prejudiced.¶

The church is an ancient structure with high and exceedingly uncomfortable pews, though the squire's was very large and square with a fireplace and looked as if made to go to sleep in, and otherwise escape the minister's observation. Just above

* The Soho Chapel, specifically, where the brothers usually attend church, and not the London district. Mr Jeffreys was evidently a leading figure.
† Three hymn tunes in the Dissenting tradition.
‡ Dissenting Conventicles were secret or unauthorised meetings of Dissenters in the 16th and 17th centuries. By John's time, an archaic phrase for a Nonconformist church.
§ Hobson's choice, meaning 'take it or leave it', was no choice at all.
¶ Ministers could buy ready-made sermons from ecclesiastical publishers.

the backs of the seats appeared the upper portion of the heads of the congregation, many of whom placed their hats where the pews joined in the middle of the church, so that there was a very fine collection of ancient and by no means fashionable head-gear, which certainly did not add beauty to the scene. About 100 people were present and the singing led by a choir and harmonium was – for a country village – very fair.

Returned to town by way of Watermouth. At first it was delightfully cool because shady, but afterwards we were obliged to travel along the dusty high road, when quite the reverse was the case. Reached Portland Street by 2 p.m. A mid-day dinner did not seem to suit us – I suppose our appetites were not so good – though lamb, peas, raspberry tart, cream etc. were all first rate. However, four decanters of water disappeared and we kept the maid in a constant state of agitation by the cry of 'More water please!'

Sunday being a day of rest, likewise on this particular occasion a day of heat, we did not feel inclined for a long walk, therefore about 4 o'clock Charles and I strolled to the famous Capstone Parade, where Joseph – after writing a letter – joined

THE CAPSTONE PARADE.

us. This is a promenade cut out of the solid rock, along which plenty of seats are provided for those who prefer to rest. The shady parts are beautifully cool, while below the sea dashes on the huge boulders; this, when it is rough, must be a fine sight. A box is placed at the end of the parade to receive donations towards the expenses that are necessary for repairs etc., and a request is made that visitors would take notice of the same. This they can hardly help doing as the seat close by is generally conspicuous for having no one on it; perhaps it is because non-subscribers' consciences will not let them rest.

The top of the hill was formerly a coastguard station. Here, a fine view is obtainable of the 'Lantern of Rock', the town and hotel; the former is surmounted by the remains of a chapel now used as a lighthouse (see sketch made on Thursday).* The latter is close at hand and is certainly a very fine building; it also seemed to be well patronised by visitors.

6 p.m. Made our way to the Baptist Chapel in High Street. When we entered – though close upon the proper time for commencing service – very few people were there, but afterwards the number swelled to near 150, which was about half the number the place would hold. The text was from Mark, chapter 4, verse 38: 'Master, carest thou not that we perish?' Here again there seemed a lack of earnestness in the preacher, though the matter was certainly good, as was also the singing led by a harmonium. A 'Bristol' was lent to us and we did our best to fill in the 'parts'. Afterwards, a collection was made in aid of the funds of the National Schools; this was also the case at nearly all the other places of worship in the town. Service concluded, we again visited the Capstone Parade and found that – figuratively speaking – all Ilfracombe was there; not a seat was unoccupied, and there are not a few. The rocks below and hill above were also covered with people, many of whom were Welsh, indeed their jargon was so conspicuous that it seemed almost like another 'competition day'.† This is to be accounted for by the fact that – Wales being only just across the channel – many of the inhabitants come

* The Clarence Hotel stood at the higher part of the town. John's sketch appears on page 98.

† The competition in question was a Welsh choir contest, which would have seen a number of choirs and their followers congregating in one small town, all speaking Welsh.

over on Saturday and stay until the following Monday. It was a beautiful evening and we promenaded till dark, then went to our apartment and soon after to bed, which event happened at 9.40 p.m.

MONDAY 20 JULY

5 a.m. Awoke and thought it rather too early to turn out, but did so three quarters of an hour later when, having dressed, Joseph and I proceeded to the railway station to see the first train of the new line start to Barnstaple. This event took place at 6.35 amidst the cheers of about 250 people. The gradient of the rail is steep, two locomotives being required to draw 12 carriages. The Ilfracombites seem to think that this new venture will bring them prosperity, but many travellers will still prefer the Bristol route.

Dream of the Ilfracombe Railway directors

After waiting some time, Charley joined us: he had chosen for his motto this morning 'A little more sleep and a little more slumber'. Then we all proceeded by a very circuitous route to The Torrs, which is a series of zigzag paths cut on the face of seven hills, where generally a capital view can be obtained. On this particular morning, a thick sea mist was rising from below so we did not benefit much in that manner. One penny is charged for admission, but as it is some distance from the town I should not think sufficient money was taken to pay interest on the sum expended in making the paths. It is proposed to build houses on a portion of the estate, though it is not every one who would care to live where there is hardly any level ground.

9.15 a.m. Breakfast, the digestion of which was aided by letters from home; these resembled angels' visits, being few and far between. Having rested a little, we started to make a second journey to Woolacombe Sands. The town was in an active state of festivity in anticipation of the celebrations in honour of the new railway on the morrow. Triumphal arches, flags and mottoes adorned the streets. One enterprising individual had hung a wooden horse above the word 'superseded', thus indicating that the coach was a thing of the past.

Passing down High Street and by Trinity Church – the pews of which (according to the guide book) were formerly seven feet high; if this is a fact the minister and congregation could have seen but very little of each other – we reached the Old Barnstaple Road then turned inland, where Mr Sol began to repeat his usual attentions.* As it seemed rather monotonous to be always saying 'Isn't it hot?', Joseph and Charles asked one or two persons if they had seen any ice or snow lately, but they only smiled grimly.

1.20 p.m. Lee. Here, seeing a notice that milk was obtainable, we entered a dairy and regaled ourselves, inspected the stock of cream etc. Joseph wished to know what they did when the supply of milk ran short during dry seasons like the present, and was glad to hear that the pigs went without instead of the human race. Having – for a consideration – borrowed a towel at a little house by the head of the bay, which we did not know of the other day, Joseph and I had a capital bathe on the sands.

3 p.m. Started off from Lee at a pretty good pace, which was nothing to that of a postman we met, who evidently did not stop to look at the surrounding scenery. The sky hereabouts came over

* *Pifferari* were shepherds from Calabria who played bagpipes (*pifferi*) in Rome each Christmas, to supplement their income.

rather cloudy, and looked so much like rain, that Charles half wished to return, but we did not see the good of going so far for no purpose, so pressed on over a rather broken country till 4.45 when Morthoe was reached. Excursionists were apparently visiting this spot, as there were five brakes waiting which certainly could not belong to so small a place. Looking seawards, on the right is the Morte Stone, which has proved fatal to many a mariner. There is a legend to the effect that it can only be removed by a number of wives who hold undisputed sway over their husbands; this I am afraid cannot be true, or the rock would have disappeared long since. To the left are the famous Woolacombe Sands; the first part consists of very small shells, but the second and by far the larger is a splendid stretch of sand about two miles in length which pleased the eye all the more by contrast with the rocky coast which we had hitherto seen so constantly.

Returned by a different route which formed one long hill; the first mile and a half was all ascent, then level for some time and the remainder downhill. Short showers fell several times, and we were obliged to take shelter more than once, which delayed us, so we did not reach Ilfracombe till 8.20. Were told that 900 people visited the place today by means of the new rail, and the town was in a state of glorious excitement. Minstrels and others, who generally assist at sea-side festivals there, even those illustrious musical foreigners the Pifferari whose strains – I say 'strains' advisedly – are only equalled by the sweet enchanting melody of the bagpipes when played by . . . *

THIS POST WAS ERECTED BY THE DUKE OF ARGYLE

a Scotchman

TUESDAY 21 JULY

For some reason unknown we seemed very tired, so did not rise till after 7 a.m. when we found it had rained a little during the night but only sufficiently to lay the dust. We had spoken to Mr Catford several times regarding the advisability of taking a photographic group of our noble selves, so having appointed to visit his studios at 10 o'clock, there we accordingly went.* Various were the ideas as to the best position in which to arrange ourselves, and Mr Catford was a considerable time posing us, Joseph's legs being a great obstacle and much in the way. However, by the aid of a country scene – which rolled down on a blind – and rustic stile we were at last formed into a group. Then came the much vexed question: 'Whether it would be better to smile or look serious?' Charley, determined it should not be the latter, narrated a short history of two men, one of whom was so short he was compelled to ascend a ladder in order to tie his boots, while the other was so tall that he was obliged to go down into the cellar to cut his corns. By this time the command was: 'Steady now gentlemen! Don't move please just for a second or two! Thank you, that will do!' And it was all over; the result may be seen below. Mr Catford is a pleasant fellow with rather a dry manner, and from what we saw of his artistic work, I do not think that anyone visiting Ilfracombe and wishing to have their photograph taken can do better than pay him a visit.

Bade our photographic friend good morning and proceeded to view the town, which was quite *en fête*; most of the shops were closed, trees planted and refreshment stalls erected in the High Street. Also five members of the Devon Constabulary – all active and intelligent of course – were especially retained to keep order, while a brass band marched through the streets playing 'Let the hills resound' to the great delight of the mobocracy.† A grand procession was arranged to take place about mid-day, but as we did not take much interest in that sort of thing, turned our backs on the festivities and strolled along the road to Watermouth.

* James Stoyle Catford, photographer of 5 High Street (studio) and 29 Portland Street (residence), Ilfracombe.
† 'Let the Hills Resound' is a quick march composed by Henry Brinley Richards, and often played by military and brass bands. The term 'mobocracy' dates from the 1750s and means government by the mob.

The Dauntless Three.

*The brothers Charles, John and Joseph Freeman photographed by
James Stoyle Catford in Ilfracombe in 1874.*

The inhabitants of Combe Martin and Berrynarbor were flocking to the centre of attraction in great numbers, clothed in hats, coats and unmentionables of a very remote fashion; doubtless many were heirlooms and only brought to light on rare occasions. Some of these gentry were mounted on donkeys, others rode in springless carts, which must have shaken all the bones in their bodies, while many simply trusted to their understanding. Huge baskets of provisions also accompanied them, and dropsical cotton umbrellas of marvellous dimensions; all were hurrying in the same direction and afforded us much amusement as each family appeared.* Not a single person did we see going the same way as ourselves.

* Dropsical here means swollen or enlarged.

1 o'clock. Watermouth Bay and Castle, the former rather a picturesque little cove but the latter is a gentleman's private residence so cannot be inspected by the tourist. Having found the man who has the privilege of showing visitors over Smallmouth Caves – which were the main object of our visit here – we placed ourselves under his guidance and were soon there. Having got us inside, the said man proffered the information that the tide was too high to obtain a good view, thinking perhaps we might come there again, but this was of course our last opportunity.

BRIAR CAVE – WATERMOUTH.

Briar Cave is the largest and best: huge slabs of rock form the sides, and the sea dashes through a chasm in the foreground. Altogether, we did not think the sight very grand.

After leaving the caves, Joseph and Charles – by way of resting themselves – indulged in an athletic duel, the object being to see who could throw large stones the farthest up, and if possible into, a deserted limekiln. When at length they desisted in a great state of heat, neither would avow himself beaten, but it seemed to me the younger one had rather the best of it. I looked on, which was not nearly such fatiguing work. Returning townwards, we passed Sampson's Caves, which were not open to inspection on account of the tide. Here the scenery is rocky and bold; we lunched and stayed a short time. The sun did not seem quite so hot as usual; perhaps it was because a strong wind had been blowing all morning, indeed the Portishead Steamer had some difficulty in making headway; wondered if we should have a rough passage tomorrow.

In nearing Ilfracombe, we could plainly hear the band accompanying the procession in full blast, but did not see it. One little boy passed us, running along as fast as his legs would carry him in order to do so, but I am afraid he was disappointed. After strolling down the High Street and seeing what was to be seen, which consisted mostly of crowds of people and clouds of dust, we hied to the Capstone Parade (4 o'clock). The wind blew strongly round the corner by the hotel and the sea rushed over the rocks in good style. This was the first day we had seen anything like a rough sea; unfortunately the tide was low, so I think we missed a grand sight.

As a part of the day's programme was to be 'Rural Sports' in the meadow adjoining the Capstone, we had an early dinner about 5 o'clock and then returned to see the same. Though we had not been able definitely to ascertain the nature of these 'sports', we had fully made up our minds that they would be of an athletic character such as running, jumping, throwing the cricket ball or leaping, not to mention 'tossing the hammer', and 'putting the caber'. So were rather surprised at seeing in the said meadow five small boys instead of a group of brawny combatants eager for the fray. As no others appeared, Joseph enquired of an individual wearing a scarlet sash, from which if he were not an 'Oddfellow' – they were engaged in the procession – he looked it, but the 'sports' in question did not appear to trouble his intellectual mind, so we went to the Parade and watched the advancing waves.*

Soon after, a military and Rhine string and brass band began to discourse sweet music in the hotel grounds, so to them we listened for some time, taking special notice of the double bass and violoncellist for obvious reasons.† Observing a crowd near, we approached to see what was the excitement and found that a man had allowed himself to be tied up with a rope from which he promised to get free when a certain sum had been collected from the benevolent public to reward his exertions. This being at last obtained, he preceded to fulfil his part of the agreement, but with very little prospect of success. For some time he tugged, twisted and wriggled till quite red in the face, but all in vain, and I do not believe would have succeeded if the woman who collected the money had not told him where the knots might be found – they were at his back. After a 15 minute struggle he liberated himself and went away a much hotter if not wiser man. On looking towards the meadow, we saw the 'rural sports' had commenced and our disgust may better be imagined than described when I say they consisted of the childish games of 'Kiss in the Ring' and 'Hunt the Slipper'. Several small rings were at first formed, but they afterwards merged into a monster, one of about 200 individuals. What other sports were indulged in I cannot say, but should not be surprised if 'Honey Pots' were fashionable later in the evening.‡

Took a last blow on the top of the Capstone, then walked towards the pier and saw the passengers land from the Portishead Steamer at 9 p.m. She was an hour behind time and had had an exceedingly rough voyage, as the looks of those on board

* The Oddfellows are one of the oldest friendly societies, which offered members insurance against injury and death, but now (as here) concentrates on charitable activities.
† The 'obvious reasons' were that John plays the violoncello (as mentioned earlier) and at least one of his brothers plays the double bass.
‡ Kiss in the Ring, Hunt the Slipper and Honey Pots are all parlour games that were popular with Victorian children.

* 'See the conquering
hero comes' (1747)
by George Frederick
Handel is a chorus
in both his operettas
Joshua (1747) and
Judas Maccabaeus
(1746, revised 1751).
The chorus was
dedicated to the Duke
of Cumberland, who
defeated the Jacobite
forces at the Battle
of Culloden in April
1746. Beethoven
composed 12
variations in 1796.

fully testified. 'Never again will I go on the sea!', 'Oh dear! Oh dear!' and other such-like remarks were heard to issue from their pallid lips, and really they were much to be pitied; just fancy looking for apartments so late at night. The High Street illuminations consisted of stars placed amidst the green of the arches, some private ones, and strings of oil lamps placed among the trees, all of which much excited the wonder of the inhabitants. It certainly was a fair show for such a small place, but what would they say to a London rejoicing?

11 p.m. Hid our diminished heads from the crowd's gaze, but our rest was disturbed more than once by jubilant outsiders, especially one gentleman on the cornet who performed 'See the conquering hero' in such a remarkable manner that it was nearly all variations.*

WEDNESDAY 22 JULY

6.15 a.m. Rose up and soon finished the slight packing which was necessary. Whilst doing this an individual outside awoke the echoes of the street by enquiring for his collars, which had apparently been left to be washed. He called out that 'he must have them done or undone', but afterwards agreed to come again. Supposed he was going off by the boat like ourselves. As all things come to an end, so did our last Ilfracombe breakfast for which we seemed to have but little appetite. Then, having paid our debts, we bade farewell to the Haynes family who had made us very comfortable during our stay. Indeed I think we may congratulate ourselves in the great facility with which we secured suitable accommodation on each occasion during this Devonshire holiday.

Having first speculated in some provisions, we marched to the pier and found the steamer waiting for its freight. The method adopted for boarding her was not by any means a safe one; instead of a proper landing ladder with rails, a few boards were laid across the intervening space and two men held a pole to guide those who wished to cross, which was all that prevented anyone who might slip from tumbling into the water. A small white dog belonging to one of the passengers, which was occupying its time in jumping about, terminated its gambols by falling into the sea. It could swim, and well too, but kept describing a circle and indeed could hardly have landed here as the platform was several feet higher than the water. Eventually, after several efforts on the part of its master, a stick was forced under its collar and the animal was then hauled on board in safety, kicking most energetically.

8.40 a.m. Took our last farewell look of Ilfracombe and steamed out of the harbour. In passing along the coast, noticed with interest all the places we had seen on last Wednesday's journey, but from this distance the sides of the hills looked exceedingly dangerous for foot-travellers. 9.40 a.m. Lynmouth. A boat brought a full complement of passengers on and relieved us of about an equal number. The four sailors who managed her must have had a good pull, and we were rather amused by the business-like way in which they put their arms around the ladies' waists in order to assist them when embarking.

The captain said yesterday's voyage was a very rough one, as the steamer heeled a good deal. None of the passengers were allowed on the upper deck, so many of them were ill. This was not the case today, as it was comparatively smooth, notwithstanding which some were quaking. One ancient-looking party of the male species, with an equally ancient umbrella of the 'Gamp' pattern, afforded a subject for merriment in the fore-part of the boat.* Enquiries were made as to the history of his gingham and he was specially warned not to open it, lest the vessel might be stopped on her voyage.† All jokes were taken in good part, and he seemed to enjoy them as well as anyone.

On nearing Clevedon I happened to go downstairs in order to obtain something from our bag, when the following dialogue ensued:

* A gamp was a large, baggy umbrella. Named for Sarah Gamp, a character in the novel *Martin Chuzzlewit* (1844) by Charles Dickens.
† Gingham is another archaic word for an umbrella; properly, one covered with gingham fabric.

Sailor, a little groggy: 'Would you give me a glass of beer, Sir!'

JGF: 'Glass of beer? No! I don't think it would do you any good.'

Sailor: 'Oh Sir, I don't think there's any harm in having a little drop.'

JGF: 'Well, is there any reason why you want it so badly?'

Sailor: 'Fact is Sir, me and my mates had a drop too much at the Combe last night, and another glass now would set me all right, I think.'

JGF, preparing to go: 'It's more than I do, then.'

Sailor: 'Well, may I have a glass, Sir?'

JGF: 'Oh yes, if you like, certainly. But I shan't pay for it.'

On relating the above to my companions, Joseph immediately went down below in order to see if the same request would be repeated, and sure enough it was, but the would-be drinker was rather staggered by the reply 'Why, that is exactly what I was going to ask you!', which effectually silenced him.

1.35 p.m. Portishead. Made at once for the train and arrived in Bristol by 2.30 p.m. Here we had hoped to have found carriages waiting to take us on our journey, but on enquiry ascertained that we should have to wait more than an hour, so repaired to a Temperance Hotel and there refreshed ourselves, during which time rain descended. This was of course very suitable for the termination of our holiday. Returning to the railway station, found to our astonishment that the train had already arrived; this was all the more remarkable as it had been the whole day on the journey coming from Penzance.

3.50 p.m. Started off punctually to the advertised time. Our carriage was pretty full, about a dozen sailors being amongst the number, some of whom must have been Red Republicans as, according to their talk, everything appeared very sanguinary. Joseph expostulated with them on behalf of the ladies present, after which there certainly was an improvement – at least outwardly. Near Bath is the celebrated Box Tunnel which takes three minutes to traverse when going to Bristol, but half as long again when travelling the other way because of the ascent. It is said that no person has ever seen nothing, but it seemed to me we accomplished the feat on this occasion; it really was so dark that we could not see our hands though held close to our noses.

Some of the sailors soon after this commenced to smoke, and neither our remonstrances nor an appeal to the guard had the desired effect, so we changed into another carriage at Chippenham where, notwithstanding that a baby was amongst our companions, we were so quiet that nothing occurred during the remainder of the journey, which terminated at Paddington by 9.25 p.m., only a quarter of an hour behind time.

Here Joseph took leave of Charles and I; we then struck for home amidst the cries of 'Quick march!' from several small boys who were astonished at our military appearance with knapsack and levelled umbrellas, and ultimately reached 134 Regent Street by 10 o'clock. Thus ended our holiday during the ...

DOG DAYS.

NORTH WALES.

1875

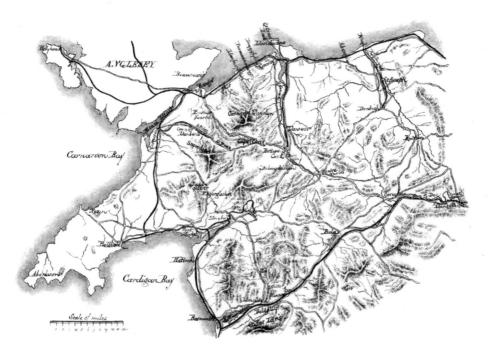

PROLOGUE

Again we were called to decide
Where we our vacation should spend;
Again we consulted the 'Guide',*
And questioned each intimate friend.

Some said: 'You should visit the Rhine,
And view the Swiss valleys and heights;
If only the weather be fine,
You see most magnificent sights.'

Said others: 'Why! How can you doubt?
To Paris go, take our advice;
Cook's tours are the cheapest now out,
With everything pleasant and nice.'

The Grants of course Scotland advised,
As judges they're partial I fear;
Yet should not at all be surprised,
To visit the Highlands next year.

South Devon, the vale of the Wye,
With Windermere's lakes so renowned;
Were talked of, with parts far and high
But each and all fell to the ground

'In many heads wisdom we find':
This proverb I fear often fails;
Still we at last made up our mind,
And finally fixed upon Wales.

---

* *Bradshaw's Descriptive Railway Hand-book of Great Britain and Ireland.*

SATURDAY 21 AUGUST

Early in the morning, three men armed with umbrellas and carrying a knapsack and bag might have been seen in Oxford Street, laughing and chatting as they walked briskly westwards. Judging from outward appearances, they certainly looked as if about to commence a holiday, and – wind and weather permitting – do their best to thoroughly enjoy it. That it was a fact, I (being one of the trio) can personally testify, and if further evidence be required please apply to my brothers, Joseph and Charles, who were my companions, and whose tour with me in 'Taffyland' I am about to record.*

5.55 a.m. Arrived on the scene of action, viz, Paddington Station, where (having purchased our tickets the evening before at Cook's agency)† we at once made for the train, and secured a capital seat by the window in an equally capital carriage with cushions and hat rack. There was one drawback to this happy state of things, and that was a man smoking; having duly warned him of his iniquity he retorted that the carriages for nuisances of his description were full, and the guard was about to convert this into another. This we found was true, so tumbled out and were soon seated in a different compartment of the same description – that is, as to the seats etc., not the smoke – and almost immediately commenced our journey.

Did not stop till Reading was reached, thus doing 39 miles in about an hour, which was not bad. Windsor Castle looked very imposing in the clear morning air and Charley made great preparations to inspect the same with his new eye-glass; however by the time he was ready it was almost out of sight. Our travelling companions were composed of a gentleman deep in study of the 'Daily Telegraph', and three persons of the opposite sex; one a servant girl, another an individual of a rather

* The term Taffyland (for Wales) has been in use since the middle of the 18th century, and is thought to be derived from the common Welsh name Dafydd or the River Taff, which flows through Cardiff.

† Thomas Cook, who began his travel business organising transport for members of a Temperance organisation in Leicester, opened a London office in Fleet Street in 1865. By 1873 this office, and the firm's head office, were in Ludgate Circus. Thomas Cook & Son were pioneers of tourism, and provided guided tours, printed guides, tourist itineraries, ticketing and accommodation services to early generations of tourists, including the Freeman brothers.

* *Oswald Cray* was
an adventure novel
in three volumes by
Ellen Henry Wood
(writing as Mrs Henry
Wood), published in
Edinburgh in 1864.
† The Black Country
is an area of the West
Midlands of England,
north and west of
Birmingham, which
became one of the
most industrialised
areas in Britain
following the Industrial
Revolution.

vinegarish expression of countenance, and a third a young lady who was trying to extract some amusement from a book entitled 'Oswald Cray'*; but finding our own company sufficiently agreeable, we did not enter into conversation with them, but kept aloof like true Britons. A wasp also essayed to journey with us. I endeavoured to stop his wild career, but the only result was I hit my hand against the seat.

8.50 a.m. Oxford. All our companions here abandoned us, except the 'reading girl'. Amid great rejoicing on our part, we were now able to move about a little. Joseph did his best to keep out intruders – mostly with success – by projecting his head from the window at every station. The next compartment – dedicated to those who smoke the pernicious weed – was quite full, which of course added to our satisfaction. At Banbury we speculated in some of the celebrated cakes of the name, and can recommend the same to anyone coming in this direction. The country round Leamington and Warwick is very pretty, especially the latter with its castle and cathedral.

On nearing Birmingham we were much surprised – though it was a fine sunny morning – to see the town was enveloped in the smoke emitted from the various manufactories, but this was nothing to what came afterwards. For the next half hour in passing Wednesbury, West Bromwich etc. as far as Wolverhampton it was really dreadful; thousands of gigantic chimneys belching forth smoke and sometimes fire which completely obscured the air. This, we were told by an inhabitant who travelled with us, was not to be compared with the state of things at night, when it really appeared that the buildings were on fire. He assured us it was healthy, but we wondered how anyone could live long in such an atmosphere. As it was, we were obliged to pull up the window and then found it very disagreeable. The ground in some places is quite honeycombed by the mining operations and the remains of the smelting furnaces in huge mounds rise on every side. All this district is known as the Black Country, and well it deserves its name.†

Llangollen from the Railway Station.

After lunching near Shrewsbury we passed Chirk. Here commenced the real invasion of Wales, and we were favoured with a foretaste of its beautiful scenery. The train passes over a viaduct from which a capital view is obtained of Llangollen's fertile valley, with the River Dee rushing below, and an aqueduct by means of which the Shropshire Canal is carried across the vale. At Ruabon we had to change carriages and after a short and pleasant ride arrived at Llangollen at 2 o'clock, the journey from London not having been at all wearisome, and performed within ten minutes of the stipulated time. From the railway station the first view is extremely favourable: below is the River Dee – crossed by a good bridge – wide, but shallow and clear, beyond which is the town while on either side are fine hills, the whole forming a most picturesque landscape. However, our first thought was to seek a place to call our home till Monday. So, having been recommended to a certain Mr Jones – chemist and Sol-fa-ist – to him Joseph applied for information on the subject. The result was that we decided on patronising the Temperance Hotel.

Having refreshed ourselves by removing the effects of our visit to the Black Country, Charley – having a slight headache – voted for a rest, so Joseph and I, seeing a notice that a cricket

BRADSHAW ON LLANGOLLEN

Llangollen lies in the hollow of the Dee, called in Welsh Glyndyfrdwy, i.e. Valley of the Dyfrdwy; and being the first glimpse of peculiar mountain scenery which the visitor comes upon, it is indebted to this as much as to its own character for the celebrity it enjoys. The population of the parish is 5,799, including some engaged in the flannel and woollen manufacture. Plâsnewydd, or New Hall, where the Maid of Llangollen, Lady E. Butler, and her friend (so graphically delineated by the late Charles Matthews), Miss Ponsonby, lived in happy retirement, remains in the same state as when occupied by them. The two former residents are buried in the old Gothic church, which is dedicated to Saint Collen, whose full name is Collen ap Gwynnawg ap Clydawg ap Cowrda ap Caradoc Freichfas ap Einion Yrth ap Cunedda Wledig. What an affliction to have to invoke the saint by his full name, or to be christened after him! A Gothic bridge in four arches is as old as the 14th century. Opposite the bridge the hills rise upwards of 900 feet high, and are surmounted by the remains of an old British fortress, which commands the pass, called Castle Dinas Bran (dinas means a fort). A little above Llangollen is Valle Crucis, or the Valley of the Cross, which may be ascended to view the striking remains of an abbey, founded in the 13th century, beyond which is the more ancient cross called Eliseg, which gives its name to the pass.

Nearby is the famous waterfall of Pistyll Rhaiadr. Here in a dark, well-wooded hollow one of the head springs of the Tanat runs down 140 feet at once, thence through a rock, and down another fall of 70 feet. There are several paths to it over the hill. It gives name to Llanrhaiadr church, in the valley below.

match was to be played at 3 o'clock, strolled down to see it wondering at the same time where a level piece of turf could be found for such a pastime. The surroundings were certainly the prettiest I have ever seen at a cricket ground. We sat and watched the game for some time, then returned and chatted with the single constable who keeps the peace of the town, but whose chief business appears to be to loiter on the bridge, swing his cane

TEMPERANCE AND TEMPERANCE HOTELS

The Temperance movement began in the early 19th century, and by the middle of the century was a mass social movement. It called on people to be temperate in their consumption of alcohol (drinking limited amounts of beer or wine, but no 'ardent spirits'), and also campaigned for restricting the availability of alcohol, especially to the working classes. At its extreme, it demanded teetotalism (total abstinence from alcohol) and prohibition of the public sale of alcohol. The movement was associated with Nonconformist churches and the evangelical wing of the established churches. Outside of the churches, groups such as the Independent Order of Rechabites (founded 1835), the Band of Hope (1847) and the League of the Cross (1873) asked members to sign a pledge to disavow drinking. The first temperance hotel opened in 1833, offering an alternative to inns and hotels where alcohol was easily available. There were also temperance pubs, where people could drink nothing stronger than coffee.

and gossip with the inhabitants. He said there would be little or nothing for him to do, were it not for the public houses of which there are no less than 29 in the place.

It being 4 o'clock, we retraced our steps, and – with Charley – took a walk by the riverside. The stream in some places is quite placid, but often rushes gurgling over its stony bottom forming pretty cascades and waterfalls, one called the Horseshoe being particularly good. Steep hills on either side, and the views at

Fancy portrait of the "chief Constable" at Llangollen.

* Llangollen Chain
Bridge, the London to
Holyhead Coaching
Road (now A5), the
'Old Road' (now
B5437) and the
Wrexham Road (now
A539), the Great
Western Railway,
River Dee and the
Llangollen Canal
(constructed as part of
the Ellesmere Canal).

each bend of the river are exceedingly fine. About two miles up is a bridge supported by chains, where for a short distance can be seen the singular spectacle of three roads, a railway, river and canal all side by side.* On enquiring, we were told that farther on was another bridge which would enable us to cross the Dee and thus return by a different route. This we essayed to do, but failed for the very good reason that the bridge was a myth; so we reached the other side by the aid of the first mentioned one and pursued our way by the canal. This is quite 100 feet above the river and does not appear to be much used, as some of the barges belonging to an adjoining slate quarry were half filled with water and grass.

Returned to Llangollen by 8 o'clock, the town being quite lively and the Welsh language heard on every side; the natives are passionately fond of and nearly always use it when speaking together, indeed some go so far as to assert that it was the tongue used by our first parents, but this surely cannot be, as the serpent would certainly have been frightened at hearing such a jargon. The tea set before us was soon attacked with more than our usual vigour, the bread and butter being especially good. Shortly after, we retired to our sleeping apartment, a very high room ornamented with busts of Milton and Shakespeare which did not however inspire us with the poetic fire of their originals; at least I am not aware that any of our number sat up in bed during the night and agonised in the throes of composing blank verse. The other two might be patient, but I do not think they would have endured this.

BRADSHAW ON THE VALE OF LLANGOLLEN

The Vale of Llangollen is said to equal any of the beauties of the Rhine, and it no doubt surpasses them in works of art, the aqueduct and viaduct being splendid ornaments to this lovely work of nature.

SUNDAY 22 AUGUST

6.30 a.m. After a good night's rest we all turned out of bed. This, however, can hardly be put to our credit, as the cocks of the neighbourhood had been for some time holding a musical competition, which had greatly disturbed me. Being Welsh of course, they displayed much energy in their proceedings; the leading soprano I imagine carried off the prize, that is if noise – as some people imagine – were the chief object. An hour later we crossed the bridge and walked on the border of the canal, closely followed by a large black dog which seemed to take a great interest in our proceedings. First he would run in front as if to lead the way, then take a bath in the water, land on the other side and vanish from view. Then, when we thought he had forsaken us, reappear in some unlooked for spot. Thus, he continued to ramble about during the whole of our walk.

Val Crucis Abbey being the object of our morning's stroll, and the road thereto not being very plain, we enquired of the only inhabitant to be seen.* He kindly directed us to the top of a hill, but finding it to be quite out of the route, we were obliged to descend. Still followed by our four footed friend, who I believe wished to act as a guide, because he was taking the correct path and only came after us when we had made the mistake. A short walk however soon brought us to the object of our search. The old abbey is said to have existed since the 12th century, and is half hidden by trees. We could not see inside as it is not opened on Sundays, but prowled about and discovered in one of the outbuilding a couple of nests containing three large eggs; these of course we did not take away.

Returning by a much shorter route, we – in company with our canine friend – reached Llangollen by 9.30 quite ready for breakfast. Two other young fellows (like ourselves bent on 'doing' North Wales) sat down at the same table. So, of course, we were soon conversing about the different sights and the best ways to see them. Found that services were held in the chapels at hours

*Now generally known as Valle Crucis Abbey. It was founded in 1201 and run by a Cistercian community until the Dissolution of the Monasteries in 1537. It is now a ruin, in the care of Cadw, the Welsh Government's heritage body.

varying from 9 o'clock till 11.15. Some were held in the native language, the Welsh Baptist being next door we could distinctly hear the singing; oh for a few such voices at Soho. Breakfast finished, we sallied forth to the English Baptist Chapel. A very small building, but quite large enough for the congregation.*

On Joseph asking for the loan of a tune book, we were seated behind the harmonium and a gentleman enquired if either of us could play it, as the lady who had been in the habit of doing so was just dead. Of course, we answered in the negative, so the singing was unaccompanied – but very fair for all that – the tunes (from Mr Binney's book) were Marlow, Boylston and Lancaster, and at the conclusion of the service the gentleman who started them thanked us for our assistance.† The sermon – from John, chapter 14, verse 6 – seemed to me very heavy; whether this arose from the preacher being a Welshman, I do not know. Curiously however, after having finished the reading he repeated the chapter and book from which it had been taken, so that all might remember it.

Service being over soon after 12 o'clock, we walked up the hill to Plas Newydd. Here there is an old house most curiously and elaborately carved in the front where formerly lived two old ladies known as the Maids of Llangollen.‡ Though ladies of title they dressed in hats, trousers and coats almost like men; their photographs are to be seen in many of the shop windows. Whether the old song which says 'the maid of Llangollen smiled sweetly on me' refers to them or not I cannot tell.§ Walked for some distance by the riverside and, on returning, finding the church door open, in we marched. It is an old building and outside as ugly as old; the interior has lately been restored. I do not remember ever having seen a church before without either organ or harmonium. This curious inscription is from a brass plate on one of the pillars:

Here lyes the purple flower of a Mayd
Having to envious DEATH due tribute payd

Whose suddaine FALL her Parents did lament
And all her friends with griefe their hearts did rent
Life's short you wicked lieves amend with CARE
And MORTALS know wee DUST and Shawdowes are.*

Returning to our abode, we expected to find a hot joint awaiting us, but perhaps our hostess thought we had joints enough of
our own; anyhow she affirmed there was not one of a suitable size
to be obtained, so had provided chops – without tomato sauce.
These we proceeded at once to chop up and with the assistance
of a custard afterwards made a very good dinner. This finished,
we asked the above named lady to tell us of a pleasant stroll to
occupy our afternoon moments. She immediately proposed the
'World's End', but we thought that would be too much of a good
thing. However, having procured various directions of a more or
less doubtful character, we decided to visit and were before long
on the summit of Castell Dinas Bran. This is the remains of an
ancient British fort on an exceedingly steep hill. A portion of the
walls are still standing and trenches are plainly discernible; our
fellow tourists making an appearance shortly after on the same
spot, we all sat down and viewed the lovely scenery all around.
Opposite is Barber's Hill, a still higher elevation with the town
and river nestling at its foot. Behind a succession of fertile fields
backed by a range of mountainous rocks to the left, the beautiful
valley crossed by the viaduct and aqueduct. The country beyond
these is rather flat; it can be seen for a distance of 20 or 30 miles.
While in the other direction, the hills towards Corwen rise one
behind another in grand style. As the sun was shining brightly,
the whole landscape looked really charming, so much so that we
remained and gazed thereon for above an hour, then began to
make downward motions.

One of our companions seemed determined not to take his
pleasures quietly. He walked up the hill so fast as to put himself
in a tremendous heat and now he must needs run down – and
some parts were very rough – with of course the same result;

* English Wesleyan chapels were affiliated to the Wesleyan Methodist movement, and delivered their services in English.

† Welsh Baptist chapels are affiliated to the Baptist Union of Wales, a Nonconformist and Congregationalist Protestant fellowship founded in 1866.

I rather think it was to show off a little. He and his companion talked of walking as far as Ruthin – 14 miles – before 11 o'clock tomorrow, but it hardly seemed practicable unless they started very early.

After tea, we all went together to the English Wesleyan Chapel, a small but comfortable place.* A good sermon was preached from John, chapter 3, verse 15, which an old gentleman in front of me did his best to spoil by making various extraordinary noises during its progress. The singing was supposed to be led by a harmonium, but it was played so badly that I did not recognise a single tune until the third or fourth line when they ultimately resolved themselves into such well known friends as Melcombe, Old Hundredth and Arabia. The last was taken at an alarming speed – it was a solemn hymn – and one individual shouted out as if he would never have an opportunity to shout again. Notwithstanding all this, the congregation sang very well. One of the hymns urged them to 'Drive out the devil and the beast!' which was enough to waken their risible faculties. Though the sentiment may be perfectly correct, I do not think this and other similar phrases are suitable for congregational singing; just fancy the above going to one of the good old repeating tunes!

In passing the Welsh Baptist Chapel, we halted to hear them sing very loudly and slowly a minor tune, giving out two lines at a time.† On coming out, the people did not waste the moments

---

BRADSHAW ON RUABON

The village of Ruabon is most pleasantly situated, and there are mansions, iron and coal works in the neighbourhood. Ruabon church is well worthy of a visit. It contains several fine monuments, particularly one to the memory of Sir Watkin William Wynne, Baronet, which is much admired. Population 7,425.

A TELEGRAPH STATION. HOTEL: THE WYNNSTAY ARMS.

---

by talking together but each went about his or her business without delay. After this we all took a short walk along the road to Ruabon, then returned, wrote letters home and went to bed.

MONDAY 23 AUGUST

6.15 a.m. Awoke and dressed; then, having packed up our extensive wardrobe, walked to the railway station, whence I endeavoured to make a sketch of the bridge and surroundings. Bearing in mind our day's journey, we merely strolled through the town, then breakfasted with our two fellow tourists who had decided not to visit Ruthin today, as one of them had a sore foot. According to their account, the coaches in this part of the world charge one shilling per mile, and in the middle of the journey the coachman comes around and demands a fee of two more for himself. We did not afterwards ascertain how much truth there was in this assertion, but I should feel inclined to doubt it. Having paid our reckoning, we soon found ourselves at the railway station, but the train was late so were obliged to exercise our patience for some time. At last it appeared with a fine assortment of natives, and we took our places therein. Our ride lay along the border of the River Dee, and few railways are I imagine more pleasantly situated; indeed it is much better in that respect than even the London Underground. Still, the iron horse did not stay in order that the passengers might view the prettiest bits of scenery, so Joseph was debarred the pleasure of continually making a halt for that purpose.

11 a.m. Corwen. Here we had hoped to find a coach or other vehicle going at least a part of the way to Betws-y-Coed, where we wished to sleep at night, but no such accommodation was provided; so having booked our bag (with clean linen etc.) for Carnarvon and purchased some of the best Corwenitish provisions, we proceeded on our journey by the 'Marrowbone stage',* which fortunately for me was in good working order.

* The phrase 'Marrowbone stage', meaning travel by foot, derives from the Marylebone Stage, a regular horse-drawn coach service in London. Similar to Shanks's pony, where shank is the lower leg.

The route lay along the Holyhead Road and a better one I have never seen, which was one point in our favour: having progressed about a mile, Charley considerably frightened us by declaring he had not the guide book in his possession, but were afterwards much relieved to find he meant the map, which was quite safe in other hands. Before long, a trap containing two men passed, and had there been room we might have asked for a lift, but such was not the case. Along the road were milestones, so that our progress could be easily marked, and on coming to the sixth we made a halt, firstly because – like nature – we abhorred a vacuum, and secondly on account of the beautiful scenery. To the right was a steep rocky hill, in the side of which was cut our road; to the left a precipitous ravine so filled with trees that the bottom was hardly anywhere perceptible. On a wall skirting this we sat, rested, and lunched. A dreadful idea suggested itself: what if our provisions were to fall into the depths below? We effectually obviated this danger – as to a portion at least – by making them disappear elsewhere. This little feat accomplished, we continued our journey.

At the end of the ravine, a fine waterfall bounds from beneath a bridge for about 80 feet over jagged rocks. This, an artist – who had descended to the bed of the stream – was trying to paint, and he certainly had chosen a very pretty subject. Near here, while changing the knapsack – which we each carried for an hour – a tourist laden with a bag appeared, but as we neither wished for his company or to have a race, we allowed him to pass. During the whole day we only saw one church, and it was evident that no service had been held there for a long time, but small chapels were very numerous, though the inhabitants were so few and far between, as to make it a matter of wonder where the congregations came from.

Near the eleventh milestone, as there was a clear running stream, we seated ourselves and dined much to our satisfaction, and having had a good rest were just preparing to start when the before named pedestrian (who had doubtless halted for refreshment) hove in sight. This time, however, we decided to take the lead and as the scenery was rather flat and uninteresting stepped out at the rate of nearly four miles an hour and at the sixteenth mile came in sight of a large range of mountains, the tops of which were in the clouds. Some of these latter indeed seemed half inclined to visit us with their contents, but decided not to, at least for the present. About 6 o'clock we were overtaken by a chaise, the driver of which offered to give us a lift. This was declined, partly because having walked so far it would have seemed as if we were very tired, but mainly on account of the fact that the scenery between here and Betws is exceedingly pretty. To our great surprise the vehicle contained the pedestrian whom we had left in the rear, and he appeared to have had quite enough walking for one day.

By the roadside saw the Conway river – shaded by luxuriant foliage on either hand – rushing and tumbling over its rocky bed.* We much enjoyed the prospect and were glad the offer of a ride had not been accepted, as in that case we could not have stopped to survey the most interesting parts. For instance, at the Conway Falls we descended to the bed of the river whence could be seen no pigmy dribbling stream, but a capital volume of water pouring over the rocks from a great height. At the side of the fall is a salmon ladder, consisting of a series of stone steps, each having a cavity for water. Up this the fish leap and are thus enabled to ascend the stream.

A little farther on is a splendid hilly view towards Dolwyddelan Castle, and Charles expressed his determination to search the dictionary for suitable adjectives so as to give vent his feelings on the subject. The shades of evening, however, warned us that the 'enemy' was on the march, so we followed his example and, on nearing our destination, sent Joseph forward to spy out the land.† This he successfully accomplished, and returned with the news that excellent accommodation could be obtained at the Waterloo Hotel. Thither we at once repaired, but Charles and I – having had our boots freshly nailed for walking purposes

* The river and the town are now spelled Conwy.
† According to the proverb, time is the enemy.

* This is an archaic use of 'discuss' meaning 'to eat enthusiastically'.

– nearly came to grief on the tessellated pavement of the hall, and I only hope our unsteady gait was not attributed to other causes.

Whilst tea was in course of preparation, we adjourned to the bathroom and indulged in the luxury of a demi-bath. This, after our walk of 23 miles, was a thing certainly not to be despised. Then going to the coffee room we found about 20 ladies and gentlemen discussing their dinner; they soon departed and we partook of our meal at a side table by the light of a very fine candelabrum.* Indeed the room was most tastefully and comfortably furnished. I am sure we did our best to let the proprietresses (the Misses Williams) know that we fully appreciated the good things set before us, and am inclined to think we succeeded. After this, a book containing remarks made by visitors to the hotel attracted our attention and we surveyed its contents with much interest. Many, not content with stating prosaic facts, had wandered into the regions of verse, which attempts were often made the subject of rather personal remarks by other critics, for instance one individual at the end of his name had put Esquire which called forth the following:

> Although 'tis right for all t'aspire,
> 'Tis vulgar to be self-styled squire;
> In future then just make amends,
> Be satisfied when't comes from friends.

Now the Waterloo had not a spare bedroom where we could sleep, and as we thought it would be highly inexpedient to do without our ordinary night's rest, the authorities had agreed to find us one in the village. Therefore, about 10 o'clock, a lad undertook to guide us to the same. Of course, gas is a thing unknown here, and what with the shade from the trees, and it being a very cloudy evening, it was as nearly pitch dark as possible, so we should have had some difficulty in finding our way alone. The necessary accommodation was soon obtained in the

Proper remedies.

house of one Lloyd Jones, the village doctor, so that had either of us been taken ill during the night he would have been close at hand with the proper remedies.*

TUESDAY 24 AUGUST

6.15 a.m. Awoke quite refreshed and not at all tired from yesterday's exertions, but on looking out of window, we were sorry to see it was raining. So instead of going for a walk, we tried to go to sleep again. In this, my companions succeeded much better than I. An hour later, as the damp atmosphere had somewhat abated, we rose, dressed and went out, but then came more rain; small, fine and plenty of it. Meeting one of the natives, we asked his opinion on the weather prospects, but he proved to be a Job's Comforter, saying, 'Oi think t'all be wet all day Zur':† and it certainly looked as if his prophecy would be correct, for on arriving at the Waterloo the barometer was found to have fallen considerably. About 9 o'clock a first-class breakfast – consisting of a joint of beef, chops, eggs, ham, fish, toast etc. – appeared in the coffee room and was at once attacked by about 20 visitors, but only two ladies were present. Outside Jupiter Pluvius remained briskly engaged and was having a capital innings. This, however, did not call forth any applause from the spectators but seemed rather to have a contrary effect, as they were quite the reverse of lively.

* The 'proper remedies' shown in the drawing were standard pharmacy offerings. Blue Pills, which contained mercury, were prescribed for 'liverishness' with constipation, and Black Draught was a powerful purgative, sometimes containing opium.

† A Job's Comforter is someone who, when trying to offer help and sympathy, merely adds to the distress. From the story in Job, chapter 16, verse 2.

Of course, it was useless to think of going out, so we again tried to amuse ourselves with the visitors' book. Also found another of more ancient date. These contained some very fair sketches and a variety of rhymes, good, bad and indifferent. Their general tenor was to praise the hotel, and especially the three Misses Williams, in fact one gentleman was said to be so madly in love with all as not to know who to choose, while another testified that the liquor supplied was very good as he had drunk 39 glasses in one day. The following I copied and think its praises well merited:

> Sturdy lads and blue-eyed lasses,
> Giddy heights and gloomy passes,
> Beetling crags and slate cliffs stern,
> Forests dark of fir and fern,
> Sparkling cascades, crystal fountains,
> Torrents thundering down the mountains,
> Rushing rivers, rippling rills,
> Rugged mountains, verdant hills,
> Bright pure water, healthful air,
> Glens romantic, landscape fair,
> Spreading valleys, shady dales,
> All are thine oh beauteous Wales.

Unfortunately, at Betws it often rains, and many recorded how for several days they had been compelled to stay indoors on that account. However, there is a very comfortable drawing room with a piano, music and plenty of books, also a croquet lawn for more propitious weather. Joseph was rash enough to propose a game with the mallet and balls, but the idea did not meet with general approval. Being exceedingly well satisfied with our experience of the Waterloo, Joseph and Charles, having duly invoked their respective muses, recorded the same in the visitors' book to which I added a small sketch. Then, as it was 12 o'clock and had ceased raining some little time, we sallied forth, determined at least to breathe plenty of pure air.

Miner's Bridge, Bettws-y-Coed.

The original plan had been to walk as far as Conway and sleep there tonight, but this – considering the state of the roads – we abandoned and proceeded along the road by the River Llugwy. Almost as soon as we had fairly started, rain began again to descend, which of course almost hid the otherwise lovely scenery: the sketch of Miner's Bridge I think fairly represents the views on this stream, which are very pretty. The bridge in question is a rickety affair with only one handrail down part of one side, and when Joseph jumped on it – the bridge, not the handrail – the vibration was such that we, not wishing to enjoy a bath just then, beat a hasty retreat. After a slushy walk of two and a half miles we came to the Swallow Falls.

Here for some hundreds of yards the river can be seen foaming and rushing over immense masses of rock. It then forms seven distinct falls and eventually terminates in a magnificent broad volume of water. The sight was very grand and well repaid us for the journey, even on such a day. Here we met an individual who was braving the elements in a mackintosh without an umbrella. We chatted and returned to Betws, where we found that little rain had fallen, though with us it had poured so much that we were obliged to stand under cover for quite an hour.

Swallow Falls, Bettws-y-Coed.

The Fairy Glen, Bettws-y-Coed.

Bettws-y-Coed, from the Llanrwst Road.

Passing through the village – which is one of the cleanest and neatest in North Wales – we crossed the Waterloo Bridge, and taking a road prettily overarched by trees, were before long at the Fairy Glen.

Some places are misnamed, but most decidedly it is not so with this lovely spot, where steep rocks covered with luxuriant foliage and the Conway river on either hand form a most enchanting scene. The best view is perhaps obtainable from a huge mass of stone (some 15 feet high) in the middle of the stream, which affords a capital prospect in both directions. Unfortunately, the sun was not shining. Had this been the case it would undoubtedly have added to the beauties.

It being now 4.30 p.m. we retraced our steps to the Waterloo Bridge – so called from the celebrated battle, being built in the same year, 1815 – then continued our journey. Hitherto, rain had been falling more or less all day, but it now ceased and I took advantage thereof to make a slight sketch, the result of which may be seen above.

The road was a complete contrast to that of yesterday, being very muddy, and we spent much time – with but little success – in trying to find which was the driest side. A walk of four miles brought us to Llanrwst, where a consultation was held as to whether we should stay here tonight or go at once by rail to

Conway, but as the sun could be plainly seen shining seawards, and the evening seemed altogether to promise a finer morrow, we determined to adopt the former alternative and by early rising do desperate deeds on the following day. Therefore – it being now 7 o'clock – Joseph made enquiries at the Glan Conwy which resulted in our staying there for the night. It is only fair here to give due credit to my eldest brother for always acquitting himself so well when performing the arduous duties – and he always undertook them – of an 'avant courier'.* Some individuals enter a hotel without asking due questions regarding prices etc. and then complain if things are not to their liking. This he never did. The consequence was that in every instance, save one – and that through no fault of his – we were well satisfied.

Wishing to take as much advantage as possible of the daylight, we strolled through the town, but were not much impressed by the sight, though perhaps the weather was in some degree accountable for this. The church is the only building I can say a good word of, being the best we had yet seen. The streets seemed irregular and dirty, the town hall also was very disreputable, but what can I say of the bank? Well, I should not care to deposit my money there. It was so rickety that, had we had occasion to enter, I should not have been at all surprised to hear the clerk say: 'Sir, it is not our interest to pay you the principal, neither is it our principle to pay you the interest.' Public houses abound everywhere. I counted no less than 22 in three streets. We did hear that the Welsh people spent most of their leisure hours either at

BRADSHAW ON LLANRWST

 Llanrwst, once noted for its Welsh harpmakers, lies on the east bank of the River Conway, about 12 miles from Conway, and is situated in one of the prettiest spots of North Wales. It ought not to be overlooked.

HOTEL: THE GWYDIR ARMS.

chapel or the ale-house. This I cannot verify, but as both places of resort are exceedingly numerous, the report would appear to have some foundations.

The names of the inhabitants, such as Evans, Roberts, Thomas, Griffiths, Williams, Owen and a few others, were of constant recurrence, but that which put all the rest in the shade was the aristocratic title of Jones, which is to be seen over the shops on every side: that of Smith in London is not to be compared with it. Like one's conscience it cannot be avoided, go where you will. Something ought to be done by Act of Parliament or otherwise. For instance, the members of this most interesting family might be forbidden to marry unless they changed their names – in order to arrest the increase of this numerous tribe. As it is, there is the greatest difficulty in distinguishing one member from another, and the method is adopted of mentioning his trade or affixing some other cognomen.

Having by this time pretty well surveyed Llanrwst we returned to the Glan Conwy and partook of a capital tea. We rather startled the Welsh girl who attended to our wants, by enquiring the road to Conway and announcing our intention to walk there early tomorrow. In order to accomplish this feat we retired at 9.30 p.m. between the sheets in a very comfortable room and were soon immersed in pleasant slumbers.

WEDNESDAY 25 AUGUST

5 a.m. Became aware of the fact that we had determined last night to rise early and walk to Conway, but thought this was rather too soon. It was well we did so, for an hour later it was raining hard. This was a misery we had not expected, so took refuge again between the sheets: however at 7.45 we rose and clothed ourselves in an anything but joyful mood, then breakfasted. Our room commanded a nice view of the river and bridge; that is, it would have done so if the clouds had not persistently emptied

* The inhabitants of
the Tower of Babel,
according to the Book
of Genesis, each
spoke one of the
very many languages
of the world. The
consequent babble
made comprehension
impossible.

their contents all around. Suddenly, we became intensely excited by a ray from the sun entering our chamber, but it vanished quite as quickly, as if sorry to have made such a mistake.

From information received, we ascertained that one of the adjoining Sunday Schools had fixed today for their excursion to Rhyl, and the authorities were now discussing if it would be advisable to go in such weather, so at 9.20 a.m. made for the railway station. Here a perfect Babel assailed our ears, for the Sunday School children and their friends were on the platform chattering with great volubility.* Such a collection of consonants I have never heard before. It seemed about as harmonious as a band when tuning up. Instead of the ordinary railway tickets, each of the excursionists was provided with a small piece of paper bearing a written number. This most primitive method would hardly be approved in London, as anybody could have made one for himself without the ticket collector being the wiser.

On the train arriving, the carriages were well filled, and a porter by way of making things more comfortable advised some of the 'thick' ones to change sides. When just about to start, a cry arose in our compartment of 'Oh! Here is Mr Jones!' (the name of course, was quite needless) so in he came and proved to be a sensible, well informed individual both willing and able to supply us with information. An English friend of his, who had been staying some time in Wales, declared that the only phrase she had been able to pick up was 'Let us have some beer', this being in constant use amongst the natives. We were also informed that Llanrwst was commonly known as the 'watering pot' of Wales, were rather glad we had not prolonged our stay there.

During our journey the rain abated, and the clouds gradually began to break when Conway was reached. To our great joy, old Sol was smiling in the most radiant manner. This town has some good streets, also the usual superfluity of public houses and the Jones fraternity, but the principal object of interest is the castle, which we at once visited. It has eight towers and is in a fair state

Conway Castle.

of preservation. The outer wall – portions of which still remain – probably once surrounded the town, but now houses are built into it. The keep affords a capital view of the country around and the Tubular Bridge crossing the river beneath. All this time the morning had been gradually becoming finer, our spirits rising in proportion, till we gave vent to the same by singing 'The March of the Men of Harlech' on the summit of the keep.*

Having thus relieved our minds we strolled through the town and then proceeded up the old Conway Road which, though bad walking, commands some very fine views. For nearly two miles, it is mostly uphill, across a bleak moorland tenanted by cows and sheep, where huge stones are constantly protruding from their mother earth. On attaining the summit a beautiful sight met our gaze: a lofty and almost perpendicular hill rises on the right, the pretty little village of Dwygyfylchi, approached by a zigzag path lies in the front, while beyond this – with a silver streak of sea glistering between – is the Isle of Anglesea.† Perhaps on account of yesterday's rain we enjoyed it all the better, and certainly did not complain because it was rather warm.

* 'The March of the Men of Harlech' is a song and military march that is believed to describe events during the seven-year siege of Harlech Castle between 1461 and 1468.
† The preferred spelling is now Anglesey or, in Welsh, Ynys Môn.

BRADSHAW ON CONWAY

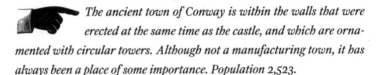 *The ancient town of Conway is within the walls that were erected at the same time as the castle, and which are ornamented with circular towers. Although not a manufacturing town, it has always been a place of some importance. Population 2,523.*

A TELEGRAPH STATION. HOTEL: THE CASTLE HOTEL.

The vale through which the River Conway flows is remarkable for its beauty and fertility. Its luxuriant pastures, corn fields and groves are finely contrasted with the bleak appearance of the Snowdon mountain, which towers in frowning majesty above it.

Conway Castle, which belongs to the Marquis of Hertford, stands on a rock which rises considerably above the river. It was built in 1284 by King Edward I to check the frequent revolts of the Welsh. The walls are of enormous thickness and defended by eight massive round towers.

The iron Tubular Bridge, erected in 1848 by Stephenson, over the Conway is one of the most unique examples of engineering skill ever imagined or carried into execution.

On reaching the village with the above unpronounceable name, we turned up a very steep glen, down which ran a stream. This, though not so large as those at Betws, was very pretty, and the brightly shining sun showed it off to the best advantage. On reaching the principal waterfall we admired its beauties, rested, partook of some refreshment, and then retraced our steps.

Another hour's walk saw us at Penmaenmawr. This is a clean, pretty and rather fashionable watering place with plenty of bathing machines, which shows that the sea is a great attraction to visitors. Here, as we wished to see the principal sights – and it was now 3 o'clock – we took a train for Aber, passing on the way Llanfairfechan (which very much resembled Penmaenmawr). A number of ladies with alpenstocks invaded our train. In Wales, the fair sex must no doubt derive much assistance from these aids to climbing. At Aber we alighted, turning our steps immediately in the direction of the celebrated water-fall. The glen leading to it – with the inevitable stream rushing and brawling over its stony bed – is at first rather confined but none the worse for that; afterwards it gradually widens, present-ing on either side a lofty hill, one rocky, the other covered with trees. This scenery continues for about two miles, when further progress is arrested by a precipitous hill, down which pour sev-eral waterfalls, the main one being nearly an unbroken sheet of water. The wind blowing up the spray in clouds was certainly a grand sight and was duly appreciated by us.

On returning, we chatted with a clerical gentleman who assured us it was only three miles to Bangor. This I did not believe as our map said five, but still hoped it might be rather less. Aber churchyard is a most melancholy place, being so damp that the tombstones are tumbling down and the odour – to say the least – is not pleasant. It was nearly 6 o'clock when, after a little rest, we started off, in order to catch the 7.20 train from Bangor to Carnarvon, and having travelled some distance came to a milestone that informed us it was four more miles to our destination. At this Joseph gave a great shout of disappoint-ment and, as it appeared to be raining hard in that direction,

BRADSHAW ON ABER

The village of Aber, celebrated as being the last place where Llewellyn contended against Edward I, is a most delightful spot, having on the right the view of the Irish Channel, in front, Beau-maris and its wooded environs, and to the left the turrets of Penrhyn Castle. From this village, a deep and romantic glen, nearly three miles in length, forms the avenue to Rhaiadr Mawr, a celebrated cataract. The prospects in the neighbourhood afford views of most picturesque beauty, comprising the Snowdon mountains on the one hand, the Menai Straits and the coast of Anglesea on the other, all together forming a rich pano-ramic view of splendid scenery.

BRADSHAW ON BANGOR

☞ *A cathedral town and bathing place, it is an excellent rest-ing place, not only for the fine mountain scenery of this quarter, but for the Britannia and Menai bridges, the Penrhyn Slate Quarries, Beaumaris Castle and other excursions. More than 50,000 persons come here in the season, so that lodgings at such times are high and difficult to be had.*

A TELEGRAPH STATION. HOTELS: THE GEORGE HOTEL, THE BRITISH HOTEL, THE PENRHYN ARMS.

things did not look very bright. However, we put on a spurt and walked the next three miles in 40 minutes, doing one of them in 11, my two confreres carrying the knapsack. During a good por-tion of this time a thick driving mist was falling and the wind blowing right in our teeth, though we managed to avoid much of the former by walking close under the hedge.

Soon after passing Penrhyn Castle, which is a noble struc-ture, with many fine entrances, the rain abated, so we slackened speed, thinking we had nearly reached our destination, but on asking the way to the railway station were astonished to find we were only in Garth and a considerable distance had yet to be traversed. 'Quick March' was therefore – to the astonishment of some of the natives – again the order of the day, but had the train been punctual we should have missed it by about five minutes. It was a matter of regret with us that we could not stay to inspect Bangor, especially the Tubular and Britannia bridges, which cross the Menai Straits at such an elevation as to allow ships in full sail to pass underneath, also the cathedral which was merely seen en route. Still, one cannot do everything, and I do not think on coming to the end of this diary the reader will accuse us of wasting time. After waiting half an hour for our train, it at last arrived and we eventually reached Carnarvon at 8.30.

Having secured our bag, which had been sent on from

Carnarvon Castle.

Corwen, we proceeded to the Prince of Wales Hotel (where we had been recommended) and were by no means overjoyed to find it was quite full. This was also the case at a temperance hotel. Here, however, a little girl offered to show us where accommodation might be obtained. To this we assented as, of course, it was quite dark, but Carnarvon seemed full of visitors and half a dozen different places were tried with no better success. At last, however, one was found which was hardly what we would have wished. Still, as it was but for one night, thought we had better make it do, so decided to stay there. Tea being served, we

BRADSHAW ON CARNARVON

It occupies the site of a Roman town called Segontium, of which there are various relics in the museum. The well-preserved castle, built between 1284 and 1320, is the most interesting object. The outer walls are ten feet thick and guarded by 13 towers, variously shaped. One of them is the town prison. Population 8,512.

A TELEGRAPH STATION. HOTELS: THE ROYAL SPORTSMAN HOTEL, THE UXBRIDGE ARMS.

managed to make a capital meal, and afterwards wrote letters home, so did not retire to rest before 11 o'clock. Just as the god of sleep was beginning to exercise his powers, we were awakened by a fearful noise as if all the wild beasts in the zoological gardens had broken loose and were engaged in a free fight on the stairs. We forgot to ask in the morning the reason, but I rather imagine, from the sounds, that they emanated from two cats.

THURSDAY 26 AUGUST

At 6 o'clock the church bells commenced ringing in a most energetic manner to warn all persons that it was time to begin the day's duties. In our case, however, this was needless as we were already awake. Having clothed ourselves, I walked through the town to make various enquiries about the train etc. while Joseph finished writing a letter, and Charley packed up the knapsack and bag. Carnarvon is the largest town in North Wales having a population of about 10,000. It is clean, contains many good streets and shops, also a fine large square beautified by a fountain in the centre. One novelty in every Welsh town is a number of what are called Temperance Houses. Some of these are not very inviting, the proprietors evidently not abiding by the maxim 'Cleanliness is next to godliness'. It is to be hoped that most of them keep to their principles better than one who lives here and informs the public that 'He is licensed to be drunk on the premises'. The chief attraction is the castle, which is perhaps one of the finest in England; it overlooks the harbour and was doubtless in times gone by a place of great strength.* By the quay in front were schooners and other craft engaged in taking cargoes of slate and, it being a fine morning, the town seemed very lively.

7.30 a.m. Had an early breakfast and then took our departure having fared no better than we had expected. There was no occasion to find fault with the charges, but things were not tidy and clean, and in a word we were not 'comfortable'. On going into a shop to buy some provisions, the lady behind the counter said: 'Nice day this, Sir, for the Eisteddfod at Pwllheli.' Of course, I replied in the affirmative, though taking no particular interest in the event which was a species of competition, musical and otherwise, held for three days in a small out-of-the-way town. With the natives, however, quite the contrary was the case. A temporary tent had been erected capable of holding several thousand persons, excursion trains ran from all parts of the country and everybody who was anybody went to listen or, failing that, talked about the affair. The amount of enthusiasm these Welsh people are capable of – especially in anything concerning their native tongue or music – is truly wonderful. I only wish we were the same in London.

After paying a small fee we entered the castle; it covers three acres of ground but only the walk and towers remain standing. The keep has 150 steps – some of which are very dilapidated – and from the summit we obtained a capital view of the town and surrounding country. Here we stayed till advancing time warned us to repair to the railway station where, having booked our bag for Ffestiniog, we waited for the train, which was as usual very late.

Lake Padarn, looking towards Snowdon.

Passing on the road seven different streams all coming from Llanberis, we arrived at Cwm-y-Glo by 10.20. Here we alighted and proceeded on foot by Lake Padarn, which is about two miles long. Such a beautiful expanse of inland water we had never before seen; on every side arose grand mountains and I have endeavoured to give some idea of the scene. Slate quarries are very numerous, and reports of the blasting operations reverberated from hill to hill; at one place we stopped and watched the men working, which was very interesting. A line of rails is laid down especially for carrying the produce of the quarries, and slate is so common that it is used for making walls and other purposes instead of stone.

On arriving at Llanberis we left our knapsack at the Alexandra Temperance Hotel and strolled through the village. It was much larger than we expected, having plenty of accommodation for tourists who resort here of course in large numbers en route for Snowdon. In one of the shop windows was some Sol-fa music exposed for sale, and we felt greatly inclined to perform a trio therefrom but desisted from respect to the inhabitant's feelings. At the commencement of the ascent to the mountain just named, numerous guides proffered their services to show us the path to the summit. One was afraid we should be lost, another thought we should like his company, while a third offered to see us safe up for three shillings. However, we laughingly refused all such kindnesses and made a similar proposal to the last for a third of

---

BRADSHAW ON LLANBERIS

Here is a pretty late English [Gothic] church, enclosing the original timber structure dedicated to St Peris. It stands near Lynn Peris, in the very heart of the mountains, which appear here in all their native majesty. From Llanberis to the top of Snowdon is 3½ miles.

HOTELS: THE VICTORIA HOTEL, THE DOLBADARN HOTEL.

---

the sum. Beggars also waited by the roadside, with piteous tales to move the heart of the unlucky tourist, and small children pestered us with a request to be allowed to sing 'The March of the Men of Harlech', expecting of course a donation for their trouble. To the latter we said we had some remembrance of having heard it before and volunteered to sing it to them if they wished.

Having at last steered clear of these nuisances, we commenced to ascend Snowdon. The road is exceedingly well defined and the idea of having a guide perfectly absurd. At first it is gentle and smooth, but this gradually gives place to loose stones which are not at all pleasant to walk on. The sun also grew less powerful, and the wind colder and stronger. Having speculated in some provisions when at Llanberis, we did not see the utility of carrying them all the way so hid them beneath two large stones. After going a little distance and looking back, I saw a lad apparently surveying the ground, and the dreadful thought suggested itself that he might have seen me and was searching for our property. However, we went on and left it to its fate.

About three parts of the way up is a house for refreshment, and past this the ascent is certainly much steeper: people who were descending did all they could to frighten us, saying we should be drenched to the skin by the mist, on the summit it was as black as night, all the ham and eggs had been eaten, and no fewer than 16 hats had yesterday been lost through the wind. Still, we pressed onwards and were soon in the clouds, which drifted past at a rate. The wind was tremendously strong, so much so that each individual was obliged to pull his hat over his head to the utmost extent, or tie it on with a pocket handkerchief, forming a rather curious picture. Some ladies who were on horseback seemed in even a worse condition, and I do not think more than two of them had the courage to persevere to the end. After some more steep climbing we found ourselves on the summit and – as we had expected – could not see many yards before us. Still, we can now boast having ascended the highest mountain in England and Wales.

The topmost pinnacle is only 800 feet beneath the perpetual snow line, and is easily recognised by a cairn of stones and two small wooden houses, or rather huts, which are built there. In the latter, refreshments are sold and sleeping accommodation provided for those who wish to pass the night there in order to see the sun rise, if possible. The charge, I believe, is five shillings per head, and the chances of seeing the orb of the day at that early hour exceedingly problematical; still, if clear, the spectacle must be very grand. It was extremely cold, hair and beards were thickly covered with moisture from the clouds and the breath could be plainly seen issuing from our mouths. I should imagine the temperature was about 40 degrees, so we thought a cup of hot coffee would not be amiss, but on enquiring the tariff found that the proprietor did not sell that article alone but only with a roll and butter, and for this he asked 18 pence and – as far as we were concerned – did not get it. Of course, everything has to be carried up here – by donkeys or otherwise – so it is necessary to charge good prices, but this seemed to me very extravagant.

As nothing was to be gained by staying on the top but a cold, we commenced to descend. The sun breaking through the clouds into the Pass of Llanberis looked exceedingly pretty, and when a little lower down we had a beautiful view in the direction of Anglesea, with the Straits, Tubular Bridge and country beyond

BRADSHAW ON MOUNT SNOWDON

Ponies and guides may be hired at Llanberis, but a stout pair of legs is the best help for those who choose to dispense with such assistants. Start early in the morning when the air is cool. For those who wish to see the sun rise, a few huts, accommodated with beds, are built on the top; but it is frequently obscured by clouds. If the weather is clear, you may see the Wicklow mountains, the Isle of Man, the Yorkshire hills etc., with above 20 lakes in North Wales, all spread out like a map.

The Pass of Llanberis.

being plainly visible. While very thankful it was not a drenching wet day, as is very often the case in these mountainous districts, we could hardly help wishing the clouds had not been so low; still, we did not grumble. Reaching the spot where our provisions were hidden we found them quite safe, so sat down and refreshed ourselves. Thus ended our day's climbing.

Not having the least regard for the feelings of the author of 'Hiawatha', I here insert a parody on one of his well-known poems, written by a 'Shortfellow'.*

* The author of *The Song of Hiawatha* (1855) was Henry Wadsworth Longfellow. The poem being parodied is 'Excelsior' (1841). The word means 'ever higher'.

The Ascent of Snowdon

Some clambered up at pace so fast,
That us 'ere very long they passed;
We did not think this method nice,
Yet still adopted the device,
        Excelsior!

The road was bad, the stones below,
Oft' very nearly stubbed my toe;
But as we onward went, we sung,
The air loud with our voices rung,
        Excelsior!

'Oh! Do not pass,' the guides first said,
'We'll take you up, so much per head,
'You may be lost in chasms wide';
But loud we laughed, and then replied,
                    Excelsior!

'Oh stay,' a maiden said, 'and rest,
'The milk I sell is of the best';
'How much is a glass?' She did reply:
'Four pence to you.' 'Oh! Oh!' said I,
                    Excelsior!

We tourists soon the summit found,
Obscured by mist was all around,
So down we rattled in a trice,
No longer having for device
                    Excelsior!

When closed that splendid August day
We on our beds serenely lay,
Well pleased to have come so far,
And murmuring as we dreamed Ah! Ah!
                    Excelsior!

On nearing the foot of Snowdon, we crossed a rapidly rushing stream to the left and viewed the Falls of Llanberis, where a fine volume of water precipitates itself into a glen below. Successfully evading a tribe of youngsters who wished to display their musical voices, we passed between lakes Padarn and Peris and took a stroll by the slate quarries on the other side. The sunset on this evening was a beautiful sight; in the direction of the sea the sky was clear with small fleecy clouds, but mountainwards all was dark and gloomy, the great contrast being very pleasing to the eye.

An inward feeling – say conscience – now telling us that tea time was near at hand, we returned to the Alexandra and partook of the meal in company with two young fellows and a large dog who had just walked from Llanfairfechan. Some fish we had – warranted fresh from the lake – were very good, and our canine friend made very short work of the bones. The hotel where we were staying was formerly called Noah's Ark, and somewhat resembled the popular idea of that vessel: perhaps the name was changed to avoid visitors being likened to various animals as they emerged. Just fancy ourselves being dubbed giraffe, billy-goat and lion! Probably we should hardly have relished the joke. 10 p.m. Retired to dreamland.

FRIDAY 27 AUGUST

6.50 a.m. Rose, glad to see it was a bright morning, and seemed to bid fair for a fine day. Breakfasted at the same table as the two young men mentioned yesterday; their dog also made a good meal from the eatables provided. This was, I think, hardly fair and they would have been rather astonished to see it charged for in their bill. These tourists – dog and all – had determined to go up Snowdon and thence to Betws today, so we bade them adieu, as our routes lay in different directions, and by 10 o'clock were fairly on our journey. After again running the gauntlet of the Snowdon guides we passed Dolbadarn Castle – merely a decayed circular tower of little interest – and skirted Lake Peris. The morning was clear and gloriously fine, so we trudged along merrily, meeting now and then a stray tourist – like ourselves – bent on scouring the country. When this was the case we often stopped to exchange ideas as to which place it would be best to visit, and other like topics.

Having proceeded some distance, we suddenly heard sounds of melody coming from an adjacent house, and on listening found it was the well known multiplication table being repeated by a number of children. Being of a curious turn of mind we drew nearer, and were just debating as to whether it would be

* The Tonic Sol-fa
Association organised
annual competitions
in the Crystal Palace,
Sydenham, London,
from 1857.

advisable to venture in when out stepped the schoolmaster himself. Now we had been recommended to one Jones, British Schools, Llanberis, as a Sol-fa-ist, so Charles at once suggested perhaps this was the very man, so I asked him if such were the case, and he at once not only pleaded guilty to the name but invited us to enter and be seated. Talking about musical topics, we of course referred to the competition two years ago at the Crystal Palace with the South Wales Choir.* He said the excitement in these more northern latitudes – though a great distance from the parts whence the singers were recruited – was intense, and the result telegraphed immediately to all parts of the principality. He had been to the Eisteddfod at Pwllheli and was proud to say the Llanberis choir had carried off the first prize of £30 for choral singing, though had not the majority of their number been Sol-fa-ists, he was certain they could not have sung such difficult music. He then finished by speaking of the great love and respect which everyone bore to Mr Curwen, who had done more for the advancement of vocal song in these regions than any living man.

During the above conversation the children had been pursuing their various studies but Mr Jones now asked if we should like to hear them sing – though he had been here but a short time, and had not been able to give them any systematic training. We of course replied in the affirmative, so the juniors were called in from the room where they had been trying to master 'seven times one are seven' and other like problems, and the whole school – about 90 in number – marshalled in singing order, boys on one side, girls on the other. They were of course a motley group, both as to size and age, many wearing clothes which had doubtless seen service on several other sisters or brothers, but they had a very healthy appearance, and rough heads and bright eyes were the order of the day, the latter often turned curiously on the visitors.

At a given signal they sang 'The Jolly Little Clacker' with great spirit, then 'Hold the Fort' in Welsh, with two of the lads taking one of the verses as a duet, 'Never Forget the Dear Ones' as solo and chorus, also several others, winding up with 'The March of the Men of Harlech'. Most of these pieces were capitally accompanied on a harmonium – without music – by a little fellow about ten years old, the last especially, in an exceedingly florid style, was rattled out with great vigour. There was no question as to the energy of the singers; such a body of sound I have never heard equalled by a juvenile choir of the same size, but very little refinement was visible and some of the high notes were very coarse. Of this however the teacher was quite aware, and with proper training, there certainly was the material for a splendid chorus. All this time Mr Jones kept on his straw hat, and beat time with a stick, occasionally tapping one of the boys on the head with it, so as to vary the monotony of the proceedings. Joseph then informed the youngsters how glad we were to have seen them, saying – and truly – this would be a red letter day in our holiday, and with a few other words of encouragement and thanks we bade them and their tutor a very hearty farewell.

It was now 12 o'clock, and soon afterwards we entered the famous Pass of Llanberis. On either side rises a lofty mountain, the one to the right being Snowdon. Down the centre rushes a torrent – cascades and waterfalls are quite common – and immense masses of rock (some weighing hundreds of tons) lie about in all directions as if they had been upheaved by some convulsion of nature. A well made road runs through all this, forming a gradual but continuous ascent, which has only been completed of late years; previous to this only the most adventurous spirits dared to traverse the pass. A walk of four miles through this grand scenery brought us to the highest point, where there is a half way house entitled The Resting Place. Here commences the ascent to Snowdon by what is known as the Capel Curig Route and, as it was such a beautifully clear day, we were debating as to whether we should again do 'doughty deeds and parlous acts', when who should be seen approaching but the two young fellows with whom we had breakfasted. They reported that the summit was as clear as possible, so Joseph wished to make another ascent, but Charles and I thought 'prudence the better part of valour', especially as we had the knapsack to carry, and the route from this side is incomparably more difficult – many say dangerous – than that traversed yesterday.*

Having thus decided, we continued our journey and on arriving in the valley fell in with a shepherd who was accompanied by three dogs. One of them gained the first prize of £50 at Bala last year, and certainly the way in which they ran after the sheep on the hillside, brought them to a certain spot, and in every way obeyed their master's call was truly marvellous. The sheep at first ran very fast, but losing breath stood huddled together panting piteously, the dogs meanwhile sitting down and looking on quite calmly. On Snowdon's top being pointed out to us, we were much surprised, having expected to see a peak almost hidden by clouds, instead of which it stood out against the sky as clearly as possible; had we been alone we certainly should have seen it and passed on without being at all aware of the fact.

Thinking both time and place highly appropriate for dinner, we said 'good-day' to the shepherd, seated ourselves by a running stream and most heartily enjoyed our mid-day meal. I

Snowdon from Beddgelert vale.

wish I could give an adequate description of the dining room. Behind was a high hill, to the right a rugged valley, in front some half dozen mountains topped by their king; a waterfall which, though nearly a mile distant, could be distinctly heard, and again below that meandered a stream leading to a most splendidly fertile valley where amongst luxuriant verdure sparkled the placid waters of Lake Gwynant. If anything more was needed to add – by way of contrast – to our enjoyment, it was furnished by two perspiring tourists, who with coats and waistcoats off in the greatest state of disorganisation, begged to know how far it was to the next house for refreshments. I made a slight sketch of the view before us.

4.20 p.m. Having had a capital and most enjoyable rest, we started off by the lake which, being surrounded by trees, presented a refreshing change of scenery. Nothing happened worth mentioning till on nearing Beddgelert a troop of small girls came out to greet us and followed a long distance forming quite a tail behind. They also wished to display their musical powers, but unfortunately gave us more than one tune at once, which had not a melodious effect. Being unable to persuade them to desist, we quickened our speed, but still they ran and sang at the same time till quite out of breath, when they most unwillingly left us and we went on our way rejoicing. This village is small, and the hotels but three in number – viz – The Royal Goat, The Prince Llewellyn and The Saracen's Head. Hearing that the first named charged very high prices, we made the latter our home, in the first place however taking a short stroll to see what was to be seen, which was very little. The houses are mostly of an ancient type, and in some cases seem as if inclined to save their owners the trouble of pulling them down by committing suicide. Of course there is a river with a bridge, and I think the inhabitants must be of a very confiding nature, as two of the youngsters came up to Charles and I, one saying: 'Please, Sir, this little girl wants a penny!' On my supposing they would divide it between them, she replied: 'Yes, Sir.' Of course, such a distressing case as

* A quotation from
*Ode on a Distant
Prospect of Eton
College* by Thomas
Gray.

this ought to have been relieved at once, so we put our hands in our pockets – and kept them there.

Returning to the Saracen's Head, we sat down to a capital tea in the coffee room, out of which I am afraid the providers did not make much capital, so successful were our stocktaking operations. Tea finished, a young man who was sitting with his brother at the same table invited us to have a rubber at whist; this we declined thinking 'Where ignorance is bliss 'tis folly to be wise'.* However we entered into conversation together, and he strongly advised us to alter our route on the morrow, and showed some very clever tricks which Joseph and Charles endeavoured in vain to find out. Whilst this was going on, one of the maids came into the room several times pretending to search for something, but really I think to remind us that it was very late. When at 11 o'clock we at last made an upward movement, no other visitors were to be seen, and two candles only remained to light us to our rooms. The one provided for us was very comfortable, and we were soon enjoying our well earned repose.

SATURDAY 28 AUGUST

Awoke at 6 o'clock and fully intended to get up but, unfortunately thinking that just '40 winks' would be beneficial, more than a minute of each elapsed before they were accomplished, thus proving the truth of what we have often written in our school copy-books: 'Procrastination is the thief of time!' Whilst at breakfast an elderly female in a tall black hat passed the window. People in London and elsewhere imagine that all Welshwomen wear this sort of head-gear, but this is a great mistake: whatever used to be the case it is so no longer, and with one exception we did not see another specimen of this ancient fashion during our trip.

9 a.m. Well satisfied with our reception, we quitted The Saracen's Head and, going to a field close at hand, inspected what is said to be Gelert's grave: the reader had doubtless heard

Allegorical sketch of the "little bill" all travellers must expect to see on visiting the "Royal Goat" Beddgelert.

during his – or her – youthful days of a certain hound which, left to guard his master's son, slew a large wolf in his defence. The father on his return seeing blood on every side, imagined the dog had killed his child, slew it and only discovered the mistake when too late. By way of atonement, he is supposed to have erected the present monument to the memory of his but too faithful Gelert; either the contents of his purse or his gratitude must have been very meagre, as only two dirty stones now stand under a tree as memento of the tragedy, which of course visitors believe or not according to the amount of faith they possess.

The clear sky above promised another beautiful day, so onwards we pressed following the course of a clear rippling stream, thus reaching the Pass of Aberglaslyn; here the distance

The Pass of Aberglaslyn.

between the hills on either side gradually narrows, with rocks, trees, river and bridge all combining to form a grand sight which I have tried to transfer to paper. Several artists were making or preparing to make sketches; one in particular ought to have placed himself in the foreground of his picture as he appeared panting up the hill, coat off and laden with his easel, sketch book and other materials.

According to our original idea, we had intended to walk hence to Ffestiniog but, following the advice of the individual at The Saracen's Head, we now kept straight ahead instead of turning to the left, and were soon in more level country. The river gradually widened and all around it was extremely fertile; mountains however still arose in the distance and Snowdon's peak could be constantly seen. On reaching The Glaslyn Inn, we crossed some fields and by following the track of a disused tramway saved a walk of nearly a mile and arrived at Porthmadog by 12.30. This town is of a fair size with some good shops, especially for the sale of provisions, as many vessels put into the harbour, which being very flat and sandy contained but little water, as it was low tide.

A train being timed to start at 1 o'clock, we now repaired to the railway station, but the clerk was so dilatory that he did not commence issuing tickets till considerably after the hour. Having duly secured three of these passes to Tan-y-Bwlch (whence we intended to walk to Ffestiniog and then return by rail to Barmouth), Joseph thought it better to enquire as to the times of the trains for coming back, and it was well he did so, as he found we could only accomplish the feat by riding all the way. This of course was vexing, but 'necessity knows no law', so for a further sum of money he procured a written pass from the stationmaster as far as Duffws.* All this complication arose from the fact that the railways here belong to several companies, who do not issue through tickets or accommodate each other in any way, and of course we were obliged to go to Ffestiniog as our bag had been sent there from Carnarvon. However, after a delay of half an hour we started amidst dire forebodings as to when we should return.

This line is certainly a curiosity in its way, the rails being only two feet apart, the carriages little more than five high and about six inches from the ground, with lengthwise seats in many so as to give a better view of the scenery, and the engine a small podgy thing quite unlike any we have ever seen. The reason for all this is that the railway winds up a series of hills to the height of quite 1,000 feet, affording a magnificent view of the vale of Ffestiniog, which for beauty rivals that of Beddgelert and what greater praise can I give? Lord Lytton said of this spot: 'With the woman he loves and a good supply of books, one might pass an age here and think it a day.'* We however had neither the one nor the other, so passed on instead. But should the unfortunate passenger sit on the left hand side of the carriage, he will hardly see anything during the journey – unless he turns round – but a stone wall, and this is so close that should he happen to put his head out the window, he will stand a good chance of having its toughness tested against an arch or some other projection. Our rate of movement was very slow, though the engine made a tremendous smoke and noise out of all proportion to its deeds, also, when about to recommence its labours after a stoppage, treated us all to a dreadful jerk.

However, in due course, we came to Tan-y-Bwlch, and there saw about 30 loads of quarrymen in open trucks. They looked anything but nice companions and possibly were carried at so much the drove or by the hundredweight. Here also we took up some passengers, who I hope and believe were not fair specimens of Welshmen: they laughed, talked and sang in a very coarse manner, three of them taking turns to smoke out of the same pipe, and one having his arms – even while smoking – round the neck of a respectable-looking girl.

On arriving at Duffws, all had to change into a conveyance of a still more primitive type, viz – open air trucks where passengers sat back to back and, being devoid of springs, jolt them

* *An Account of a Journey into Wales,* by George Lyttelton, 1st Baron Lyttelton (1781). John has evidently misremembered Lytton for Lyttelton.

in a most unmerciful manner. Two working men near us had some sheet music printed in both Sol-fa and Old notations, from which they were singing most tunefully. One might go a long way in London before seeing a thing of this sort among the same class of people. Discussing the probabilities of our getting to Barmouth tonight with my opposite neighbour, he informed us we *might* do so, but only the other day the train went away without waiting for another which was overdue, and 200 passengers were left behind to shift for themselves. This was pleasant intelligence, and of course our hopes rose accordingly.

On nearing Ffestiniog, the train stopped whilst the engine driver – an extremely grimy fellow who reminded us forcibly of that gentleman who is never mentioned in polite society – came round to collect the fares, as tickets are not issued for this branch line.* To my surprise many of the quarrymen did not stay for him, but took a short cut by climbing along the embankment: as my time was short I suggested the propriety to my vis-à-vis of our doing the same, and as he volunteered to show me the Post Office off we went together. It being close at hand, I soon obtained the three letters which were there waiting for our perusal, and then returned. We had of course when in London arranged where we should be on each succeeding night, and our friends directed their correspondence accordingly.

During my absence, Joseph had agreed to secure our bag, so on returning I was of course overjoyed to learn that the authorities had no idea of its whereabouts, and declared it had never come to hand. Dismal thoughts arose of having to wander about in dirty linen during the remainder of our holiday. Even the stationmaster – if a man who seemed to perform the duties of every railway official can be so called – only gave us the information that he 'supposed it was somewhere between here and Carnarvon'. He however was about to return to Duffws, and promised to make further enquiries, so back we all went. When the black man came round again for our fares, Joseph flourished our written passes in his face, but it might have been a receipt for Income Tax for all he could make of it, so the stationmaster came to the rescue and we then had to disburse, though he was exceedingly mystified by the fact that three of us were now present while only two paid for the up-journey; this was of course because I had gone to the Post Office.

Duffws Station. A.D. 1975.

At Duffws we found the train was waiting, so Charles and I secured seats while Joseph enquired respecting our missing property. Judge his horror then on being told: 'Mr Freeman had taken it.' Now, at Carnarvon, the clerk would not give a receipt for the article in question as it was to be forwarded by three different companies, so it would have been very easy for anyone to have said 'that is my bag', paid the carriage and walked off with it. However, the facts were not quite so bad as this; it appeared that notwithstanding the label was distinctly marked 'Ffestiniog Railway Station, to be left till called for', the officials knowing a person of the same name in this village had actually sent it to him. It was of no use wasting time in talking, the train ought to have started, but Joseph said it must be detained while I procured the missing article. So, having obtained a porter as guide, off I started. This individual was not to be hurried; I wished him to show me the way so that I might run on, but he said no doubt the train would wait and plodded on as if time were no object. However, after going a short distance, I spied my well known name gleaming over a shop door, so off I rushed and rather startled the nerve of the good lady behind the counter and a native whom she was endeavouring to supply with goods, by asking for my property. She acknowledged having the bag, and paying ten pence for the carriage, but as to why it had been left here when directed to another place, or why not returned when the mistake was discovered she 'did not know indeed!', and was about to give it up when the customer hinted that it might not be mine after all. Upon this I produced the key and offered to open it; this settled the case and without further parley I repaid the carriage, shouldered the bag and scampered off, leaving the astonished porter – who had but just arrived – to reflect upon the 'baksheesh' he had lost by not being sharper. As I fled through the street, the villagers opened their eyes in amazement evidently thinking something had happened, and on arriving at the station I found the train had been kept specially waiting for me nearly a quarter of an hour – just fancy this! As may be well imagined I was now hot, breathless and very glad to seat myself in the train, which started off immediately. As all is said to be 'well that ends well', suppose we must not grumble at this little adventure, especially as it has enabled me to fill so large a space in this diary.*

The question now was, should we be able to catch the 4.20 train at Minffordd Junction for Barmouth? The whole journey being downhill, we of course went much faster and arrived there with a little time to spare. The expected train was also half an hour late and when it did come was so full that we could not find three vacant seats in one compartment so were obliged for once to be separated. The line is along a flat sandy coast, the only place of interest being Harlech where is an old castle, but the 'March of the Men of Harlech' would not now I think be a very extensive affair. By 6 o'clock we were at the end of our day's journey, viz, Barmouth, having been during the last five hours either in a railway carriage or station nearly the whole time. For this we had to thank the Beddgelert tourist, and I do not think after all we gained much by the change of route, as the walk to Porthmadog was certainly not so magnificent as he made out, and one journey on the Ffestiniog railway would have been quite sufficient.

Our first care now was to search for a place to call our home until Monday, and as suitable hotels seemed scarce Joseph made an attempt to secure private apartments, but people did not care to 'take us in' for so short a period. However, at the fourth attempt, he succeeded and we were soon located in a house opposite the church. As it was still early, we went for a stroll by the seashore, enjoyed the breeze, listened to some instrumental music in front of the grand hotel, and in passing the Presbyterian Chapel heard sounds of singing. So we stopped and listened, thinking it was probably a Welsh service, but on being informed that they were about to practise some of Sankey's pieces and that visitors were quite welcome, we entered and a commencement was made with 'Hold the Fort'.* As nearly all who sang from music used Sol-fa, we readily obtained a copy; a lady presided at the harmonium and we had some of the best known pieces such as 'Sweet By and By', 'The Gate Ajar' etc. The sopranos and alto voices were very powerful, but they seemed to have no idea of singing softly, and went from one verse to another without hardly any pause. One of the gentlemen, when he heard were Sol-fa-ists from London, asked if we knew Mr Proudman, and on being told we were members of his choir was highly delighted and shouted out the news to a certain Mr Jenkins who was some distance off.† In fact they seemed quite glad to see us, and gave us a cordial invitation to come on the morrow. Returning to our apartments we found another individual was to his meals in our sitting room; to this (if necessary) we had agreed beforehand as we were staying for so short a time. Retired to bed about 10 o'clock.

* Ira David Sankey (1840–1908) was an American gospel singer and composer. He often toured with the evangelist preacher Dwight L. Moody. Sankey's hymns include 'Oh tell me the story that never grows old', 'Who is on the Lord's side?' and 'Sometimes I hear strange music'. He produced a number of hymn books; his most popular, *Sacred Songs and Solos* (1896), is still in print.

† Joseph Proudman conducted the London Tonic Sol-fa Temperance Choir, which was founded in 1860, and which comprised 70 male and female singers.

SUNDAY 29 AUGUST

7 a.m. Turned out of bed, and – in company with the individual who was staying at our house – directed our steps towards the beach, where we all (save Charles) had a capital bathe, which

the soft sand beneath and warm sun above rendered doubly enjoyable: then, having re-dressed, we strolled through the town. Barmouth – little more than one long street of some 200 houses – appears to have but lately sprung into existence: in one direction is the River Mawddach across which runs the rail, and in the other a splendid stretch of fine sand, along which doubtless ere long a parade will appear. Altogether the place is very prettily situated.

Breakfast finished, we went to the Presbyterian Chapel and seeing the gentleman who welcomed us last night, seated ourselves again near the harmonium at which presided a Miss Davies who played in a ladylike manner, not 'showing off' as did her substitute last night. The hymns were all chosen from Mr Sankey's edition and the singing went very well. Nearly all the congregation were English, the natives having had a service all to themselves previously. We heard a good sermon from Matthew, chapter 10, verses 32 and 33, but the minster had a peculiar manner of waving his bible in the air; I do not know how he would have managed had it been a very large one. Before this, a collection was made in a species of shovel which was poked in front of each individual, and an announcement given that Miss Davies would sing one of Mr Sankey's solos at the afternoon service. This young lady is a professional vocalist at the Royal Academy of Music in London but was now home for her holidays. Her native townspeople are very proud of her as indeed they have some reason to be.

Service being over by 12 o'clock, we went for a short stroll. It was a magnificent day; just my *beau ideal* of what a Sunday by the seaside should be, sun brilliantly hot, a gentle breeze, sea almost without a ripple and everything of course exceedingly quiet. On the railway is the following notice: 'Persons crossing this line are requested to look sharp after passing trains!' As there is hardly one per hour I should not have thought this warning necessary, but suppose 'prevention is better than cure'.

A capital dinner having been provided by our landlady, we

made a desperate attack thereon and came off victorious with much booty, after which we rested a little. Then, wishing to take a short stroll, we consulted the above lady who was doing her best to direct us to the Panorama Walks, when a lady staying in the rooms beneath ours offered to lend us her 'Guide', which we thankfully accepted.* It was one of Abel Heywood's, who publishes others of a similar character of all the principal places in North Wales, and if the explicit information contained therein was a fair criterion they must be a very cheap two penny-worth. The gentleman who had bathed with us, being quite by himself, intimated that if we had no objection he should like to accompany us, to this we assented but, not wishing him to make a similar request on the morrow, marched off at a pretty good pace, so that by the time we reached the top of a moderately high hill he – not being at all robust – was quite out of breath, and voted for a rest. Of course we left him to imagine this was our usual speed, and having gained the summit of our ambition seated ourselves, and quietly enjoyed the prospect around from the heights not inaptly called the Panorama Walks. The splendid expanse of water in Cardigan Bay and the winding Mawddach enclosed by lofty mountains, chief among which towers the majestic Cader Idris, forms a sight said to equal the famous Drachenfels on the Rhine, but we hardly saw it at its best, as the tide was low and the river consequently not half full. Here we sat, gazed and mused, deeply thankful for the glorious weather with which we were favoured and which enabled us to enjoy tenfold the splendid works of our Creator spread out on every hand.

Returning, we had an early tea and then repaired to the Wesleyan Chapel. On entering, the harmonium was grinding and three or four voices shouting 'Hold the Fort' to the utmost of their power. When asking if we could be accommodated with a tune book, we were told they only used Sol-fa; this of course was rather an advantage so we were conducted upstairs to the choir. The singing was entirely spoilt by the harmoniumist who sang as well as played. Whether he was in the habit of eating files

* The Panorama Walks is a group of trails set out in the Victorian period for the use of tourists. They offer views of the Mawddach estuary and Cardigan Bay. *Barmouth and Harlech* was one of a wide range of guides to tourist destinations in the UK published by Abel Heywood of Manchester.

* The brothers attend Soho Chapel when at home in London. This Baptist chapel stood at 406 Oxford Street, near Soho Square, according to *Dickens's Dictionary of London* (1879).

† 'Hold the Fort' (1870) is a hymn by Philip Bliss. The chorus in English is: 'Hold the fort, for I am coming,' / Jesus signals still; / Wave the answer back to heaven, / 'By Thy grace we will'.

or swallowing nutmeg-graters I cannot say, but his voice was fearfully harsh in fact the worst – for one who pretended to be musical – I have ever heard, and that all who attend Soho Chapel will admit, this is saying a good deal.* The chapel was small but well filled, Mr Brown of Bedford preaching from Acts, chapter 3, verse 10, and immediately after the benediction the harmonium and choir – without any announcement – again struck up 'Hold the Fort', which appears to be a great favourite here on account I suppose of its warlike words and music.† This time it was in Welsh, which caused us to beat a hasty retreat. I have appended the chorus and appeal to the unprejudiced reader if it is not sufficient to frighten any civilised being:

> Dalich afael medd yr Ieeu
> Deuaf atch chwi
> Bloeddiwn rianw'n ol ri ddalwin
> Yr dy all u di

During service time, it being warm and the doors open, a number of people could be seen prowling about outside, and the children were I think playing at 'touch' or some other juvenile game; these individuals all trooped in directly we were done for their Welsh service. It being only 7.20 p.m. we crossed over to the Presbyterian place of worship and hearing a sermon was being delivered in the native tongue, we entered entirely of course from curiosity as not a single word could we understand. The minister was a sallow-looking man with very long hair, and spoke in a peculiarly melancholy voice, more like intoning than anything I know, but towards the close he became more energetic. We were afterwards told the subject was the crucifixion, and it was considered a very eloquent discourse. This being finished, a hymn was read and during the singing thereof – as it was now quite dusk – a queer old fellow near the pulpit struck a Lucifer match and then, walking amongst the congregation, threw a light upon the subject. This hymn was a curiosity in its way, consisting of eight verses sung nearly in unison and very slowly to a minor tune, with one of the elders who started the melody continuing the key-tone between each verse. This perhaps he thought was necessary to sustain the pitch, since some of the old people here are so prejudiced that, though they have a harmonium, they will not use it for their own services. Though a large chapel it was quite full, so much so indeed that an unpleasant frowsy odour was perceptible, which did not speak well for the cleanliness of the congregation and made us glad to be once more in the open air.

After a short communion service, a meeting for singing was held similar to that last night, to this about 150 people stayed and seemed thoroughly to enjoy it: as before, the treble and alto voices were capital but those of the men very coarse as if they were never in the habit of singing softly. The English words were also articulated very indifferently. On my opinion as to their singing being asked by one of the tenors, I told him plainly what I thought, and rather to my surprise he coincided with me (this was the more singular as he was one of the greatest transgressors) saying that though they had much more powerful voices than those belonging to our London choirs, he knew they were wanting in expression, which is of course the soul of music. Miss Davies sang the solo 'Come home Father', with much taste and feeling, her unobtrusive and ladylike manner pleasing us greatly.

The nightmare.

part-songs for choral
singing. Many schools
and colleges had
Glee Clubs, the first of
which was established
at Harrow School in
London in 1787. The
word first started to
be used as a musical
term in the 17th
century. The song they
are singing here is
from *The Haymakers*
by George F. Root.

The services held at the chapel were as follows: Welsh 9 a.m., English 11 a.m., Sunday School 2 p.m., English 4 p.m., Welsh 6 p.m., Communion 7.35 p.m. and the meeting for singing at 8.30 p.m., so the authorities cannot be accused of belonging to the 'do nothing' race. The gentleman who lent us tune books and made us so welcome had attended all save one, and that (the one at 4 o'clock) he could not manage. After chatting some time we bade him goodbye, expressing our hearty thanks for his kindness. Then returning to our apartments we were occupied for an hour or more letter writing, but retired to bed about 11 o'clock to sleep and renew our strength for the morrow.

MONDAY 30 AUGUST

Owing to the late hours kept last night, we did not rise till 7 o'clock, and an hour after were fortifying ourselves for the forthcoming day's pleasure by a substantial breakfast. On settling our little bill, we found the expenses were not much more than half what they would have been had we stayed at a hotel; it also suited us much better, as we were able to spend the Sunday in our own manner, not mixing with persons whose habits would clearly clash with ours.

Bidding our landlady good-day, we booked our wardrobe for the last time to Llangollen, taking special care to write the directions on the label clearly, then enquired if there were any boats going to Dolgelly – this being a capital way to view the scenery – but finding we ought to have gone up with the tide at 7 a.m. determined to walk instead and by 9.30 were out of Barmouth. As usual, the morning was fine and, being nearly full, the River Mawddach, with the grand Cader Idris range of mountains, presented a glorious spectacle. 'Light hearted were we and free from care' as onwards we merrily went, ever and anon carolling some well-known part-song of glee to give vent to the exuberance of our spirits.* Though it is some time since we first learned to sing – I am afraid to say just how long – neither of us have ever had to regret it, and on such an occasion as this its utility became specially apparent: if one learns to play an instrument, say the pianoforte, bass-viol or drum, they cannot well take it with them on a walking tour, but God's own gift – our voices – we always have and should learn to use as He intended. That this can be so easily done and yet persons with low voices will persist in vainly trying to reach the upper notes or grovel on with 'hideous moan' in the lowest depths, is a marvel which I leave the reader to solve.

A pleasant walk of about eight miles brought us to Llanelle-tyd, where we enquired at the Post Office and general warehouse as to the direction of two celebrated waterfalls which were found to be nearly seven miles distant: we had intended to dine at Dolgelly, but finding it to be quite out of our route purchased some of the best provisions this small village afforded. Unfortunately, there was nothing to choose between biscuits and a 7lb tin of Australian mutton, to which we hardly felt equal, so laid in a stock of the former. It had hitherto been a matter of wonder with us how the inhabitants obtain their letters in some of these remote districts, but the postmaster here informed us that those who did not live within 70 yards of the main road had to send for theirs. This of course solved the difficulty of the letter carrier having to deliver a communication to, say, the man who lives on the top of Snowdon, which we thought would be rather awkward especially if the day should be wet.

1.30 p.m. Resumed our journey, passing by some very fine orchards, where trees laden with plums grew within arm's reach of the road. These soon gave place to wilder scenery: the Mawd-dach rushing nosily over its extremely rocky bed and lofty hills rearing themselves on either hand, sometimes covered with trees so close together that it was quite dark beneath and they looked like a forest of sticks, others assuming a rugged aspect or covered with short furze. Streams and waterfalls were of frequent occurrence, these being at times utilised by water mills, but very few houses were to be seen. No help is given to the traveller in

* Fingerposts
are signposts
with the name of
the destination,
sometimes the
distance, and the end
of the sign shaped
like a hand with the
index finger pointing
in the direction of the
destination.

Wales by fingerposts or otherwise, and people are only to be met with at long intervals and even then their directions are often exceedingly foggy.* Nevertheless, having walked about four miles – and they seemed to be very long ones – we turned to the right up a rugged footpath through thick overhanging foliage, but still keeping to the river's side; many a time the sound of its rushing waters was so loud that we thought the falls were close at hand, but were each time doomed to disappointment.

Hereabouts Charley – having hurt his ankle, of which we were not aware – lagged behind so we, on reaching the end of our journey, seated ourselves and waited for him, but all in vain for no Charley appeared. I ran back, shouted as best I could, and fancied I heard a reply, but the noise of the falling waters was so great that it was of very little use so doing; to make matters worse for us he had the provisions which, for all we knew, he might be quietly enjoying behind some rock close at hand. We even might not again see each other till we arrived in London. However, after a short interval of suspense, I saw the well-known puggaree waving some distance above, and once more we were together, though Charles could never make it clear as to where he had been wandering.

The two waterfalls here – called Pistyll y Mawddach and Pistyll y Cain – are situated in a glen, and though both are well worth seeing, the latter is by far the finest having an unbroken fall of water about 130 feet in depth. After the winter rains it

Muid y Matter

must present a splendid sight as it would then be about four times as wide; we were much more fortunate than the majority of summer tourists as July had been an exceedingly wet month, in consequence of which all the mountain torrents and rivers presented an exceptionally fine appearance for this time of year. Two gold mines are to be seen near here: one close by the falls and the other some little distance away. The precious metal is obtained by crushing a species of quartz, but the machinery was at a standstill and not a single person to be seen, though we heard it was a very paying speculation. At the foot of Pistyll y Cain we consumed our provisions, rested about half an hour and then (5 p.m.) started back for Dolgelly.

Though the morning had been very fine, since leaving Llanelletyd the sky had been gradually becoming more and more cloudy, and now at last rain began to descend, valleys and mountains looked very gloomy and we hurried along sheltering ourselves as well as possible under the trees. Notwithstanding several smart showers – which fortunately were not of long duration – we did not get wet and arrived in good condition at Dolgelly a little before 8 o'clock, having traversed quite 23 miles, and as part of the distance was over a very rough road I consider this our best walking performance. Having been recommended to Ellis' Temperance Hotel we were before long discussing a first rate tea in the coffee room.* Here there was a piano, harmonium and visitors' book to amuse ourselves, but nothing worth copying was to be seen in this latter.

Just opposite our abode were the Assembly Rooms, where a concert was taking place. We had seen it advertised at Barmouth and had thought of forming a part of the audience, but of course arrived here much too late. There was evidently a good number of persons and – judging by the fearful yells (applause is not the word) which were uttered at the close of each song – they fully appreciated the singer's efforts. The tenor Eos Morlais, at the conclusion of a Welsh piece, finished on the high A; to say this 'brought down the house' would hardly be correct, since a

* The Temperance Hotel stood in West Street, Dolgelly (now known as Dolgellau).

* Richard Davies
(Mynyddog) (1833–
77) was a popular
Welsh language poet.

prolonged 'Yah!' broke from the assemblage and their shouts must have been heard over a good portion of the town.

An individual called Mynyddog did the comic business with great effect and, as we had a programme and the windows of the hall were opened, we could hear the whole concert very well.* At last the end came; everyone sang 'God save the Queen' in stentorian strains and the streets were flooded with people, some of whom came from long distances and must have had some difficulty in reaching their homes as the last train had departed long ago.

TUESDAY 31 AUGUST

6.30 a.m. Anxiously looking out of the window, we perceived the sun had risen earlier than ourselves and had already commenced business. Last night being very cloudy, we had half feared a wet day and now hoped it might not be too fine to last. Walking to the railway station, I enquired for the best scenery in the neighbourhood and was strongly recommended to 'do' the Torrent and Precipice Walks, and then go by rail to Bala on the road to which there was very little worth seeing. The houses in Dolgelly are mostly built of stone, and of an ancient type; the inhabitants also I should say are rather 'behind the age', as even the time of their clocks is very slow.

After a good breakfast, my brothers occupied (I will not say wasted) a considerable amount of time in composing and writing some rhymes in the visitors' book stating their opinion of our reception. Then, leaving our knapsack here, we walked down to the bridge and obtained from the chief – because the only – constable, full directions for our morning's walk; these Joseph transferred to paper, after which we started off. Having travelled about half a mile we came to a halt in the middle of some field, with no path to guide us, and were informed by some workmen that we were trespassing. However, being assured we wished for nothing better than to be put in the right direction, they endeavoured to direct us but with little success.

At last we were again on the high road – from which we ought never to have wandered – and soon found ourselves at the gates of the Nannau estate. Here a lady and gentleman accompanied by a guide were going on the same errand as ourselves, so we followed them and thus avoided any further mistake. This estate is a splendid wooded park through which runs a carriage drive to the house, and a little farther on commences what are known as the Precipice Walks. Here on the face of a steep hill is cut a capital path about two miles in length and in many places not more than the same number of feet wide, but the views at every step are most magnificent: at first, hill behind hill – to the number of about 30 – rises in front covered with purple furze, grass or trees. Then comes the splendid valley we traversed yesterday, with its silvery stream and pigmy houses just visible amidst the luxuriant foliage, whilst in the far distance (about 25 miles) rises a lofty range of mountains. Progressing onwards, Llanelletyd lies at our feet and the whole length of the River Mawddach, the railway which crosses it at Barmouth and the sea beyond are plainly visible. Dolgelly nestling in the beautifully wooded landscape and the Cader Idris mountain in the background bring the panorama to a close. As the sun was shining brightly, I need hardly say we greatly enjoyed this truly picturesque bird's eye view, my brothers averring it was so beautiful that it would be of no use to travel farther, and we had better return to London with these last pleasant recollections in our minds. Certainly it was the prettiest sight I have ever seen.

On nearing Nannau House again – for we had described a complete circle – a gentleman walking behind us asked if a certain little book was our property. Joseph at once gave a negative answer, but Charles immediately after claimed it; it proved to be his notes for a diary similar to this which he had dropped: I fear to picture the calamitous results to his diary-reading friends had it been lost. Though the contents only related to one day, perhaps he would have drawn largely on his fertile imagination and the reader been none the wiser, perhaps he has done so in the present instance; time alone will show.

Returning to Dolgelly well satisfied with our morning's walk, Joseph again· interviewed the constable regarding the route to the Torrent Walk, whilst I purchased some provisions and Charley went for the knapsack, then (2.30) we all set off again and were before long ascending a steep road under a very hot sun. Having gone a little distance, a small urchin volunteered to show us the way, and then asked for a subscription towards buying a ball so that he and his friends might play at cricket on the green. Much as we like this game we did not put our names down as subscribers, for we had not even seen such a place and had little doubt but it was only an 'idea' to impose on unwary travellers.

Two miles from Dolgelly commences what is known as the Torrent Walk. At first it is almost the counterpart of the River Lyn in Devonshire. A small stream rushing and foaming over many large stones, with trees growing on either side casting a refreshing shade and sometimes meeting together overhead. Here, having found a suitable spot, we pitched our camp and rations were duly served out. The 'Adam's Ale' which flowed at our feet being stimulant sufficient for us, notwithstanding all some people say about the absolute necessity of having so much beer per day.* On resuming our journey, the ascent became very steep, the river descending by waterfalls 20 or 30 feet at a time, then dashing along at a rapid rate only to repeat the descent again and again. This scenery continued for about two miles and then terminated most fitly in a calm pool of water, an utter con-trast to all that had preceded it. The day being beautifully fine, the views at every step we took were charming and (though this was the last day of our tour) we enjoyed ourselves amazingly and could not well have chosen two spots more lovely and at the same time so totally different as the Precipice and Torrent Walks.

From here we had intended to make for Bont Newydd and

thence take the train to Bala, but after having walked a long distance enquired at a cottage and found that somehow we had missed the proper path, so pressed forward again for the station. The road was rough and extremely bad walking but, being at a great elevation, the views all along the valley were very fine, the River Mawddach sparkling in the far distance like glass. Descending to the vale below, we strolled leisurely along, thinking there was ample time and on reaching a lodge (which belonged to the Nannau estate although so far from Dolgelly) we refreshed ourselves with some capital milk, then thinking we might as well ascertain how far it was to Drws-y-nant enquired, and were exceedingly astonished on hearing it was nearly two miles. Quick march therefore was the order of the day, thinking perhaps for once the train might arrive in time. This however was not the case by 20 minutes and it was 7.30 before we were off again. Passing on our journey Bala Lake, a splendid expanse of water four miles in length, we arrived at the station of that name and found the town was quite a mile distant: here we had been advised to patronise a certain Mrs Griffiths, and though she appeared to be of the 'Tartar' breed and we were not particularly elevated at the appearance of the house, we decided to stay there, as it was by this time quite dark, and it was quite possible to 'go farther and fare worse'. The results proved our wisdom, and we had no reason to regret our choice.

* Bala Calvinistic Methodist College was founded in 1837 with Lewis Edwards and David Charles as tutors. The statue is actually to Thomas Charles (1755–1814), a founder of the British and Foreign Bible Society, and grandfather of the above David Charles.

WEDNESDAY I SEPTEMBER

6.15 a.m. For the last time this holiday we rose, dressed and then took a short stroll well knowing that for at least two of us the end had almost come. Bala is mainly formed of one very long street and has several churches and chapels with some pretensions to architectural beauty, a fine handsome college and a statue erected to the memory of its founder, the Rev. John Charles.* In recording our doings at Llanrwst, I mentioned the great numerical superiority of the Jones tribe, and though I have not since said much about it, the same fact was noticeable in every village we visited, but here, as if to crown the absurdity, a clock is erected to the memory of John Jones Esq., but neither his native place or previous occupation is stated. Perhaps it is a joke and intended to serve as a memorial to a large number of the inhabitants, which it certainly does.

Having made a good breakfast, we departed for the railway station, passing Bala Lake, a beautifully clear piece of water, and though the morning was dull the reflection of hills, houses and sky was almost like a second edition below. The train was late as usual, and during the journey a curious quacking noise was heard, which could not be accounted for until one of the passengers on alighting drew a basket of ducks from under the seat. Passing various spots which seemed now quite familiar to us, we arrived at Llangollen by 10.40 a.m. thus finishing our tour in Jonesland which – owing to the splendid weather – we had enjoyed far beyond our expectations. In the description I have endeavoured to give of the scenery, it may be thought I have been too enthusiastic, but this really is not the case and I can only advise any disbelievers to go and see for themselves before passing such an opinion.

As we had about an hour and a half to spend at Llangollen, Joseph wanted to utilise the time by climbing Barber's Hill. This idea was abandoned as a heavy mist hung around and would have spoilt any view we otherwise might have had. Instead of this, we each speculated in some photographs of the surrounding

country, then calling at the Post Office found four letters waiting to cheer us under the trying circumstances. One of these was from Zeph and amused us as it contained a graphic account of how during the service at Soho on the previous Sunday the musicians had endeavoured to adapt a 148th metre tune to a common metre hymn, but notwithstanding the harmonium was playing with an amount of force worthy of a better cause the two could not be made to agree together and the attempt was eventually abandoned in despair.*

Took a short walk up the Holyhead Road but, as it began to rain a little, we turned our style towards the station, once more was the train behind time but we all eventually arrived at Ruabon where it was necessary to change carriages. Whilst waiting here, three gentlemen near me were talking together, when one of them suddenly said to his companions: 'Do you know each other?' On receiving a negative answer, introduced them as 'Mr Jones of Barmouth' and 'Mr Richards of Dolgelly'. I almost burst out laughing, and am sure it was a great wonder they did not both bear the former name.

2.12 p.m. Started off and, not hearing anything to the contrary, concluded we were now fairly on our way to London. However, on reaching Shrewsbury we stopped for some time. Thinking it could do no harm to ask if we were 'All right', I did so, and finding if we stayed in our present position we should soon be in Aberystwyth, changed carriage very expeditiously. What a pleasant termination it would have been to our holiday to have found ourselves towards the evening in South Wales instead of London! Resuming our journey, we had for travelling companions two Welshmen, one of whom tried to enter into conversation with us but his knowledge of English was rather limited. However we ascertained he was a native of Harlech from which place he started at 8.30 a.m. and hoped to reach his destination sometime during the evening, having already changed carriages five times with one or two more in prospect. He seemed pretty well tired on bidding us 'Good-day' at Oxford,

* 148th metre takes its name from Psalm 148, which has verses of eight lines; the first four have six syllables and the second four have four. Common metre has verses of four lines; the first two have eight syllables and the second two have six.

we first confiding him to the tender mercies of a porter as he seemed rather foggy as to what ought to be his next step. From here the iron horse quickened his pace considerably and brought us to the great metropolis within five minutes of the stipulated time, this event being celebrated by our singing 'The March of the Men of Harlech'. And what more can I say?

Calling the marrowbone stage once more into requisition we soon arrived at the palatial mansion of the Freemans, were cordially received by the inhabitants thereof, and before many hours had – figuratively speaking – our noses again at...

THE GRINDSTONE.

SCOTLAND

AUGUST 1876.

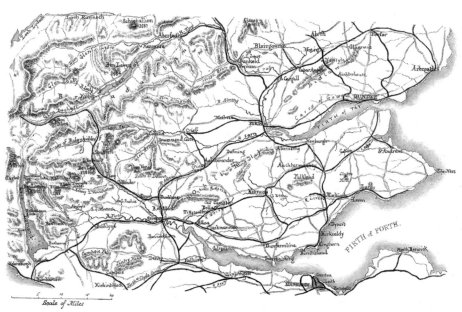

Scale of Miles

Map showing the line of route travelled.

Saturday to Monday	London	to	Edinburgh	Friday	Callander to Killin.
Monday	Edinburgh	.	Stirling	Saturday	Killin . Dunkeld.
Tuesday	Stirling	.	Callander	Sunday to Tuesday	Dunkeld.
Wednesday	Callander	.	Balloch	Tuesday	Dunkeld to Edinburgh
Thursday	Balloch	.	Callander	Wednesday to Friday	Edinburgh . London.

PROLOGUE

In years now gone by, when Charley and I
Were arranging our peregrination;
Each time with much pains we worried our brains
As to where we should spend our vacation.

But summer came round this year, and we found
Our ideas on the subject agreeing;
Resolved we would go to Scotland, and know
If her mountains and lakes were worth seeing.

Then all whom we knew, and they were not few,
Who had ever crossed over the border,
Were asked what they saw, and many things more,
For we like to do all in good order.

By aid of these friends, on whom much depends,
We planned out the route after travelled;
With maps at our side, we studied the 'Guide',
And its legends perused and unravelled.*

The captain and crew all told, numbered two,
Who were destined to make this invasion,
There used to be three, but that could not be
On the present momentous occasion.

---

* Alongside their trusty Bradshaw, the brothers may have consulted *Black's Picturesque Tourist of Scotland* (Adam and Charles Black, Edinburgh, 20th edition, 1875) or *Murray's Scottish Tourist* (Thomas Murray & Sons, Glasgow, 8th edition, 1875).

For Joseph you see is married, and he
Now goes in for domestic attractions;
So cannot well roam any distance from home,
On account of the infantile fractions.

And so to the north we two sallied forth,
Ever hoping for beautiful weather;
For always the wet – which seldom we get –
Throws a damper on everyone's pleasure.

SATURDAY 19 AUGUST

Towards mid-day, passengers were fast assembling on board the General Steam Navigation Company's screw steamer 'The Libra'.* Many however – ourselves among the number – had arrived in good time, and were watching the stowing of the cargo in the hold, which was executed by several men aided by a large steam crane, with great rapidity; one of these individuals having used bad language, as sea-faring men so often do, the captain gave him a piece of his mind, and admonished him in such a style that the culprit was glad to get out of sight. Some of the passengers were already making themselves comfortable for the voyage, and the pilot having taken his position on the bridge, those who were not bound for 'merrie Scotland' made for the shore; these included a fruit woman who was selling pears and lemons, though what these latter were for I cannot say, unless they are supposed to be a preventative against sea-sickness.†

12.15 p.m. Steered off from the wharf and commenced our voyage, the sun gleaming forth, which was of course put down as a very satisfactory omen. The steamer – which we trusted would take us safely on our journey of 470 miles – usually trades to Hamburg, but goes to Scotland during the summer months for the better accommodation of the tourist traffic. She was a capital specimen of her class, standing 15 to 20 feet out of the water, with a raised deck fore and aft, double funnels and generally in so trim and sea-going like an appearance, that as we passed through the fine shipping which abounds on the Thames, her equal was rarely seen.

Mr Glover, the honorary secretary of the Tonic Sol-fa Association, was to give us the benefit of his company during the voyage.‡ There may be certain cases when the saying 'Two is company, but three is none' is true, but it decidedly did not

* The General Steam Navigation Company, founded in London in 1821, specialised in routes between London, other British ports and north-west Europe. It was bought by P&O in 1971. The *Libra*, a twin-screw steamer which was built by Gourlay Brothers in Dundee and launched in 1869, was 250 feet long with a gross tonnage of 1,030. The vessel sailed from St Katharine's Dock, Wapping.

† 'Merrie Scotland' is John's version of the usual phrase 'Merrie England', popularised by William Hazlitt in an essay of the same name in 1819, and referring to an idealised version of the country that existed at some un-specified 'golden age' in the remote past.

‡ Given their commitment to Sol-fa singing, it is likely that the brothers were members of the association.

apply on this occasion, and we were only too glad to have such a genial companion. Having all booked saloon berths some days previously, we at once took possession of the same, and while so doing the steward presented each passenger with a card containing a list of the various refreshments supplied and asked if we desired to 'contract'. Stout gentlemen might consider such a question little short of a personal affront, but what he meant was this: those who wish to give their names at the commencement of the voyage and agree to pay the sum of 12 shillings for breakfast, dinner, tea, etc. during that time, which would otherwise be rather more. For many this is a very bad speculation, as if ill, they are still bound to pay for that which they saw but could not partake of. Trusting that we should not be reduced to such a miserable plight as this, we put our names amongst the list of 'contractors', and then came again on deck.

On passing the Foreign Cattle Market at Deptford, we took a turn in the front to enjoy the breeze, which was tempered by the various odours for which Father Thames is famous. Shortly after, it rained sharply so were obliged to descend once more into the lower regions. The saloon measured almost 70 x 12 feet, was ornamented with stained glass, much gilding and ornaments, and being well supplied with good sofa seats, presented altogether a very comfortable appearance. Here, some were having lunch but we did not wish to spoil our appetites for dinner. Glover wanted some soda-water and a lemon, but of these latter articles there were only three on board: these the waiter thought would be required for whisky toddy in the evening, which he imagined would be in great request.

After half an hour, we ascended again on deck, when old Sol was shining brightly and enabled us to have a good view of both banks of the river. The passengers for the most part walked to and fro, as the only fixed seats on the promenade were a few on each side of the saloon skylights, but plenty of camp-stools were obtainable from below, and were freely used by those so inclined. About 2 o'clock we passed Erith, just before the captain called our attention to the Seamen's Institution at Belvedere, enlarged on its merits, distributed circulars respecting it, and ended by passing round a collection box for its benefit.* Our commodore was certainly an oddity: imagine a short, thick-set, weather-beaten man, with the bumps of arguments and obstinacy very strongly developed, crowned by that most un-nautical of head dresses, a chimney pot hat (and one too which had evidently seen many a storm) taking short walks backwards and forwards, and talking all the while, and you will have some idea of Captain Wilson of 'The Libra', whom I shall have occasion to make mention of again before reaching Edinburgh.†

2.30 p.m. Gravesend. Here a boat came out and took off our pilot, also two ladies who had accompanied their friends thus far on their journey. One would almost think a captain who so often navigates the river had no need of a pilot, but we were told that the articles of insurance made it necessary. Soon after, the ship's bell sounded 'Prepare for action': this was the warning note for dinner, to which half an hour later we sat down in the saloon cabin. The menu consisted of salmon, soles, beef, mutton, lamb, pastry, fruit etc. About 40 were present, and nearly all seemed determined to make at least a good commencement. We wondered how many would present themselves at tomorrow's mid-day meal, and whether we should be among the number. Some of the ladies merely played with that which was set before them, being probably under the impression that it is a bad thing to eat much when commencing a sea voyage, we on the contrary thought there was nothing like making a good foundation, but avoided all kinds of intoxicating liquors, which some people seem to regard as preventatives, but which we do not patronise.

After an hour spent transferring some of the before mentioned eatables to more eligible quarters, we again reappeared on deck and found we had passed Southend, were rounding the Mouse Light, and going along at a fine rate.‡ Visited the forecabin arrangements and found them very inferior to ours; curious odours enough to make one feel queer haunted the

* The Royal Alfred Aged Merchant Seamen's Institution was opened at Belvedere-on-Thames in January 1867 by the Shipwrecked Fishermen and Mariners' Royal Benevolent Society, with accommodation for 80 retired seafarers.

† John's reference to the 'bumps of arguments and obstinacy' on Captain Wilson's skull indicates a knowledge of phrenology, a so-called science that asserted that personality could be read from the bumps on someone's head. A chimney pot hat is a type of top hat with slightly convex sides.

‡ The Mouse Lightship was moored off the Mouse Sand in the Thames Estuary.

neighbourhood, so we beat a retreat, well satisfied with our quarters. The company appears to cater more for first- than second-class passengers, and really the additional comfort is quite worth the extra money. Enjoyed a good blow in the front and counted the number of persons on board: there were not more than 100, though I should think the boat would have taken at least three times as many. Some were reclining, so as to avoid all possible motion. We rolled but little and all were as yet 'good sailors'. The day had hitherto been rather dull, the sun not often cheering us with his presence, but in passing the Mouse Light he produced some very pretty effects on the clouds.

7 p.m. Tea (beef, ham, toast etc.) at which we 'assisted'. Not so many present as at dinner, and the rolling of the boat was much more perceptible, owing to which ladies opposite as were no sooner seated than they retired. On going above again, it was so chilly that we were glad to don our overcoats, and march arm in arm to and fro to keep ourselves warm. Of course, it was now quite dark, and the lights of Aldeburgh town showed very plainly as we passed along. Overhead, the stars were shining brightly, but landwards it was very sombre with flashes of lightning at intervals. Tried to do a little singing, but as neither of us knew the treble part perfectly, this effort was not very successful, so after staying on deck till 10.45 p.m. we thought it was about time to retire to rest, and therefore descended to our berths. These measured six by two feet, and were situated in small cabins running parallel with and opening into the saloon. Each cabin was illuminated by a large lamp, provided with washing conveniences, and in fact everything requisite except perhaps a little more elbow-room, but regarding this I suppose we must not grumble when on board ship. Usually I manage to go to sleep almost immediately, but then our house at Regent Street is a stationary one, and I did not seem to take kindly to the continued motion of the boat. However, after what appeared to me a very long time I did eventually fall into the arms of the sleepy god Morpheus.

SUNDAY 20 AUGUST

I was awakened several times during the night by the uneasy motion of my bedroom, which persisted in rolling first to one side, and then to the other; the sheets and blanket also showed an inclination to part company, and generally speaking I was rather uncomfortable. Nevertheless, our berths being on the inside and at some distance from the screw, we were in as good a position as possible, and doubtless had as much sleep as most, and a great deal more than very many of our fellow passengers. About 7 o'clock, having been awake some little time – remembering my former episode on the Jersey voyage – I turned out very carefully but the same result occurred viz, I felt an inward rising sensation. Being aware of the proverb 'Out of debt, out of danger', I immediately paid toll to Father Neptune, though it must be confessed not in a very generous manner, however doubtless he was appeased as he did not again trouble me.

After performing our toilettes we appeared on deck, where the sun was shining brightly, and a splendid breeze blowing. Glover, having brought one of Sankey's books, commenced singing, whilst Charles and I filled up the harmonies to the best of our ability. At first I thought some of the passengers might object to our displaying our musical propensities in this manner; on the contrary, however, many listened attentively, while if there were any possessors of 'savage breasts' which could not be 'soothed', well I suppose they walked away. Having thus pleasantly passed a considerable time, Charles declared he could not do any more before breakfast, and at 9.15 a.m. the bell rang for that necessary meal to which we at once hastened with great alacrity: ham, eggs, fish etc. appeared at the table and disappeared again with marvellous celerity, but the number of combatants were reduced to 25, which suggested the idea that all on board had not passed the night in happy demands.

Captain Wilson sat at the head of the tables, and seemed able to talk and eat at the same time. One old fellow – whom we

* Many Non-
conformists –
evidently including
John – rejected
vestments and clerical
collars, believing that
preachers should
not differentiate
themselves from
their fellow church
members. The 'all-
round dog-collar' was
in fact introduced
by the Church of
Scotland, and only
later adopted by
the Roman Catholic
Church. The Rev.
Dr William Brock
was minister of
Bloomsbury Chapel,
a Baptist church, in
Bloomsbury Street,
West London.
† The Bethel flag was
a blue flag, with the
word Bethel (House of
God) in white capital
letters across it. In the
top left corner was
a white star and in
the bottom left (also
in white) a dove with
an olive branch. It
was the symbol of
the Bethel Union, a
seafarers' missionary
organisation.

named Crabapple – did his best to find fault with everything: he grumbled about his berth (would doubtlessly have done so at his birth if possible), the sailing and speed of the vessel, and especially complained that the captain was so late that he had lost all appetite for his breakfast. At last he found a real grievance in the shape of a bad egg, which – being very anxious the waiter should inspect – he waved about with such vigour as quite to terrify his neighbour, who evidently thought that it had better remain in its egg shell and remonstrated accordingly. Still, all things come to an end, and so did Mr Crabapple's fault finding, but only because everyone else had quitted the breakfast table.

Ascending again, we asked the skipper if he intended to hold service – as we understood he generally did so – but he said 'there was too much swell on'; this was an excuse, as he afterwards acknowledged that his real reason was that he did not feel well enough. A clergyman being among the passengers, we suggested him as a fit and proper person to officiate, but the captain retorted he did not know what 'ism' he might preach and as he wore an ultra-clerical costume with an all-round dog-collar, perhaps he might be a Roman Catholic. It seems to me certainly unadvisable for evangelical and even dissenting ministers to adopt such a style of dress; it is funereal and ugly, especially the collar, and why they should imitate in appearance those from whom they so materially differ in doctrine I cannot understand, but would prefer to see them look like men (vide Dr Brock) not parsons.*

However, the captain said he would hoist the Bethel flag so that everyone might be reminded it was the Lord's Day, which ought to be sermon sufficient for all.† Then away he went, but shortly after returned and ordered the sailors to put the awning alongside so as to 'keep off the weather', bring up sofa seats from the saloon, see how many hymn books they could muster, tell the passengers to come from the front and ring the bell for church. All this was soon accomplished, but the bell gave forth such a mournful peal that someone suggested we were to have a funeral, whereupon the ringer had orders to make it more cheerful. The congregation began to assemble; one came smoking a pipe, another with a 'Daily Telegraph' under his arm, and several brought yellow covered novels, all of course laid aside when service commenced, but equally showing the true bent of their owners' minds.

The question now arose, 'Where is the minister?' and as Glover had been absent half an hour, I had almost determined in my own mind that he was preparing an address. However, the hymn books having been distributed amongst the congregation, who were seated in anything but church-like regularity, our indefatigable captain gave out a hymn, and asked us if we could 'raise Russia's Dream'? Not knowing a tune named 'Constantinople', we were rather startled at this request, but thinking he meant 'Rousseau', we sang that with very fair results.* A portion from Isaiah was then read, very liberally interspersed with remarks, and succeeded by a second hymn. Prayers then followed and another hymn was sung to 'Belmont'. The manner of giving out these hymns was highly original, as there were but few books the verse by verse system was adopted, so the captain accompanied his readings with observations and anecdotes, illustrative or not as the case might be; consequently we were always at a loss to know when to commence the next verse.

A sermon was duly preached from 1 Corinthians, chapter 15, verses 3 and 4. Our minister soon wandered from his text; still, he spoke earnestly and sincerely, pointing out that Christ and Christ only could save sinners, and urging his hearers to rest their hopes on Him. The discourse being concluded, 'Begone unbelief, my Saviour is near' was announced as an exceedingly suitable hymn for a termination, and duly commented upon when the preacher all at once changed his mind and said we would have 'Sun of my Soul' instead, which having been sung to 'Hursley' and the benediction pronounced, the congregation dispersed.† To me it was a very enjoyable service, though I fear it was regarded with mixed feelings by many, who attended more

* Some political satire here, suggesting that 'Russia's dream' was to capture Constantinople (now of course called Istanbul), the then capital of Turkey. The song 'Rousseau's Dream' is the popular name for a tune composed by Jean-Jacques Rousseau for his opera *Le Devin du Village* (1750).
† The hymn 'Begone unbelief, my Saviour is near' was written by John Newton and first published in 1779; 'Sun of my Soul, Thou Saviour Dear' was written by John Keble and first published in 1827.

* The monument
to Lord Collingwood
(1845), by the
sculptor John Graham
Lough, stands in Pier
Road, Tynemouth.
Cuthbert Collingwood,
who was born in
Newcastle in 1748,
was Admiral Lord
Nelson's second-
in-command at the
Battle of Trafalgar.

from curiosity, or because they had nothing else to do than any other motive. Next to Charley had been sitting a lady who sang a very good contralto, so after lunch we mustered all our copies of Sankey's music and by asking her to join formed a quartet and sang a number of his best pieces, the sun shining brilliantly the while and adding much to our enjoyment.

3.00 p.m. In answer to the dinner bell we seated ourselves in the salon to a repast consisting of salmon, chicken, beef, mutton, lamb, pastry etc., but the company exhibited a considerable falling off compared with that of yesterday, only 25 being present. As usual, the captain was engaged in an argument, this time with a Roman Catholic lady on the subject of confession. About 5 o'clock we came abreast of a fine range of hills on which could be distinctly seen a monument erected to the memory of Lord Collingwood, and soon after passed Tynemouth.* Hereabouts, Captain Wilson came round to examine tickets, and while doing so asked the clergyman if he would conduct evening service. He declined, having being affected by the sea voyage, and not feeling able to preach.

7.30 p.m. Tea. As the captain was not present, no one took upon himself to say grace, but each commenced without any audible preface. On reappearing above, we found it quite light, the fact being that at this time of the year the days lengthen as one travels northwards, which during the holidays is certainly a great boon. As it was rather cool, we put on our overcoats and paced to and fro, then went below and wrote letters, after which took a last survey above before turning in. To our surprise, we found two ladies and four gentlemen had made themselves beds on deck and intended to pass the night there. The latter were lying on their backs and singing 'Hold the Fort' with not a very charming effect.

11 p.m. Retired to our berths.

BRADSHAW ON GRANTON

 Here is an excellent pier, 1,700 feet, built by Walker, and a floating railway for luggage across to Burntisland, erected by Napier.

HOTEL: THE GRANTON HOTEL, THOMAS MARTIN

Had a much better night's rest: either the boat did not roll so much or else I was more accustomed to it, or perhaps it was a little of each. Arrived at our destination about 5 o'clock, and many of the passengers immediately rose and departed by the 5.45 train. We, however, voted for more slumbers, but obtained very little in consequence of the noise made on deck by those engaged in unloading, so we soon after followed their example, had a cup of coffee, paid for our 'contract', and then took leave of 'The Libra'. Granton has a fine harbour, close to which is the railway station. Here we essayed to take tickets for Edinburgh,

Princes Street, Edinburgh, Calton Hill in the distance.

BRADSHAW ON EDINBURGH

This city, which has not unaptly been termed the 'modern Athens', is one of the most ancient in this country. Its schools for the acquirement of useful knowledge have long held a high rank amongst the universities of Europe, and have supplied some of the most distinguished statesmen, warriors, poets and divines who have graced our annals.

It contains beauties and peculiarities which give it a high claim to attention amongst the capitals of Europe, and is the capital of Scotland, in a superb situation on the north slope of the Pentland Hills, fronting the Firth of Forth, two miles from it.

It covers a space of from two to two and a half miles square, and contains the Old Town on the east between the Castle, Holyrood Palace and the Abbey; the South Town, round Heriot's Hospital, Newington and Morningside; and the New Town on the north and north-west. Both the South and New towns have been erected within the last 100 years; the latter especially comprises many noble streets and squares, built of the beautiful stone from Craigleith Quarry.

In the Old Town, along the High Street, Canongate, Grassmarket etc., many houses are of Queen Mary's time, divided by narrow dark closes (or alleys), and from six to ten stories (or flats) high.

Between it and the New Town are East and West Princes Street Gardens, beautifully laid out, and through which the Edinburgh & Glasgow and North British railways pass; this was formerly called the North or Nor' Loch, a sheet of stagnant water. There are the North and Waverley bridges, and Mound, forming connection with the Old and New towns.

Edinburgh Castle: On a hill, 383 feet above the level of the sea, is surmounted by modern batteries, the state prison and arsenal, Queen Mary's room (where she gave birth to James VI) and the regalia room (admittance free by order from the City Chambers). [Queen Mary is better known as Mary, Queen of Scots.] Mons Meg, a large cannon, said to be cast at Mons, in Brittany in 1486, is mounted on a carriage on the Bomb Battery. The castle ought to be visited on account of the magnificent prospect it offers.

Nelson's Monument, on Calton Hill, is 102 feet in height; on the top is a time ball, which is lowered at one o'clock, Greenwich Time. National Monument, on Calton Hill, unfinished, consists of 12 great pillars, and erected at a cost of £13,000; it is a model of the Parthenon at Athens. Close by is the Royal Observatory, shaped like a St George's Cross, 62 feet long.

John Knox's House, foot of High Street, open on Tuesdays, Fridays and Saturdays (6d.), consists of three rooms, the principal object being the chair which belonged to the Reformer.

Holyrood Palace (open daily, 6d., Saturday, free) and Abbey, the latter being founded for Augustine Canons by David I in 1128. The present palace is for the most part a building about 200 years old; here Queen Mary was married to Darnley in 1565; the Gothic tower, doorways and Chapel Royal still remain. Queen Mary's bedroom and cabinet, with the mark of David Rizzio's blood.

HOTELS: McGREGOR'S ROYAL HOTEL (FIRST CLASS, FOR FAMILIES AND GENTLEMEN), PRINCES STREET; MURRAY'S LONDON HOTEL (FAMILY AND COMMERCIAL), ST ANDREW'S SQUARE; MACKAY'S HOTEL (FOR FAMILIES AND GENTLEMEN); BARRY'S BRITISH HOTEL (FOR FAMILIES AND GENTLEMEN); DOUGLAS'S HOTEL (FOR FAMILIES AND GENTLEMEN); RAMPLING'S WATERLOO HOTEL.

STEAMERS FROM GRANTON PIER AND LEITH HARBOUR; EDINBURGH OFFICES FOR ABERDEEN AND INVERNESS AT 6 SOUTH ST ANDREW'S STREET; GENERAL STEAM NAVIGATION COMPANY, FOR LONDON, 21 WATERLOO PLACE; LEITH AND EDINBURGH COMPANY, FOR LONDON, 9 WATERLOO PLACE; STIRLING, 10 PRINCES STREET.

TELEGRAPH STATIONS AT 68 PRINCES STREET AND AT THE PARLIAMENT HOUSE.

* The terms Scotch,
Scots and Scottish,
while being used
interchangeably by
many, have different
uses in modern
English – from whisky
to dialect and the
people of Scotland. In
the 1870s, however,
Scotch was more
widely and generally
used. *Murray's
Timetables for
Railways, Steamers
and Coaches
throughout Scotland,
North of England and
Ireland* was published
annually by Thomas
Murray & Co. Ltd. of
Glasgow.
† 'Auld Reekie'
is Scots for 'Old
Smokey'.
‡ Robert Burns
described Scotland
as the 'Land o' Cakes'
in his poem 'On the
Late Captain Grose's
Peregrinations thro'
Scotland' (1789).
Francis Grose was a
captain in the Surrey
Militia.
§ The 'lake' was
known to the locals
as the Nor' Loch
(North Loch) and
the 'gardens' are
called Princes Street
Gardens.

but the clerk was so exceedingly slow (perhaps he had only just turned out of bed) that we were kept waiting some time. As he had but one arm – being possibly engaged at half salary – I suppose he could not well be so expeditious as an ordinary mortal.

Soon after 7 o'clock we found ourselves in the Scotch metropolis, and our first care was to purchase one of Murray's timetables, which as it contained full particulars of all the trains, steamers and coaches in Scotland, we afterwards found of great utility.* The next thing was to dispose of our luggage, so this we left at Darling's Hotel, and then trusting ourselves to Glover's guidance (who is no stranger here), ascended the Calton Hill. Here is the National Monument, a structure erected to commemorate the heroes who fell at Waterloo. It was intended to be a reproduction of the Parthenon, but having proceeded as far as the foundations and twelve columns – on which £12,000 was spent – the work came to an ignominious end for want of funds, and now has the appearance, from a distance, of being some last remains of some ancient temple. Here are also the Observatory and Nelson's Monument; from the latter an especially fine view of the city is obtainable, but on the occasion of our visit it was much obscured by mist and smoke, the historical portion well meriting its soubriquet of 'Auld Reekie'.†

Descending the hill by Greenside Church, we passed through Saint Andrew's Square, which contains a monument erected in memory of Lord Melville, and some fine buildings, mostly of a commercial character, and then returned to Darling's and sat down to breakfast in the Commercial Room. This was our first meal in the 'Land o' cakes', and were greatly astonished at seeing no less than ten different kinds of fancy breads, scones etc., as well as meat on the table.‡ Having duly paid our respects to these, we paid for them, and then sallied forth on a tour of inspection.

Edinburgh is certainly a most picturesque city, formerly a lake existed in its midst, but this within the last century has been drained and converted into gardens.§ One side of these are the gigantic houses of the High Street, which they divide from the modern part, and on the other Princes Street, one of the best thoroughfares, but the smoky railway station being at one end rather mars the prospect in that direction. The streets are mostly wide, and as stone is largely used for building purposes they have a cleanly appearance; splendid bird's eye views of the whole city are obtainable from Arthur's Seat, Calton Hill and the castle, all of which rise to a great elevation. Temperance hotels appear very numerous, but as we heard a gentleman at Darling's talk of a 'brandy and soda' of which he had partaken, perhaps they do not confine themselves strictly to Temperance principles. Proceeding along Princes Street, we saw Mr Crabapple for the last time, evidently grumbling at something or other, and soon after which the castle was gained, and we at once put ourselves under the care of a guide who was waiting for prey.*

Formerly this fortress was of great strength, being built on the summit of a rock 380 feet above sea level, and almost inaccessible save by the drawbridge. The prospect all around is very

* Guides formerly waited at each tourist attraction, offering their services to travellers.

Heriots Hospital and tall houses, Edinburgh.

* 'Princes Gardens'
are now known
as Princes Street
Gardens.
† Mons Meg is now
believed to have been
constructed by Jehan
Cambier at Mons in
1449. It fired cannon
balls with a diameter
of 20 inches (510
mm), making it one
of the largest guns by
calibre in the world.
The projectiles each
weighed 400 pounds
(180 kg).
‡ As the New Town
was developed from
1765, the rich moved
there, leaving the Old
Town to the less well
off.

fine, Heriot's Hospital and the old city being on one side, and in the opposite direction Princes Gardens, the more modern buildings, and – in the distance – the Firth of Forth.* Unfortunately for us, the atmosphere was very gloomy, so we did not enjoy its full beauty. The best view perhaps is from the Mons Meg battery which overlooks Princes Street; here is a large gun which takes its name from Mons in Brittany, where it was made in 1476.† It carried shots – which lie at the side – 4½ feet in circumference, but it is now totally useless, having burst when firing a salute in 1682. Just here, the castle was scaled and taken by Earl Moray in 1313, but it must have been difficult work as the face of the rock is exceedingly steep. The Regalia of Scotland – crown, sceptre etc. – which did not look very magnificent, and Queen Mary's room having been visited, we had seen everything worth seeing, so took our departures.

The castle was garrisoned by the Highlanders, a fine body of men, all of course wearing kilts, many of whom were being drilled in the courtyard. When near Mons Meg battery, we were suddenly startled by a most discordant noise, and soon perceived that it rose from the pipers who were coming forth to practise – which they do daily on the hill side. We could not distinguish the least semblance of a tune, and were informed by our guide that each man played according to his own sweet will. The effect may be better imagined than described. Leaving the castle behind, we strolled down the High Street and Canongate, the houses of which are remarkable for their extraordinary height, many having nine stories; some were even taller than this but, being unsafe, have been demolished. The lower portion of those now standing are modernised, but the upper remain as formerly and are let out in flats, access to each being had from a staircase common to all.

This part of the city is very interesting, as it is connected with events remarkable in Scottish history; here were formerly the mansions of the nobility, but they are now inhabited by quite the other end of society.‡ Especially the part near

Holyrood Palace: what was once the residence of the Marquis of Queensberry is now a 'Refuge for the destitute', and other changes equally great have taken place.* St Giles and the Tron churches are worthy of note, the latter so called from the Tron or weighing beam which formerly occupied its site, to which it is said bad lawyers and knaves were nailed by the ears. Had this custom been maintained, I fancy the natives would have had to grow a species of gigantic tree solely for the purpose. John Knox's house is also an object of interest, and is often inspected by visitors, but Monday was not of the days when they are 'taken in'.† Farther down is the Tollbooth or prison, which is a good specimen of old architecture.

In two things Edinburgh seems rather behind in civilisation: firstly regarding the mode of watering the streets, which is done by means of large barrels fixed on a species of framework; and secondly the appearance of the children, most of whom have not yet learnt the use of boots and socks. This is not confined to the rag, tag and bobtail of society, as we saw many evidently belonging to the middle class in the same condition. However surprised we were at their costume, they were still more so at ours. The preceding month having been exceedingly hot, we – as usual during our holidays – wore puggarees round our hats. If we had arrayed ourselves in tartan kilts etc. with Charley discoursing sweet sounds on the bagpipe, no notice would have been taken of us, but our white and flowing head dresses created a general sensation, and some of the less enlightened made rude remarks thereon, one small urchin crying out: 'Yah!, yah! Look 'ere!' Perhaps they gave us the credit of being distinguished foreigners (we heard a suggestion that we were probably Americans), so we did our best to bear our newly acquired honours with dignity.

It being now mid-day, we had exhausted the time arranged to be spent on Edinburgh, so after leaving our large bag – with overcoats etc. – at the General Steam Navigation Company's office till our return, we proceeded to the Waverley railway station,

* Queensberry House was once the townhouse of the First Marquess (note spelling) of Queensberry. It is now part of the Scottish Parliament complex.
† John appears to share the view of most historians that the house has no connection to John Knox, the leader of the Reformation in Scotland. Visitors were indeed 'taken in' only on Tuesdays, Fridays and Saturdays at the time of John's visit.

obtained tickets and entered the train, bade Glover goodbye, and at 12.30 p.m. were en route for Stirling. The line at first traverses the Princes Gardens valley and then, passing through a tunnel, soon reaches the open country. The Almond river is spanned by a fine viaduct, after which we successively passed Niddry Castle, where Queen Mary stayed in her flight from Lochleven, Linlithgow with its old palace and church, Falkirk and Bannockburn, both so celebrated for the battles there fought, and eventually reached Stirling by 2.20 p.m.

I cannot say much in praise of the railway, for we had been nearly two hours travelling 30 miles, and the noise made in accomplishing the same seemed to me almost intolerable; certainly the atmosphere was heavy and close, all the more so perhaps to us as we were so recent from our sea voyage. Therefore I must say the journey was not a very enjoyable one, but am rather anxious to see what description Charley will give of it in his diary, as he was asleep the best part of the time. After some little search we decided to stay at Dowdy's Temperance Hotel and, having refreshed ourselves, directed our steps to Albert Place, where friends of ours – the Misses Gibson – were

Stirling Castle.

BRADSHAW ON STIRLING

 Stirling, a county and garrison town, is built on an eminence in the centre of a fertile plain, which is watered by the River Forth, and above the town rises the Castle of Stirling, so celebrated in Scottish history.

This ancient seat of the Scottish kings, and capital of Stirlingshire, is situated on a beautiful part of the Forth, about half-way between Edinburgh and Perth. Population about 12,837.

The best [i.e. greater] part of the palace, or castle, was begun by James V. It offers one of the most splendid prospects in Scotland, especially of the rivers Forth and Teith, and the distant Highlands.

A TELEGRAPH STATION. HOTELS: THE GOLDEN LION (LATE GIBB'S) HOTEL, THE ROYAL HOTEL.

* Dowdy's Temperance Hotel stood at 5 King Street and was managed by William Dowdy.

† The 'lions' of any place are its tourist attractions.

‡ The Valley Cemetery was opened in 1857.

spending their holidays.* On enquiry however, their aunt – with whom they were staying – said they had gone to Edinburgh for the day, and invited us to come to tea, which we promised to do.

The principal object of interest in Stirling is its castle, so thither we went without delay. It is built on the summit of a rock, one side of which is very precipitous, and the other well wooded forming a prettily shady walk. It is in good repair and garrisoned by Highlanders, though now of course quite useless as a fortification. The 'lions' are King James V's Palace, a curious specimen of architecture, profusely ornamented with grotesque carving, a room containing John Knox's pulpit, and the place where a certain Earl Douglas was killed and then thrown from the window and, last but by no means least, the panorama which can be seen from the battlements on a clear day.† Unfortunately for us, the atmosphere was still very misty, and consequently the view was strictly limited.

Determining to come here again in the morning if fine, we repaired to the cemetery which is close at hand and well worth a visit.‡ It contains monuments erected to the memory of Knox and other reformers, a huge pyramidal stone called The Salem

* The monuments
to the reformers
were paid for by
local Presbyterians,
including William
Drummond, a
nurseryman. The
Martyrs Monument
commemorates three
women who were
sentenced to death by
drowning: Margaret
MacLauchlan,
Margaret Wilson
and her sister Agnes
Wilson.
† John Erskine, Earl
of Mar, began to build
what is now called
Mar's Wark (a Scots
word for work, here
meaning building) in
1570, intending it to
be a townhouse for
his family. The work
is now an A-listed
building and a
scheduled monument.
‡ Henry Stuart, Lord
Darnley, married
Mary, Queen of Scots
in 1565. Within two
years, he was killed
by persons unknown.
Mary and her second
husband, the Earl
of Bothwell, were
both accused of the
murder; he was found
not guilty, and her
separate trial ended
without a definite
verdict.

Rock, as being typical of the stability of Bible truth, and last but most beautiful of all, a group of marble statuary commemorative of the death of Margaret MacLauchlan, who during the persecution of the Covenanters, was tied to a stake in the Solway Firth and drowned by the rising tide.* It is shielded from the effects of the weather by a screen of glass and iron, the latter being painted blue, which gives it a very pretty effect.

Descending, we walked round the foot of the hill and through the town – which is not worthy of much remark – to King's Park, which is merely an open space devoted to public recreations. The most popular sport is golf, which game consists in trying to knock a ball into a number of small holes, the players being accompanied by lads who carry a large assortment of sticks of various weights, which are used according to the nature of the hit required. As the holes are sometimes a quarter of a mile apart, I fancy the game must be rather wearisome to those who are not enthusiastic admirers of it.

On perusing our guide book, we found there was still one object of note in Stirling still unexplored, so we mounted again to the cemetery, close to which is an old gate called Mar's Wark, which is said to have been the commencement of a palace projected by an Earl of that name, who to save expense utilised the remains of a neighbouring abbey, which act of sacrilege called down divine wrath.† He died and the building was never allowed to be finished. It is ornamented with many grotesque heads, figures and inscriptions, in fact is altogether a curious relic and, though nearly 300 years old, is still in a good state of preservation.

Near here is a house bearing an inscription which informs the public that it was formerly the residence of Earl Darnley, who played so important a part in the history of Mary, Queen of Scots.‡ It is now a pawn shop, but had evidently not adhered to the pawnbrokers' motto 'Always keep advancing', as both its appearance and that of the surrounding neighbourhood is quite the reverse of fashionable, all the children and many women being quite destitute of any covering for their feet, and every one stared at us as if they had never seen two respectable people before. So much was this the case that we were glad to escape from their presence. Proceeding on our tour of inspection, we came across a hospital erected by a tailor – in which we of course took a great interest – bearing the following rather curious inscription:*

THE LIBERAL man deviseth Leberall things ✂ 1320.

It being now 7.30 p.m. we directed our steps again to Albert Place, but the Misses Gibson had not yet returned. Their aunt invited us in the drawing room, and entertained us in conversation till about 8 o'clock, when the truant young ladies made their appearance. Tea *à la Écossaise* being laid, we were invited to assist thereat, which we did with mutual pleasure and profit, and then discussed together various topics, mentioning among other things the places we intended to visit.

At 10 o'clock, having passed a very pleasant evening with these hospitable Stirlingites, we bade them farewell and returned to our hotel, where we went to bed amidst dire forebodings, as it had just begun to rain and there seemed every prospect of a damp night.

TUESDAY 22 AUGUST

During the early hours of the morning there appeared to be a competition of engine whistles taking place at the railway station, which of course awoke me. I do not know the reason of the clamour, as no trains ran at that un-business-like time, but my duty is to record facts, not account for them. At 6 o'clock the waiter – by order – beat a tattoo on our door, but Charley proposed another half an hour snooze, at the end of which time we dressed and then sallied forth. Having almost expected a wet

* Robert Spittal, who prospered as the tailor to King James IV, left money to build a hospital (not an infirmary, but an institution or home) for the poor in the 16th century. The domestic block known as Robert Spittal's House, at 82 Spittal Street in the Old Town of Stirling, dates from the 17th century, and is likely a replacement for the original institution, rather than the abode of Spittal himself.

* The National Wallace Monument was funded by public subscription, designed by the architect John Thomas Rochead, and opened in 1869. It commemorates William Wallace, a 13th-century Scottish hero, probably best known as the inspiration for the film *Braveheart* (1995).

morning, great was our gratification at finding it was bright and beautifully clear, so off we went at once to the castle and were amply repaid by the magnificent view from the ramparts. The Bridge of Allan and Wallace Monument (of which mention will presently be made) seemed close at hand, Edinburgh was just visible in the distance, and the River Forth with its numerous windings glistened like silver in the morning sun.* Congratulating ourselves on having made such good use of our time, we returned to our hotel and sat down to an exceedingly substantial meat breakfast. One thing certainly deserves mention here, and that is the Scotch butter: it is put on the table in small rolls or balls and kept in water; the quality is also first rate, and this we found to be the case everywhere.

9 a.m. Shouldered our knapsack, bade goodbye to Dowdy's, made at once for the railway station, duly booked our bag for Callander, taking care – in lively remembrance of our adventure at Duffws last year – to obtain a receipt, and then commenced our walking tour. Crossing the Forth and continuing along the road we soon came to Wallace's Monument, a baronial tower 220 feet in height, erected on a rocky eminence 560 feet above the sea's level to perpetuate the fame of the celebrated Sir William.

Wallace's Monument, near Stirling.

BRADSHAW ON BRIDGE OF ALLAN

 Bridge of Allan is denominated the queen of Scottish watering places, and is a place of great resort in summer. There are several places of worship, and good medical advice. There are mineral springs close to the village, pronounced by high authority to possess strong purgative qualities.

A TELEGRAPH STATION. HOTELS: THE ROYAL HOTEL, THE QUEEN HOTEL.

It does not appear nearly so high as it really is, and as we did not think a better view would be obtained than that seen from Stirling Castle, we did not mount to its summit.

Two miles farther is the Bridge of Allan, nestling in trees and protected from cold winds by a hill; neat and clean, with many pretty villas, in fact rather a fashionable watering place. It is noted for the healthful properties of its waters, which are mostly drunk hot, and rejoices in a pump room, but neither of these had any attraction for us. We wished to visit the dyeing and bleaching works of Messrs Pullar and Sons, with whom Charley transacts business through the celebrated St Martin's Lane firm.* After several enquiries we found the object of our search, and, sending in a card to announce our presence, we were ushered into the counting house and duly welcomed. Here I grieve to say my confrere talked 'shop', which I regarded as time wasted and was only too glad when Mr Pullar offered to show us round the works.

The goods here produced are twilled cottons, so first viewing the cloth in the grey, we then inspected the various processes of dyeing, dipping in boiling oil, singeing over hot plates, rolling by machinery and papering, all of which much interested us. The dye sent forth a very unpleasant odour, and in one department men protected by mackintoshes were in constant danger of being soused by water – not a delightful prospect I should think during the winter. However, that which most astonished us was the 'beetle finishing', this was not at all connected with the

* John Pullar began a dyeing business in Perth in 1824, which was soon offering its services nationally (thanks to cheap parcel post and railway freight rates) and in 1852 was awarded a Royal Warrant as Dyer to the Queen. The firm moved to the Keirfield Dye Works, Bridge of Allan in 1858. The Freemans were likely shown round by James Pullar and invited to dinner by Robert Pullar, the sons of the founder, who had become partners in the firm. The business – known in the 20th century as Pullars of Perth and famous for dry-cleaning – had a network of agents throughout Britain, including three in London.

* Beetling is the
pounding of linen
or cotton cloth (by
wooden blocks known
as beetlers or fallers)
to give it a flattened,
glossy finish. Paviours
are tradespeople
who lay pavements,
and employ heavy
implements to bed
and level the paving
stones into the
supporting sand or
other material.

death of insects of that name, but consisted of several hundred wooden blocks continually bumping down – after the fashion of paviours' rammers – on cloth beneath; the noise was really fearful.* So much so that it was quite a relief to quit the room. A large proportion of the hands employed were girls and women, very few of whom wore boots; to these our puggarees – as usual – seemed to afford much amusement, as we saw them constantly laughing together at our approach.

Returning again to the counting house, we were introduced to the senior partner, who invited us to dine at his house, as however it was now only 11.30 a.m. we declined with thanks and elected to push on. His brother did his best to alarm us by saying it had been very wet in London, and we were sure to have rain in a day or two. In vain we protested that as the wind blew from the north such could hardly be the case. Thanking the Messrs Pullar for their courtesy and hospitality, we once more resumed our journey, accompanied by the senior brother who – before parting – advised us as to the best route to Dunblane.

The scenery along the River Allan, with its clear stream and well wooded banks, greatly reminded us of last year's trip in Wales, and as the sun was shining brightly, added much to our enjoyment. About 1 o'clock we came in sight of Dunblane, and were rather startled but somewhat comforted to see a lad wearing a puggaree, as probably the inhabitants having seen one

BRADSHAW ON DUNBLANE

This city, though it has only a village population, is well worth visiting. The cathedral is much admired, and in good preservation. Tannahill's beautiful song 'Jessie, the flower of Dunblane', has given it popularity. The River Allan runs through the village. A beautiful foot road by the riverside runs between Dunblane and Bridge of Allan.

TELEGRAPH STATION AT BRIDGE OF ALLAN. HOTEL: DEWAR'S HOTEL.

before would not regard us with such curiosity as in other places previously visited.

Dunblane is now merely a small town, though as it possess a cathedral I suppose it was once of more importance. This edifice is very old, the tower dating from the Norman period; one half of the building is in ruins but the remaining portion was restored two years since, and is now used for public worship.* It is chiefly remarkable for its double windows, between which – as they are quite three feet apart – one can walk round the walls. Some stone effigies and fine oak carving still remain as a memento of the ancient order of things, also the plate formerly used for collections which measures about 18 inches in diameter. Poles with bags attached to the ends have now taken its place, but these our guide regarded as a great innovation, saying they were 'poked under people's noses so that they were obliged to give whether they wished to or not'. This lady – after receiving her fee – pointed out the house where 'Jessie, the Flower of Dunblane' formerly resided; who she was I really cannot say, but hope she was more attractive than her supposed residence, which is a very rickety affair.†

Upon quitting the cathedral, we seated ourselves on the bank of the river to lunch, and while so doing – though the sun was still shining brightly – a few drops of rain fell, as if to remind us that we could not always expect such beautiful weather. Resuming our journey, we endeavoured to take advantage of a short cut, which the above mentioned lady had pointed out, but twice came to a standstill where two roads met, and each time had we been left to ourselves should have taken the wrong one, but fortunately natives were near and directed us into the proper path. On reaching the high road we found milestones, which gave the always desirable information as to how far we had to travel. I hardly know why, but when this is the case much more progress is made than when it is otherwise; perhaps it is because one naturally takes more note of the time, and soon finds out if the pace is deteriorating.

* The earliest part of Dunblane Cathedral is the base of the bell tower, which was built in the 11th century. The remainder is largely from the 13th century. John and Charley visited before it was fully restored around 1890 by the architect Robert Rowand Anderson.

† 'Jessie', the subject of the song by Robert Tannahill, was Jenny Tennant, who was born in Dunblane. Windyhill Cottage was built in 1808 on the site of her birthplace, and can still be seen.

BRADSHAW ON DOUNE

👉 *This place is remarkable for its castle, now in ruins, cresting the top of a lofty eminence, overlooking the River Teith. It affords a fine opportunity for the rambler.*

TELEGRAPH STATION AT BRIDGE OF ALLAN. HOTEL: MACINTYRE'S HOTEL.

3.20 p.m. Doune, which though it rejoices in a castle, river and bridge – and what Scotch village does not? – is a very second rate place. It has three churches, but hardly any good houses, so I do not well understand how the inhabitants manage to support so many places of worship. In the centre of the main road stands a curious upright stone surmounted by a lion, probably a relic of feudal times, on the occasion of our visit however it was utilised by the local school board who had attached a notice thereto. If the lion could speak, I wonder what he would say regarding this wonderful change.

Having rested for a little while, we started off again at 4 o'clock but had not made much progress when two roads again confronted us, and as we were debating which we should patronise, two tourists approached and enquired if we could direct them to Callander. Of course we confessed to being strangers in these parts, but choosing that which seemed to be the better road – the right one for a wander – we all walked on together and

How some people enjoy a walking tour.

Tailoring under difficulties.

were soon engaged in conversation. They, like ourselves, were brothers but much younger, and consequently (I suppose) less experienced, or they would hardly have carried their overcoats – which were strapped together in a bundle – in their hands instead of on their backs. They came down with us in 'The Libra', and were about to make the tour of the Trossachs, returning to Edinburgh via Glasgow.*

Our route lay along the high road which was flat, dusty and not very interesting; in fact the only thing we saw to amuse us was a native who was seated at the side mending his 'breeks'.† To accomplish this task he had made bare his understandings, which when we passed were dangling in the ditch.‡ Perhaps the sketch will give some idea how the tailoring business is carried on in these out-of-the-way Scotch villages.

Reached Callander soon after 6 o'clock, and then parted from our pedestrian companions; they went in search of a suitable hotel, we for our luggage. Success soon crowning our efforts, we then thought it was quite time to follow their example. On seeing them, however, we ascertained they had made no further progress than ordering tea at McGregor's, the proprietor of which could not at present guarantee them a bed, but promised to find one if possible. The only other large hotel is the Dreadnought – so named probably to encourage intending visitors who might perchance fear the scale of charges – and as they are both under the same management we thought it better to make

* The Trossachs is the name for a region of undulating woodland and scattered lochs in west central Scotland. Callander and Aberfoyle are the chief settlements, and Loch Katrine the largest body of water. It is now a protected area, and part of the Loch Lomond and The Trossachs National Park.

† Breeks is the Scots word for trousers.

‡ 'Understandings' is a humorous word for legs.

BRADSHAW ON CALLANDER

👉 *This place is perhaps mostly noted as being the centre of a most beautiful and highly picturesque district. It is the station for the Trossachs and Loch Katrine, and of course via Inversnaid to Loch Lomond and the Western Highlands. There are several communications daily during the season by coach, between this, the Trossachs and Loch Katrine.*

TELEGRAPH STATION AT BRIDGE OF ALLAN. HOTEL: THE DREADNOUGHT HOTEL.

a further search. The choice was extremely limited, one good woman actually asking if we would like to sleep in a cupboard where someone was evidently in the habit of passing the night, but this we declined, not being at present willing to submit to such novel quarters.

Eventually, we put up at a Mrs MacFarlane's who offered to make up sofa beds for us in different rooms, which we thought it best to accept under the circumstances, as a train was overdue which would doubtless bring a fresh influx of visitors, so tea was at once ordered. This was soon ready, and that we without delay made ourselves 'at home' may be easily imagined. After a little rest, we sallied forth to inspect Callander. The village itself is one long street with but few good houses; it is sheltered from the cold winds by a verdant hill, close at hand runs the River Teith, Ben Ledi can easily be seen, and it is the usual rendezvous of tourists for the Trossachs, and consequently generally has plenty of visitors. Meeting our afternoon companions, we strolled up towards and intended to visit the Pass of Leny, but having gone two miles and ascertaining it was at least as far again, we turned back. It was a beautifully starlit night, and not dark till nearly 9 o'clock, but both Charley and I prefer to take our rambles in the daytime.

Returning to our hostelry, we entered our notes of the day's journeys and then engaged in conversation with two individuals who like ourselves were bent on 'doing' the Trossachs. As a proof of their friendship they invited us to have some whisky, and on our declaring in favour of Temperance principles, they said there was no doubt we were right, but they had acquired the habit of having a 'refresher' and could not well desist. Did not retire till late, and when that feat was accomplished sleep was chased away by a group of natives who were having a discussion with their fists in the street, and indulging in bad language. But eventually they went to their homes and we to the lands of dreams.

* Bodies of water in Scotland are called lochs, not lakes. The only natural body of water breaking this convention is the Lake of Menteith. There are a small number of artificial creations that have been given the title of lake.

WEDNESDAY 23 AUGUST

About 6 o'clock the Callanderites were up and doing, accompanied by a dog which was up and barking. Some time later we followed the example of the former, and then sat down to breakfast with the two tourists mentioned on the preceding page. They indulged in chops, we in steaks; in fact when possible we always endeavoured to do so at our morning meal, having great faith in laying a good foundation before commencing a day's pleasure. As we intended returning here tomorrow night, we left our luggage with Mrs MacFarlane and requested her to reserve a room for us; this she promised to do and then tried to point out a short cut over the hills to Lake Menteith.*

9.30 a.m. Quitted Callander, and had not proceeded far before we enquired of a native as to the desirability of taking the above mentioned 'short cut' – having by experience found out that sometimes this is only another name for 'the longest way round' – he said he should not like to try, and strongly advised us not to do so as we should very probably lose ourselves. Though very interesting from a diary point of view, we of course did not wish for such a calamity, so continued along the main road. Here we soon overtook a regular old Scotchman, who with a spade was engaged in clearing all the loose stones from the highway. As he volunteered to guide us, we gave him the benefit of our company, extracted as much information as possible – coupled with a prophecy of fine weather – from him, and finally parted company when our routes lay in contrary directions. Crossing several fields, we next encountered the district postman, who lamented the decadence of the present generation of tourists: formerly, visitors came on foot to view the scenery, but now they rush through by rail or coach and miss the best of it, at least so he said, and he was old enough to know.

The morning was beautifully bright, Stirling Castle being plainly visible, and as we gradually advanced along a pretty lane shaded *à la* Jersey, Loch Ruskie appeared on our left, and Loch Venachar glistened between two hills on the right. Then came the ruins of Rednoch Castle, but so little now remains of this once feudal stronghold that, had it not been for our map, we should have passed it and been none the wiser.* We reached Lake Menteith by mid-day, when we sat down, rested and held a council of war. The question under discussion was: having intended to walk to Port of Menteith station and then proceed by rail, we now found there was no train till 3.20 p.m. and – it being only three miles from here – we did not wish to loiter about. So we considered whether it would not be better to go

Lake Menteith

round the lake and, by taking a road which appears on our map, reach Buchlyvie in time to catch the above train. This we calculated could be easily done, but to make assurance doubly sure we resolved to consult the nearby toll keeper.* Perhaps this individual had been a soldier, perhaps he was in training for a race, perhaps he had a perturbed conscience which would not let him rest, or perhaps he was endeavouring to solve the problem of perpetual motion; but, whatever the reason, he was engaged in pacing up and down the road – much to our amusement – in a very energetic manner. In answer to our question, like many other wise gentlemen, he seemed disinclined to give away any decided opinion on the subject, saying it would no doubt be a very fine walk, so we bade him good morning and resumed our travels.

The sun was shining brightly, causing the waters of the lake – which contains several pretty little islands – to glisten beneath its rays, and the landscape here being rather more open, with mountains looming in the distance, it is altogether a very delightful spot. On reaching the end of the lake, we looked out for the road to the left, but could not see any signs of it, so after walking for some time we enquired as to its whereabouts of a postman who chanced to be passing that way, and gained the delightful information that it was nearly two miles farther. Thinking he might perhaps be wrong, we asked him to direct us by the aid of our maps, but his eyesight being bad he could not see it clearly, so offered instead to draw one on the ground with his stick. This he essayed to do, but his ideas were so gigantic that he was soon in a ditch and was compelled to commence again on the other side of the road.

He succeeded in making it pretty clear that we could not reach Buchlyvie by 3.20 p.m., so we determined to take it easily, and go by the next train which was nearly three hours later, and by way of carrying out this resolve at once sat down by a stream, lunched and then rested for three quarters of an hour. Of course, we might have tried a short cut across the heather, but having read in the guide book that travellers sometimes come to grief amongst the thousand and one bog holes – please to notice how extremely particular the narrator is to a single hole – which abound on the Scotch moors, we thought it better policy to keep to the beaten track.

From here to Buchlyvie no startling events happened, nor, as the country is flat and our route lay mainly through pasture land, is there any occasion to comment on the scenery. Added to this uninteresting state of things, my companion was troubled with the toothache and felt more inclined to sleep than do anything else, so I am compelled to state that we did not enjoy this afternoon's walk as much as those on the succeeding days. Still, the weather was beautifully fine, for which we had every reason to be thankful.

Nearing our destination, a very stout individual minus his coat and weighing quite 16 stone, and about 60 years of age, accosted us, desiring to know 'why we wore those white things on our heads?'. On being informed it was to protect them from the sun's rays, he seemed to think it was a splendid idea, saying it was quite time he did something in that direction, having suffered very much from the late extreme heat. If the reader should at any time happen to be passing near Buchlyvie, and sees a very obese individual wearing a puggaree, he will of course at once know how to account for so singular a sight.

Reaching the railway station about 5 o'clock, we found there was no train for an hour and a half, and the nearest hotel was more than a mile distant, so we could not even indulge in the luxury of tea. Five trains pass here per day in each direction, and the staff employed consists of a man and a half – that is to say a boy – whose time seemed mainly employed in chatting with such of the inhabitants as chanced to be passing. So, as may be imagined, we did not have a particular lively time of it whilst waiting; more especially as my companion was still troubled with toothache, and consequently felt much more inclined to be quiet than to enter into conversation.

BRADSHAW ON BALLOCH

 Here are several mills, and an old castle of the Lennoxes. Steamers up and down the loch daily in summer.

HOTEL: THE RAILWAY HOTEL.

'All things come to him who waits,' and so did our train to us, but it was much behind time, and we did not reach Balloch till 8 o'clock. Gladly jumping out of the carriage, we crossed the bridge which spans the river – paying of course for the privilege – and enquired for the Temperance Hotel which we had been told was to be found here. I suppose it existed only in the imaginative brain of our informant, as the toll keeper said the Balloch Hotel was the only place of accommodation for the benighted, who when there could be as temperate as they pleased, so thither we at once repaired, and though the tariff was rather high – which perhaps was only natural at a hotel which boasts of having been patronised by the late Empress of the French – we were extremely comfortable during our short stay.

Adjourning to the spacious coffee room, we were before long discussing tea in a manner which soon made us more satisfied with things in general and ourselves in particular. The few guests present were silent as ghosts, only one crusty old fellow breaking the solemn stillness to order a glass of whisky-toddy. Tea being concluded, a visitor's book attracted our attention, but it merely consisted of the names and addresses of those who had patronised the hotel and contained nothing interesting in the way of rhythmical effusions. One thing was noticeable: though Scotland was – as a matter of course – largely represented, also Manchester and northern cities, while even many foreign countries sent their quota, very few hailed from London.

Having perused the metropolitan newspapers, and read of the bad weather they had experienced down south during the last few days, we retired to bed devoutly hoping it would not come northwards, at all events for the present.

THURSDAY 24 AUGUST

* Knockour Hill or Mount Misery is a 577-foot (176-metre) mountain peak overlooking Loch Lomond. The alternative name comes from the tradition that the women of Clan Buchanan observed their men being massacred by Clan Gregor at the Battle of Glen Fruin in 1603.

During the night I dreamed I was back at business in the City, but awoke and was not at all sorry to find myself in bed at the Balloch Hotel. 7 a.m. Turned out and anxiously examined the appearance of the sky. The view from our window – embracing lake, river, and bridge – was very pretty, and there seemed every prospect of another fine day, at which we certainly did not feel inclined to grumble.

Tourists staying at the Balloch Hotel are allowed the privilege of visiting the Mount of Misery (which is I presume a gentleman's mansion).* Perhaps this is sometimes necessary, as it is well not to be too hilarious, but we rather preferred to patronise the Hall of Plenty, better known as the coffee room, where we arrived in time to hear the waiter ring such a peal with a large bell that we expected quite a numerous array of combatants to present themselves, all ready to commence an attack on the morning meal. However, only a solitary one, and he a Japanese, appeared, so we at once seated ourselves before a plentiful supply of ham and eggs and steaks. Our friend the Asiatic, who presided over the first named dainties, seemed to think the eggs particularly good – and we did not venture to contradict him – as he distributed the whole of them amongst us, leaving ham alone for those who happened to have overslept themselves. He, however, did not seem to possess a very good appetite, so we tried to make amends for his laxity by turning our attention to the steaks, which with a few other et ceteras soon made us feel ready for the day's travels.

Having first discharged our pecuniary liabilities, we then crossed the bridge, and as the train had not yet arrived essayed to walk down to the pier; in order to accomplish this it was necessary to traverse the lines, and the railway authorities – having an eye to the main chance, the fares – objected to such a proceeding, so we were taken by train in the ordinary manner, and – after paying pier dues – at once boarded the steamer which

BRADSHAW ON LOCH LOMOND

👉 *Loch Lomond is justly considered one of the finest lakes [sic] in Scotland. Boats can be hired at Balloch, for visiting the islands and points of interest on the loch. A steamer is provided for places more remote. At Inversnaid there are ponies ready (make a bargain beforehand) to take you to Loch Katrine, five miles, passing through Rob Roy's country.*

* Loch Lomond (27.45 square miles) is the largest body of fresh water in Great Britain. Lough Neagh (147.87) and Lower Lough Erne (42.28) in the north of Ireland are far larger.

was in waiting. Shortly after, about a hundred persons arrived by rail from Glasgow; when no more passengers were expected, we departed from Balloch and forthwith commenced our trip upon Loch Lomond.

This is the largest lake in the British Isles, being 25 miles long by five miles broad in the widest part.* The mountains which rise on both sides commence in many places almost from the water's edge; the surface is dotted with islands so verdant that they have the appearance of floating masses of trees; plenty of wild fowl are visible; and a fine day only is wanted to make even Mr Crabapple enjoy so picturesque and lovely a spot. This we so fortunately had, though it was a trifle chilly and those who possessed overcoats were glad to seek their protection. The sun's rays soon became more powerful, and while making us more comfortable at the same time cast an additional charm on everything around.

Our complement of passengers was certainly rather a motley group. Scotchmen were of course numerous, but besides these were several north-countrymen, Frenchmen and Germans, the before named Japanese and a party of Americans. One of these was a veritable Yankee, tall, thin and shrivelled, and I think the person who wished to 'take him in' would have had to rise uncommonly early in the morning. He was silent and left all the talking to one of his companions, who certainly did not require any assistant, as he managed to keep up a running conversation during the whole voyage, of which the following is a fair specimen.

'Yes, it is a pretty piece of water, we should call it a small creek out west.'

'You should see our lakes: one of them is 1,000 miles long and 300 miles broad and one of the waves would fill Loch Lomond.'

'These mountains are like mole-hills to ours; they are miles high I reckon, one has a large lake near the top and the wind blows so strong it does, that the house up there is anchored down to prevent it being blown away.'

'Can you get on out there? I guess and calculate you can if you will work; why one of our leading men is worth more than all Scotland put together, his income is so big that he really can't guess what it is.'

In this manner he rattled on from one thing to another, having quite a knot of listeners, and though he had rather an inflated way of talking, in many things he was undoubtedly of a practical turn of mind, and a man of sound common sense.

After calling at Luss, Rowardennan, and Tarbet, each of which possess a hotel, that at the last named place being an especially lovely spot, we arrived at Inversnaid by 11 o'clock – 20 minutes late – and at once disembarked. Here those who had circular tourist tickets – which includes rail, steamer and coach – made a rush for the last named, five of which were waiting, in order to ensure the best seats, and at once took their departure. It is only five miles to Loch Katrine, and the fare by coach is two shillings and sixpence besides the driver's fee. This seemed rather too much of a good thing, so we determined to walk there, the only reason against so doing being that there was not much time to spare, as the steamer was supposed to start from Stronachlacher at 12.30 p.m. By the side of the Inversnaid Hotel is a pretty little waterfall caused by the River Arklet descending precipitously over its rocky bed, but in consequence of the late dry weather it was seen at a great disadvantage. Having duly admired it and its surroundings, we retraced our steps and began to follow in the track of our late fellow passengers.

At first, our route lay up a steep and very dusty hill; here however the sky suddenly became overcast and rain fell heavily for about five minutes, but this was rather welcome than otherwise as it partially laid the dust. On arriving at the top, we saw about five and twenty other individuals who, like ourselves, were walking, but we had now a great advantage over them, for the sun was shining in all his splendour. Many had overcoats and some even bags whilst we, having nothing heavier to carry than our umbrellas, passed them all one by one and before long led the way. The view all along was wild and grand, mountains looming up majestically on either side.

When about half way, we met the two brothers who had walked with us to Callander; they had been staying at Stronachlacher, were now bound for Inversnaid, and evidently had curious ideas of enjoyment, as by their united efforts they were engaged in carrying a heavy iron-bound portmanteau, which gave rise to the thought: 'What a day they are having'! Near here a gate crosses the road, which we found to be locked; a woman on the other side muttered something which we conjectured to be an application of baksheesh, but on further enquiry it proved she only said: 'Say please then'! Which magic word being uttered, she loosed the barrier and we passed on, wondering at her singularity in making such a request.

12.20 p.m. Arrived at Stronachlacher Hotel, having accomplished the journey of five miles in 72 minutes, which was not particularly bad. This hotel, which is near the head of Loch Katrine, is very prettily situated, the pellucid lake and surrounding wooded hills combining to produce a charming effect. So beautifully clear is the water that the city of Glasgow draws its supply of that necessary of life from this quarter; it is conveyed there by means of an aqueduct, and when it is known that the consumption averages nearly 50 gallons daily to every individual amongst a population of half a million, it might be thought that before long the lake would be

Loch Katrine by moonlight

considerably diminished in size, but this does not appear to be the case at present.

After waiting for some time, the steamer appeared and discharged a cargo of passengers, who as usual made a rush for places on the coaches, and we at once walked on board. Travelling by boat here is very popular and certainly is the best way of seeing the lake scenery. Loch Katrine, though smaller than Loch Lomond and not so grand, is exceedingly beautiful, and being on a more diminutive scale its loveliness is perhaps all the more appreciated. An attempt was made to run a steamer on this lake in 1843, but the native boatmen strongly opposed the scheme, and after it had made a few voyages it suddenly disappeared during the night. No one was ever punished for the deed, and the idea was abandoned for the time being, but has since been revived with much success.

Those who visit Scotland would always do well to read beforehand the words of Sir Walter Scott, as many of his tales refer to places seen by the tourist.* Loch Katrine is especially interesting as being connected with 'The Lady of the Lake', and here is supposed to have been sung the celebrated chorus 'Hail to the Chief', with which we might have favoured the passengers, but not knowing if their tastes were musical, we thought it better not to run the chance of irritating them.†

1.30 p.m. Arrived at the end of our water trip, and found ourselves once more on terra firma. Here commenced some of the most lovely scenery imaginable: trees rose on each side of the road, densely covered with foliage and surrounded by ferns, yet not placed so closely together as to obscure the view of the rocks and mountains which towered behind; the sun was wearing his most brilliant aspect, and every conceivable shade of green met the eye, forming a really beautiful spectacle. This continued for more than a mile, as far as the Trossachs Hotel, a fine castellated building in the baronial style. Many people when passing spend a day here, and some are rash enough to make a prolonged stay, but the tariff is very high and we had been warned to pass it by, but before doing so sat down, lunched and rested ourselves.

* John seems to be suggesting that Scott wrote about places that people were flocking to. In fact, the opposite is true, and it was the locations and their stories that Scott wrote about that attracted visitors and then organised tourism. Scott's Romantic worldview re-presented wild landscapes and dangerous mountains as dramatic spectacles and awe-inspiring landscapes.

† Rather than 'irritate' the American passengers, a rendition of 'Hail to the Chief' would have impressed them considerably, for the song is their country's Presidential Anthem. The lyrics were taken from Scott's poem *The Lady of the Lake* (1810), set to music by James Sanderson (1812) and first associated with the American presidency in 1815.

Loch Achray from the Trossachs Hotel.

While thus employed I endeavoured to make a sketch of the scenery before us; in former years I have generally managed to put on paper some of the views which seemed especially deserving of remembrance, but when in Scotland the requisite scenery never appeared to present itself when leisure was at hand, consequently this is the only picture which can lay any claim to originality. I do not think I can be accused of laziness when away for my holiday, but am free to confess that had it not been for the zeal of my travelling companion and another kind friend (who seems to take an interest in this diary nearly equal to that of its author) in procuring me 'copy', I am afraid many of the pen and ink etchings here annexed would – to use an Irishism – have been conspicuous by their absence.

2.45 p.m. Having had a long and enjoyable rest, we started away on foot, having Loch Achray on our right and a well wooded hill to the left, soon after which we reached Glenfinlas. The sun about this time shining tremendously hot, and passers-by generally relieved their minds by saying 'Wa-r-r-m day, Sir!', in which sentiments of course we acquiesced. The flies were troublesome, but we were not likely to complain while there was no rain.

Continuing by Loch Venachar, the country became flat and comparatively uninteresting: on nearing the end of the lake, having been especially advised to see 'Samson's putting stones', we kept on the lookout for them, but not being successful enquired

Highland sports _ "Putting the stone".

of two Scots who were passing in a cart. One seemed half daft, and the other very deaf, as when Charley had asked three successive times, making a capital crescendo in the effort, he said to his companion: 'Ah p'haps he wants Coilantogle Ford'; this so aroused my confrere that he made a final endeavour, fortissimo, which had the desired effect and some time after we passed the object in question. It consists of one large boulder on the edge of a hill, which seems as if it were about to roll down, and a smaller one by its side: in ancient days when a Scotchman wished to become a warrior, he was requested to lift the latter stone on to the top of the large one, a feat requiring much strength. If this could be done, he was adjudged worthy to shed his blood on behalf of his country, hence the name 'Samson's putting stones'.

Near here is Coilantogle Ford, made celebrated by Sir Walter Scott as the scene of the conflict between Fitz-James and Roderick Dhu, when the latter uttered the famous lines:

> See, here, all vantageless I stand,
> Armed, like thyself, with single brand;
> For this is Coilantogle Ford,
> And thou must keep thee with thy sword.

Arrived in Callander soon after 6 o'clock, having spent a very pleasant day, though I must acknowledge having been rather disappointed with the latter part of the journey; as far as Glenfinlas it was all that could be wished, being by turns grand and majestic, or peaceful and lovely, but from thence to Callander there really was hardly anything worth seeing, and I had expected the Trossachs scenery to continue the whole distance, so we resolved for the future – to prevent disappointment – to restrain our fertile imaginations. Repairing at once to Mrs Macfarlane's, we found her still doubtful as to whether she could give us sleeping accommodation, but eventually she agreed to do so. Tea then followed, and a perusal of letters from home – which we found waiting for us at the post office – also an account, which

Joseph had sent by way of encouragement of a traveller who had lost his way and died on Helvellyn. After answering these communications, we retired to bed about 10 o'clock, feeling that we had fairly earned a good night's rest.

FRIDAY 25 AUGUST

I had intended to rise early and visit the Falls of Bracklinn, but my boots having been taken away to be cleaned, was not able to do so; perhaps I was only too glad to have an excuse for not turning out, as being in the air all day is rather calculated to make one feel sleepy. 8 a.m. Breakfast and then took our departure, the morning being cloudy and not having a very promising appearance. First visiting the railway station, we booked our bag for Aberfeldy, but the clerk refused to give us a receipt, saying they had not such a thing in place, and as it would travel on the lines of two companies they could not be answerable for its safe arrival. I expostulated with him but in vain, and with many misgivings – well remembering the episode at Duffws last year – we left it to be forwarded in due course.

Now we proposed sleeping at Killin tonight – a distance of 23 miles – and thought if we arrived at Strathire in time to catch the train there at 11.32 a.m. we could then have a lift to Lochearnhead and accomplish the journey easily. According to map calculations, Strathire was only seven miles distant, so we determined to adopt this plan, and having first purchased some provisions, we were fairly on our way by 9.20 a.m. About two and a half miles from Callander is the Pass of Leny, a spot well worth remembering. Mountains, not bare and rocky, but profusely covered with trees rise on both sides, between which runs the River Teith, railway and high-road, while behind is Callander just peeping out of its leafy surroundings. As we advanced, the views constantly changed, but the richness of the vegetation still continued and I must again note the beautiful greens of the trees, grasses and ferns which contributed in so large a measure to our enjoyment of the scene.

Proceeding onwards, Loch Lubnaig appeared and gradually opened to our view, showing a magnificent stretch of water; sometimes the mountains descended precipitately to the edge of the lake and in many places had at their base large groups of trees, the whole forming a beautiful and – owing to the constant winding of the road – ever varying prospect. On reaching the fifth milestone, a horseman overtook us and, in answer to our enquiry, said the distance from Callander to Strathire was at least nine miles. Our faces lengthened considerably at this intelligence; nevertheless, as Scotch trains are not at all noted for their punctuality, we trudged on trusting we might still arrive in time. Fortunately for us, the road was well made – as they always are in Scotland – and though a fine day it was not very hot, so we made fine progress.

As the time specified for the train to arrive drew near, we met the equestrian returning, and he said the station was a good mile farther, so onwards we pressed, but soon after passing the eighth milestone heard to our great dismay a train approaching on the other side of the lake. At first, we thought it might only be the wind, or the result of our imaginations, but 'nearer and clearer' grew the sounds, until at last we could see the carriages advancing rapidly in our rear. As a last chance I proposed to run, but my brother – who was carrying the knapsack – thought it was useless, and politely declined, as the railway station was not yet even in sight. Some distance off was a house, so onwards I ran but only to discover it was a farm; from here I was shown the desired-for haven where the train, by this time, was standing. Waving my umbrella to my confrere as a signal to hasten, off I rushed – unfortunately it was all uphill – and soon reached the goal.

Notwithstanding frantic signs on my part, Charley did not seem to be coming much faster, but I thought it would be as well to procure tickets, so hammered away at the window of the booking office to the amusement of the passengers who were in the carriages, but with no other result. On investigation, the room proved to be empty, and not seeing a single individual on my side of the platform, I gave one last despairing flag to the rear guard – who was now coming at the 'double quick' – and darted round the train to the other side. Here the guard, who was just about to give the signal to depart, said we were rather late and, as he had no tickets, took our money without giving any equivalent, saying that it would be all right. Just as this was settled, I saw Charley's white puggaree waving on the platform, and – all hot and breathless but victorious – we seated ourselves in a carriage and the train moved out of Strathire.

Elsewhere we always found Scotch trains very late, but on this occasion – though coming from Glasgow – the iron horse was only three minutes behind time; however it waited five more at the station (probably the stoker had gone for some whisky), which just enabled us to reach it. Here is a sketch of my companion coming at the 'double quick', but as it was not taken on the spot I cannot guarantee its correctness in every particular.

The final charge at Strathire.

After a quarter of an hour's ride we arrived at Lochearnhead, when three coaches – which were waiting – were at once filled with passengers who rode off to survey the surrounding country, which is very grand, hill rising behind hill in every direction. Here we rested, lunched and then at 1 o'clock resumed our walk, passing the head of Loch Earn. Here there is a hotel which I can certainly recommend for seclusion to those who wish to pass their holiday in perfect quietude, the houses for miles round being very few and far between. Here we posted the letters written last night.

Leaving Loch Earn behind, we entered Glen Ogle, a romantic defile very like the Pass of Llanberis. Down the centre runs a stream, and on each side rise mountains gloomy and stern, huge masses of rock projecting in all directions and dried water courses suggesting to the imagination the manner in which the torrents come thundering down during the winter. Midway up the hill to the left runs the railway, but really it does not look at all safe, as stones from above fall on the line, and it appears as if the carriages might at any moment topple over; doubtless a close examination would prove this to be a fallacy. When about half way up the glen we heard unearthly noises, and soon became aware that someone near at hand was practising on the bagpipes, so we did not rest here, but hastened our steps considerably.

4.30 p.m. Being by this time near the end of the pass, we were greatly astonished to see written up in large letters the name 'Killin', but as not the least vestige of a habitation – save the railway station – was to be seen, I enquired of an ancient dame, and ascertained this was the nearest point by rail, the village being still four miles distant. Certainly a coach always meets each train to convey passengers thereto, but just fancy arriving here late in the evening, after that conveyance had departed and then finding out these facts for the first time! Some idea of the loneliness of the country may be formed when I say that since leaving Lochearnhead – about seven miles distant – we had only seen two houses and four inhabitants.

On arriving at the end of this road, we halted by the tollgate to admire the surrounding prospect, which was very fine: behind lay Glen Ogle, to the left Glen Dochart, all around and beyond which lowered giant mountains, Ben More and Ben Vue being especially conspicuous. In the opposite direction the Breadalbane Hills, and country round Killin. Here we chatted for a time with the toll keeper, who thought the distance from the last named place to Aberfeldy was 28 miles, which – as we intended to be there by 5 o'clock tomorrow – rather alarmed us, and we hoped that he had made a mistake, which indeed afterwards proved to be the case.

After an enjoyable ramble by the side of the Dockhart, a river very like the Dee at Llangollen, having a stony bed over which the water gently rippled forming a very pretty sight, we reached Killin about 6 o'clock. In our guide book this place was mentioned as a capital specimen of a Highland village, but if so I can only say I should not care to live in the houses, or rather huts, nearly all of which are merely two rooms thatched over to keep out the rain. Here is the burial place of the celebrated McNabs, one of the descendants of which illustrious clan now supplies the Killinites with groceries, so of him we enquired as to the various hotels, and learnt that only one – which was very expensive – existed in the village, but that by walking another mile we should come to The Bridge of Lochay, where everything was comfortable and reasonable. As this coincided with our ideas, and at the same time would moreover help us on tomorrow's journey, we thanked the intelligent McNab, followed his advice, and soon arrived at the above mentioned hostelry.

Mountains, rivers, lakes, glens and trees all combined to render today's ramble one of the most, if not the most, enjoyable during our trip; though not hot it was fine, and a glorious sunset formed a fitting climax to the many pleasures of our walk. Whilst waiting for tea we inspected the Visitors' Book, which contained many poetical effusions. This sample was written by an individual whilst staying at Lochay in December, and gives a good idea of the surroundings during the winter.

> The Dochart stream rolls thund'ring down,
> Dark Lochay threats, its surges frown,
> Loch Tay's huge billows hoarsely roar,
> And proudly heave their foam on shore.

Tea was rather a long time in making an appearance, but as our appetites increased with the delay, ample revenge was taken on the ham, eggs and various other et ceteras when they at last were spread before us. At the close of this entertainment it was 7.30 p.m. so without farther delay we strolled to Finlarig Castle, about half a mile distant.* As a castle it is hardly worth seeing, being little more than a heap of stones overgrown with ivy, the latter from its luxuriant growth being by far the more interesting sight. That which most attracted our attention was the magnificent trees which grew around: larch, sycamore, spruce, box, holly and oak were all well represented, the last two deserving special mention as being superb specimens of their kind supposed to be several hundred years old. As may be imagined, the *tout ensemble* formed a beautiful spot for repose in hot weather. Returning to The Bridge of Lochay, we retired to bed shortly after 9 o'clock as we had rather a long journey before us on the morrow.

* Finlarig Castle was built in 1629 by Duncan Campbell of Glenorchy. It was abandoned in the late 18th century.

SATURDAY 26 AUGUST

6.30 a.m. Rose and, having dressed, left Charley to pack the knapsack and sallied forth for a short stroll towards Glen Lochay. The morning did not look by any means propitious: heavy misty clouds were hanging over all the surrounding hills, things generally wore a very gloomy appearance and, before long, rain began to descend. I soon retreated to our hotel, where I heard a native prophesy that 'it might clear off', which I devoutly hoped would be the case.

Breakfast had been ordered for 7.30 a.m., but it did not appear at the appointed time. I expect the host's daughter was flirting with some of the guests who in the visitors' book describe her as the one bright particular star without whom Lochay would be excessively dull. When at last this damsel appeared with our morning's meal, we were informed that no steak had been killed

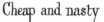
Cheap and nasty   Clean and comfortable.

in the village during the week – just as if there were animals
of that name – so therefore were obliged to be contented with
chops. Being at last well-fortified for our walk, we shouldered the
knapsack and prepared to depart, but even then great delay was
shown in relieving us of our spare cash. The Bridge of Lochay is
a comfortable hotel, and moderate as regards expenses, though
the hostess cannot be recommended for punctuality. This perhaps may be accounted for by the fact that visitors as a rule are
not in a hurry, and indeed sometimes hardly know what to do
with their time; it is placed in the midst of some of the prettiest lake and tree scenery, and we might well have stayed there
another day.

8.35 a.m. Bade adieu to Lochay, and commenced our day's
pleasures. We had intended to sleep tonight at Aberfeldy, and
stay there till Monday, but now determined if possible to spend
the Sunday in the neighbourhood of Dunkeld. In order to do this,
it was necessary to be at the first named place before 5 o'clock
as the last train left about that time, the distance is 22 miles,
and the only means of conveyance is by a coach which starts
daily. As the fare is something like sixpence per mile besides the
driver's fee, we decided to go by that much more economical, if
somewhat less expeditious, mode of travelling, the 'marrowbone
stage', which we trusted would take us to our place of destination
in safety.

Of course there was time to perform the journey, but we did
not wish to be hurried, besides which the very serious question

of the weather troubled our minds, for though it was not actually raining, all around and especially behind whence blew the wind, heavy misty clouds were hanging over the hills, reminding us no time was to be lost. Our road commenced with a gradual ascent cut in the side of the mountain, till it reached the height of about 500 feet. It bore a great resemblance to that of The Hobby at Clovelly, being well wooded both above and below, only instead of the sea the smooth expanse of Loch Tay was seen beneath, beyond which rose another range of hills. Had the weather only been propitious, I am certain the sight would have been well worth remembering. As it was, I am sorry to say, though actual rain held off for some time, its beauty must have been greatly obscured by the low hanging clouds, which before very long began to favour us with their contents.

About seven miles from Killin is Ben Lawers – nearly 4,000 feet high – but as the rain began to descend in earnest, we did not profit by a nearer acquaintance with his mountainship. Shelter too was nil, so we had no alternative but to walk on, which we did as much under the trees as possible. The road was good but no milestone was visible until 12.10 p.m. when we came to one with the information '3 miles to Kenmore, 12¾ miles to Killin', so we had been travelling at the rate of three and a half miles per hour, which considering the uphill road, rain, umbrellas, knapsack and slight stoppages, was I think pretty fair. Seeing by this that we could now – weather permitting – easily reach Aberfeldy by the required time, we rested under the shelter of some trees for about 20 minutes, and then resumed our journey.

Near here commence the grounds adjoining Taymouth Castle – the residence of the Marquis of Breadalbane – which are many miles in extent, and once more were we reminded of Clovelly. Thousands of trees lined the sides of the road, sometimes larches straight as masts towering above, but more often the foliage of the spreading branches meeting overhead and forming a charming canopy. By this time Jupiter Pluvius had ceased to send down his gifts, and when the end of the lake was reached

Rustic entrance to Taymouth Castle.

* Russell Square, in Bloomsbury, London, is approximately 6 acres (2.5 hectares) in area.

our friend Sol had dispersed some of the darkest clouds, so hope once again revived in our breasts. Crossing a bridge where we stayed to admire the splendid *tout ensemble* of loch, trees and hills, we came upon a very pretty sight.

Imagine a block certainly not more than half the size of the floral part of Russell Square.* At one end is a church surrounded by trees, at the other the fine iron gates of the grand entrance to Taymouth Castle, behind which are the splendid park-like grounds belonging thereto; on one side a good hotel – The Breadalbane Arms – and two cottages, opposite to which are five houses. Imagine this, and you will have some idea of Kenmore, as picturesque a village as I have ever seen and which much took my fancy. I should have liked to have made a sketch of it but time forbade, as we did not know but that the railway station of Aberfeldy might be as distant from the village as that of Killin. The clouds by this time had broken up, and there seemed indications of fine weather, so having made some further progress we rested, lunched and at 2.25 p.m. started off again. Our route lay by the side of the River Tay, beyond which lay Breadalbane Castle, surrounded by its magnificently wooded grounds which alone form a sight worth coming a long way to see.

4.20 p.m. Reached Aberfeldy, by which time the sun had fairly broken up the clouds, edging them with gold as they hung in scattered patches above, forming a very pretty sight. Having still some time to spare, we inspected the village which possesses a curious bridge, a small church, only one hotel and streets paved with knobbly stones, and is altogether a charming little place. Procuring a budget of letters which were awaiting our arrival, we repaired to the railway station, and made enquiries for our bag, which seeing on the floor I claimed at once. The clerk seemed so anxious to be rid of the article that he handed it to me immediately, saying there was nothing to pay. This I knew must be a mistake, as I had only prepaid for its journey on one line but, notwithstanding this assertion, he seemed to think I was wrong, and it was not till after a long search that he found a memorandum to the effect that 16 pence was required, from which he refused to make any deduction as a reward for my honesty.

At the booking office there was quite a crush for tickets, those present seeming to be under the impression that these could be obtained much more expeditiously if they jostled each other. One lady asserted she had 'missed two trains already and was now nearly killed', but it is only fair to state she was alive when we last saw her. This condition of affairs was not improved by the clerk who, after he had taken the money for tickets often replied – as gentlemen do sometimes to those of the gentler sex on whom they wish to fix their affections or afflictions, whichever it may be – 'You'll find no change in me'. He was also minus first-class tickets, and altogether in a state of general confusion, which the crowd before him did their best to aggravate, so the scene was of rather a lively character, especially for so quiet a spot.

Having at last obtained our tickets, I took my place in the train – where Charley had already secured seats – and at 5.30 p.m. we started from Aberfeldy. An ancient Scotchman who sat

BRADSHAW ON DUNKELD (BIRNAM)

☞ *Situated at the pass into the Highlands, from which there is a splendid view; also an old cathedral, and the Duke of Atholl's seat, at which are the fine falls of Braan, and the two first larches brought to England [i.e. Britain] in 1737; there are upwards of 30 million planted now. Population about 1,104. Distance from station, seven miles.*

A TELEGRAPH STATION. HOTELS: THE ATHOLL HOTEL, THE BIRNAM HOTEL.

next to me indulged in the vice of snuff-taking by helping himself to that article out of a box with a small spoon and, being of a generous disposition, he invited us to partake of his store, but we declined with thanks. Upon which he – like many others who have acquired the habit of smoking, drinking or snuffing – advised us not to begin it, to which we replied that we had no intention of so doing.

After a pleasant ride through some very fine wooded scenery we arrived at our journey's end by 6.30 p.m., when we immediately proceeded to seek a place which we might call our home for the present. Tomorrow being Sunday, we determined it possible to secure private apartments, and at the first application found exactly what we required at the house of one Mrs Lorimer, to whom we gave orders for tea, and then strolled to inspect the neighbourhood. To our surprises, we found ourselves not in Dunkeld but Birnam, the railway station being nearly a mile distant from the former place. The houses are all good, being built in quite the modern style, and it can boast of a splendid hotel – The Birnam – with fine grounds attached thereto. Whilst admiring this edifice we observed a procession of people headed by a band approaching from Dunkeld, and it was at once suggested that they might be a deputation from that place coming to invite us to reside there, but this of course was now out of the question.

As they came nearer, bearing a banner on which was inscribed 'Success to Keiller', we ascertained they were the workpeople of the celebrated marmalade manufacturer of that name from Dundee who had been enjoying a 'bean feast', and a cart brought up the rear which without doubt contained the remainder of the 'beans' on which they had been feasting.* I am afraid they must have had something stronger than either beans or marmalade, as they were rather excited and particularly wished to know 'Who were our hatters?' As we ourselves were not quite certain of the identical individual, we allowed them to pass without the required information, and then adjourned to tea.

Afterwards we wrote letters home, and eventually repaired to bed about 10 o'clock, having every reason to congratulate ourselves on our first week in Scotland.

SUNDAY 27 AUGUST

7.15 a.m. After a good night's rest, with which we were generally favoured, we rose and took a short stroll round the foot of Birnam Hill, which we determined to ascend later in the day. The natives seemed quite aware it was the day of rest, and were in most instances – I suppose – taking an extra snooze, as we did not meet more than half a dozen persons during our walk. 9 a.m. Breakfasted – for the first time since leaving London – by ourselves. Our sitting room was very comfortable, having among other ornaments a globe containing goldfish which seemed to have solved the problem of perpetual motion.

10 a.m. Strolled towards Dunkeld, to reach which it is necessary to cross a fine bridge which spans the River Tay; this means of communication was built by one of the Dukes of Atholl.† To make it prove a good investment, a toll is levied on everyone who passes, not only the living but even the dead, as there is a special fee for hearses. We expostulated with the toll keeper, stating it was the Sabbath, and of course we wished to respect Scotch scruples regarding Sunday trading; nothing would satisfy him but a 'bawbee', which we were obliged to pay.‡ It certainly does

* The term 'bean feast' originally meant an annual dinner held by employers for their staff.
† The 4th Duke of Atholl commissioned the pioneering engineer Thomas Telford to build a bridge across the Tay at Dunkeld, which opened in 1809. The duke decided to charge pedestrians and carriages to use the bridge, which led to the bad feeling and vandalism John describes. The tolls ended in 1879 when the bridge was taken into public ownership.
‡ A bawbee was a Scottish halfpenny coin.

Dunkeld, from the bridge.

* The Atholl Memorial
Fountain was built by
public subscription in
1865; Dunkeld Free
Church was built in
Boat Road in 1874;
Dunkeld Cathedral
dates from the 14th
century. All are still in
place.

seem a little hard on the inhabitants, for they not only have to pay a toll when crossing the river, but also in returning. Some think the duke ought to throw open the bridge for free, and a short time since they endeavoured to enforce their opinions by pulling down the gates which were of wood, but the only result was that strong iron ones are now substituted, and the chief offender was prosecuted and sent to jail for his trouble.

Dunkeld is much older and somewhat larger than Birnam. The principal objects of note are: a fine fountain erected by the inhabitants in memory of the late Duke of Atholl; the Free Church, a new and very ornamental edifice; and last, but much the most important, the cathedral.* Here we had determined to attend morning services, but on arriving found the gates closed; after a few minutes the clerk issued from a side house laden with the pulpit bible and books, when we all entered together. Like Dunblane Cathedral, more than one half has only the walls standing, the remaining portion being restored and now used for public worship. The ruinous part has also been utilised as a burying ground, and the old tombstones are remarkable for being mostly ornamented with a skull and cross bones or in some instances a coffin and hour glass; this we also found to be the case in other places. It must be a matter of wonder to all thinking persons as to where all the bad people are buried. If one might judge by graveyard inscriptions, they do not rest there. Perhaps there might be some difficulty in deciding who belonged to that class, so we had better leave the subject alone.

At 10.55 a.m. the bell began tolling for service, so we entered the cathedral and waited to be shown into a seat. No one appeared to perform this act of courtesy but, after standing some time, a stranger (like ourselves) pointed to a pew and we at once sat down. Looking round, we found the interior was rather narrow in proportion to its length, the pulpit being placed about midway at the side; opposite this – enclosed with ornamental woodwork and surrounded by a coat of arms – was a large elevated dais, which was reserved exclusively for the Duke of Atholl and his servants, with curtains partially protecting its occupants from the gaze of the vulgar. Nor did the service begin until the butler

Dunkeld Cathedral.

had locked the door, and the retainers of the ducal house were all seated. When we go to worship God, surely all are on an equality; it cannot be right that anyone should thus seem to assert on such an occasion their superiority over their fellow creatures.

The service was almost identical with that to which we are accustomed in modern dissenting chapels, save that instead of hymns a metrical version of the Psalms was used.* However, no one had the common politeness to offer us a book, so we were obliged to hum the tune or stare about us according to our fancy; nor were we the only persons thus seated, as in our pew were four more strangers in the same condition as ourselves, while in the adjoining one were six natives, all of whom were provided with books, which they greedily kept to themselves. We could not even make a silent protest by refusing to stand, as the whole congregation remained seated whilst singing. I have always heard the Scotch mentioned as a kindly, hospitable race, and when I narrated the above facts to a friend who hails from Nairn, he suggested that it must have been the English and not the Scotch service which we attended, but of course we knew better than that.

The singing – led by a precentor whose upper notes were harsh and strained – was pretty fair, but did not have the aid of a musical instrument, as many of our Scotch friends hold that organs and harmoniums are inventions of Satan.† This doubtless may be so when they are badly played, but not otherwise. The minister – a stranger and substitute for the stated pastor – chose for his text Deuteronomy, chapter 30, verse 19: 'Choose ye now this day, between blessing and cursing.' Having first divided his congregation into the following classes – those who came from love, curiosity, duty or habit, to criticise or for intellectual enjoyment – he made an earnest appeal to those present to choose the right path, and altogether preached a good parochial sermon. At each door of the cathedral was a tremendous plate about a foot and a half in diameter to receive the offerings of those who felt disposed to give; under ordinary circumstances we certainly should have felt so inclined, but being of opinion that our reception was the reverse of civil, we kept our contributions for a more deserving object.

In the portico of the main entrance is a splendid marble bas-relief erected to the memory of the soldiers of the Black Watch who fell at the battle of Waterloo.* It represents a Highlander in full costume mourning over his fallen brethren, and is very finely executed. Near at hand is a stone, full-length effigy of the Wolf of Badenoch, one of the fiercest of the race of Celtic warriors.† After having inspected these, we strolled through Dunkeld and then by the side of the River Tay. Many people are I think under the impression that Scotchmen are for the most part dressed in kilts and tartans, but this is quite a delusion and until yesterday we hardly saw a single specimen of this costume. Here however – the Perthshire Highlands – it is much commoner, and we came across many, mostly strong, brawny men, who were thus clad. Still, our appearance created a much greater sensation than theirs, and as we had left all our go-to-meetings clothes in London, I must say our *tout ensemble* was the reverse of what is generally considered Sabbatical.

Returning to Mrs Lorimer's, we dined, rested till 3 o'clock and then went out. Crossing the railway, we began to ascend Birnam Hill, which is 1,580 feet high and covered with trees the whole distance till near the top, when a splendid heather – the like of which I had never seen – takes their place.‡ A winding path cut in the face of the hill tends to make the ascent easier for ladies; this we followed for some time, and then took a shorter but much more precipitous route leading straight to the summit, which was gained by 3.40 p.m. Here, as may be imagined, a splendid bird's eye view met our gaze, Dunkeld, Birnam, the River Tay and Loch Lows all lying at our feet, behind which stretched a beauteous landscape of hill and dales.§ Perhaps better than any description I can give will be a representation of the scene in black and white.

Ascending again to a slightly more elevated position, we could see behind Birnam Hill a splendid succession of mountain

* The marble memorial to the Black Watch was sculpted by Sir John Steell in 1871.
† Alexander Stewart (1343–1405), the Earl of Badenoch, was the son of King Robert II. He held extensive lands in the north of Scotland, and was notoriously cruel to his wife, his servants, his tenants and everyone else he came into contact with. After a row with the Church, he sacked Elgin and destroyed its cathedral, and for this he was excommunicated.
‡ Birnam Hill, made famous by the play *Macbeth* (1611) by William Shakespeare, is now believed to be around 1,300 feet (400 metres) in height.
§ Loch Lows is usually given as the Loch of the Lowes.

View of Birnam from Birnam Hill.

beyond mountain for about 20 miles, Ben Lawers, Ben More and many other minor bens being plainly visible. Though perhaps not prettier, or more varied than the Precipice Walks at Dolgelly, the views here are of much greater extent and exceedingly grand. Having spent some time here, and duly admired the prospect in every direction, we descended by the circuitous path so as to avoid the tremendous jolting which otherwise would have occurred, and were soon in Birnam sitting down to tea.

We had intended going in the evening to the Free Church at Dunkeld, but on enquiry ascertained that service was held there morning and afternoon only, so having to choose between a church with an Anglican service and the parish kirk, we decided in favour of the latter.* First, taking the precaution to borrow a book of psalms and paraphrases from our landlady, so as not to be again dependent on Scotch hospitality, we sallied forth and were soon seated in a long narrow building with windows on one side only, viz, behind the pulpit, before which sat the precentor in the midst of what might not inappropriately be termed a 'waste howling wilderness' as not more than 70 people were in the whole place, and no one within 20 feet of him in either direction.* Notwithstanding this, he sang very well, and the congregation supported him better than I should have thought possible under the circumstances.

After an opening psalm and the Lord's Prayer, the minister read selections from the books of Joshua, Daniel and Revelation, with copious expositions of his own; then, having sung another psalm, he proceeded without selecting any text to discourse on certain passages in the second mentioned prophecy, which he was confident referred to the destruction of Rome and Turkey.† He made many historical allusions, giving dates enough – had they been eatable – to have fed the whole congregation. The discourse was not a sermon at all in the general acceptation of the word but a lecture, and by no means a good one. Those present seemed very little interested; some fell asleep, and by the time the sermon was concluded it was past 8 o'clock and I was wondering how the service would terminate, as it was by this time quite dusk and the kirk very gloomy.

The preacher was determined that we should have all that was our due so – leaning over one side of the pulpit so as to obtain all the light possible – he gave out a psalm, which the congregation proceeded to make comical efforts to sing. Many who had their faces towards the windows turned around so as to see the better, and one individual near me leant over into the front pew, thus nearly describing a half circle, and produced sounds of a most extraordinary kind when he attempted to sing. The benediction followed and then the minister said 'Let us sing a paraphrase', which appears to be the Scotch method of concluding service. This, after what had passed, seemed such an absurdity that I could not refrain from laughing and I am afraid some of those present must have heard me. It was however 'the last feather which breaks the camel's back', for the precentor

* The quoted phrase is from Deuteronomy, chapter 32, verse 10.
† The minister may mean Rome as the seat of the Roman Catholic Church and Turkey as the most important state in the Ottoman Empire, representing Islam.

commenced to expostulate on the subject, probably saying that he could neither read music or words, so 'Sun of my soul' was substituted, and being well known was sung and the service brought to a termination.*

After a short stroll we returned to Mrs Lorimer's, and before long went to bed, the day having been fine and dry, though not very bright.

MONDAY 28 AUGUST

6.30 a.m. Rose and dressed. Having previously arranged to go by early train to Pitlochrie, visit the Pass of Killicrankie, and then walk back to Birnam, we discovered it was raining in a most persistent manner. As it was necessary to do something, we proceeded to discuss our morning meal, hoping that the moisture might abate, but instead of doing so it came down with redoubled vigour, and we were compelled to abandon our proposed day's enjoyment.

Anticipating weather of this description, Charley had put in the knapsack a set of dominoes which now proved very useful, for we played games in all imaginable kinds of ways with them, at the same time sitting by the window so as to be aware of the least indication of fine weather. Nothing of the sort was destined to be seen that morning, as the clouds completely hid the surrounding hills and discharged their contents in a continuous thick drizzle. As, whether it be wet or dry, dinner is usually found to be a necessity, we summoned Mrs Lorimer to ascertain what she could suggest for that meal. After looking very sagacious, she gave it as her candid and unbiased opinion that meat was scarcely ever obtainable on Mondays, but intimated that rabbits might be procurable, so we gave her full permission to obtain the latter delicacy, hoping it might not prove to consist of a lively little dog we had seen playing near the house a few minutes before.

Having amused ourselves by watching the hotel fly go to the railway station and return with one melancholy victim – who doubtless was mercilessly fleeced – we wrote letters home, played dominoes again and Charley read a book of 96 pages, but still it rained as persistently as ever. We were becoming desperate when dinner appeared, though we could not conscientiously say we had earned it. Still, we did our very best, and when I say the whole dinner did not cost half a crown, it will I think be admitted that it was as cheap as it certainly was good.

Simultaneous with the appearance of the rabbits came a cessation of rain; and a ray of sun, combined with a patch of blue sky, put us into a state of indescribable rapture. At 2.30 p.m. it still held up, though not particularly bright, and we ventured out, puggarees and all, which not only showed our faith in a continuation of the improved state of the weather but amused the natives. On reaching Dunkeld Bridge, rain began to descend once more, so thinking it the wisest plan not to go far, we inspected the photographs and other curiosities in the shop windows, and then went some distance down the Perth road but, finding this very uninteresting, we returned again – the rain by this time had ceased – crossed the Tay and took the road towards Blairgowrie, which was very muddy, though elsewhere the continuous downpour had only just laid the dust.

A change now took place which we certainly had not anticipated: from the west arose a few white clouds, which gradually became more and more numerous, blue sky appeared, the sun shone forth, at first fitfully, then with full power dispersing all the dark clouds. The rain drops sparkled like pendant diamonds from every leaf and branch, each tree and shrub seemed fresher and greener for its recent shower bath, birds began to sing, and all nature seemed to rejoice at the welcome transformation. Nothing on earth is quite perfect, so even this state of things had just one drawback: the flies, which tormented my companion most unmercifully. It was a mystery as to what became of them during the rain, but no sooner did the sun begin to shine than

"Bother these flies"

out they came in swarms. This was a small matter compared with staying cooped up indoors, and we rather welcomed them as harbingers of fine weather.

Having no particular object in view, we walked as far as Loch Lows – a pretty piece of water – then sat on the roadside and basked in the sun, Charley nearly falling asleep while so doing. After which we returned to Dunkeld and spent some time inspecting the stock of a fancy shop. Pretty brushes, boxes and other articles, ornamented with views of the neighbourhood, are made here from a light coloured tree said to be from the plantations of Atholl, and called Birnam or Dunkeld wood according to the locality in which they are sold. In some of these we speculated, and then directed our steps Birnamwards. When crossing the bridge, a small boy called out to us at the top of his voice, 'Ah! I saw you at Callander last week!' which will give the reader some idea of the sensation we everywhere created.

Returning to Mrs Lorimer's, we partook of tea at 7 o'clock, after which we did not again venture out, but retired to rest at 9.30 p.m. when the stars were shining brightly, and all seemed to promise favourably for the morrow.

TUESDAY 29 AUGUST

6.20 a.m. Alas, the promise which seemed so fair last night was not fulfilled in the morning, as on looking out the window, heavy rain and muddy roads met our gaze, so in despair we turned again into bed and indulged in another snooze. Eventually, we arose and breakfasted in a not very contented state of mind, after which our landlady treated us to a graphic account of things in general; her volubility reminded me of the epitaph said to be written on the tombstone of one of her sex:

> Beneath this silent stone is laid
> A noisy antiquated maid;
> Who from her cradle talked till death,
> And ne'er before was out of breath.

Of course, I do not mean to say many ladies deserve such a description as this, which might apply equally well to some of my own sex; as a rule I think they do rather more than their fair share of talking.

We had intended to visit the Rumbling Bridge Falls in the morning, and then depart for Edinburgh by the 2.50 p.m. train, but as there seemed no probability of the rain clearing off, we decided to go three hours earlier, so meanwhile played at dominoes and amused ourselves as well as possible under the circumstances. When the time drew near for departing, we were pleasurably surprised by the rain ceasing and the sun shining forth, so we changed our minds, reverted to our original plan and at once proceeded to put it into execution.

Opposite The Birnam is a small stream, the bed of which two days since was perfectly dry, but now there was a considerable flow of water hastening towards the Tay. If this is the case after comparatively so little rain, what must it be like when the winter floods begin? I should like to come here then; it must be a magnificent sight. Leaving Dunkeld Bridge on our right, we proceeded along the road for about two miles and then came to a splendidly wooded glen down which rushes the River Braan. The two principal points of interest are the Rumbling Bridge and Hermitage Falls, the first being the finer of the two; here, huge masses of rock impede the progress of the stream, which rushes foaming along and at last falls seething and boiling about 80 feet. From the bridge – situated just above the cascade – a fine view is obtained both up and down the river.

The second falls are of a similar character, but hardly so grand; near at hand is the shell of a house formerly called The Hermitage, whence the onlooker could see the surroundings with great advantage. A short time ago, it was partially blown up during the night, though from that day to this the offender has never been discovered.* These waterfalls were the only ones we saw during our trip which approached those of Wales, and we were glad we had not hastened off to Edinburgh by the morning train.

The weather still kept tolerably fine, though every now and then as we made our way through, and caught hold of the trees to assist us down the banks of the river, which were rather steep,

Rumbling Bridge Falls, near Dunkeld.

we experienced a shower bath from the branches overhead. On nearing Birnam, we were overtaken by a heavy fall of rain which obliged us to take shelter. On its cessation, we procured our knapsack and bag, bade farewell to Mrs Lorimer and repaired to the railway station. Here, of course, the train was very late, so we amused ourselves by reading the wall advertisements and inspecting the travellers who happened to be on the platform. One individual wore a ginger coloured coat ornamented with an enormous check. Why tourists should wear such extraordinary suits passes my comprehension; it is almost enough to make one feel ill merely to see them.

A neat thing in checks.

The train having at last arrived, we at once seated ourselves therein and were immediately informed by one of the passengers that the inhabitants of Dunkeld were mainly celebrated for having in times gone by:

> Hanged their pastor, drowned the precentor,
> Rang down the steeple, and fuddled the bells.*

If this be the case, I doubt if any minister would consider they had a 'call' in that direction unless indeed the natives have somewhat improved since this saying was first quoted.

I cannot say much in praise of Scotch railways if that by which we were travelling was a fair specimen of them, for most of the carriages leaked from where the lamps hung, and

* The story of Jacob's ladder appears in Genesis, chapter 28, verses 10–17.

consequently the seats were very wet. At Perth we waited a long time, but afterwards travelled 33 miles in 50 minutes without stopping then, passing Dunblane, the Bridge of Allan and Stirling, we at last reached Edinburgh by 7.15 p.m. having had quite enough railway travelling for one day.

Now, having seen advertisements of several hotels in the neighbourhood of the High Street which offered inducements in the way of economy, we decided to go and judge for ourselves if they were worth patronising, and after one futile application we at last found suitable accommodations, and were soon enjoying a substantial tea in the coffee room, where a number of other guests were similarly employed. Here also for our amusement were all the leading London newspapers, illustrated journals, and serials as well as those published in Scotland. The natives of this country are well known to be great readers, but they prefer to obtain their information rather by reading the books of their friends or others to buying for themselves, so all this food for the mind was provided free of charge. This was by no means the case with the food for the body, as we were required to pay for everything as soon as it appeared, by which system the proprietor did not stand much chance of making bad profits.

The hotel seemed to be mainly patronised by canny Scots, who were so constantly ascending and descending the staircase that it seemed to resemble Jacob's ladder, save that there were not many angels amongst them.* On reading the newspapers, we learnt that during our absence the weather had been exceedingly stormy in the south of England and was now very cold for the time of year, so we had good cause to congratulate ourselves on that which we had experienced.

Going out for a short stroll, we crossed North Bridge and viewed the city by night. The many lights on each side of the valley, especially those from the tall houses, have a curious appearance to a stranger and form a pretty sight at dusk. As it was a cold evening we soon returned to our hotel, and were before long reclining in an old fashioned four-post bedstead, which had such a heavy-looking top that it reminded me of medieval legends where the upper part of the bedstead screws down and crushes the unfortunate occupants thereof during their slumbers. Notwithstanding the pleasant sensation produced by this idea, a very short time only elapsed before we were once again wrapped in the arms of Morpheus.

WEDNESDAY 30 AUGUST

5.30 a.m. I was awakened by a tremendous noise, and soon became aware it was caused, not by the descent of the top of our bedstead, but by a bell in the neighbourhood which was pealing loudly to warn all 'early birds' that the 'worms' had already begun to take their morning walks or – in other words – that it was time to get up. Had the atmosphere been clear, we might have ascended to Arthur's Seat, but as such was not the case we indulged in a little more slumber, then turned out of bed at 7 o'clock, dressed, fortified ourselves with a meat breakfast, and afterwards took our departure with the impression that though everything provided was of good quality, and we were without doubt money in pocket by our stay, yet somehow we had not felt 'at home', and if we had remained another night in Edinburgh should certainly have changed our quarter.

9 a.m. Repaired to the General Post Office, where we found quite a budget of letters awaiting our arrival.* First calling at the office of the General Steam Navigation Company – where we had deposited our luggage on our first arrival in Edinburgh – we left our knapsack etc. in safe keeping then strolled up Princes Street to Charlotte Square, where stands the equestrian statue of the late Prince Consort which was unveiled by the Queen only a week previous to our visit and was the talk and general admiration of all the citizens for the time being; bas-reliefs round the pedestal represent the prince in the principal acts of his life, and at the corners are groups of statuary of the different classes

of Scotch society; altogether it is a capital memorial of one who fully deserved it.*

From here we walked through some of the principal streets, and crossed the Dean Bridge which spans the River Leith at a great elevation; a stream which looked precisely like soapsuds ran by the side of, and eventually discharged itself into, the river, the name of which from its general appearance might be appropriately changed to Lethe.† Returning down Princes Street we passed an individual whom we thought we had seen before and, as each of us turned round just to have another look, we recognised a gentleman named Dick who belongs to Mr Proudman's choir. He arrived from London in 'The Libra' last Monday and, according to his account, had a fearful voyage: notwithstanding the name of the steamer, hardly any of the passengers had been able to preserve their balance. It was scarcely a matter of wonder that he was unwell, as he had passed a great portion of his time trying to rest on a barrel and was now quite sore from rubbing against its sharp edges. Mr Dick's manner of speaking even when joyful is very mysterious and ghostly, so I will not attempt to describe the way in which he related his sufferings. We bade him adieu, hoping most devoutly that we should have a more agreeable return voyage.

In Princes Street are a number of shoe blacks, two of whom polished our boots, and rather surprised us by a demand of two pence per pair for their labour, on our saying the London charge was only half that amount they retorted that no shoe black society existed here, so they fixed their own tariff. In the midst of Princes Gardens stands the National Gallery, which we inspected and found to contain a very good collection of pictures. Those which pleased me more especially were 'The Quarrel and Reconciliation of Oberon and Titania' by Sir Noel Paton, a copy of Rubens' 'Crucifixion', and 'The Death of Holofernes by the Hand of Judith', but strange to say there was only one example of Landseer, and very few of Scotch historical subjects.‡

Once more, we repaired to the castle and took a final view

Holyrood Palace, Arthur's Seat in the distance.

of Edinburgh and its environs; it was a better day than on our previous visit, and we could see across the Forth as far as Burntisland, but still it might have been clearer, and when we again visit the modern Athens I hope the atmosphere will enable us to enjoy the prospect at its very best. Hurrying past an old man, who was seated on a chair at the castle entrance and playing the bagpipes with a vigour truly appalling, we walked down the High Street and entered Holyrood Palace in front of which is a pretty and very ornamental fountain erected from a design by the late Prince Consort.

This palace was formerly the residence of Scottish royalty, and is more celebrated for its historical connection with Mary, Queen of Scots, than for anything that can actually be seen there now. The picture gallery is a very long chamber containing a number of portraits supposed to represent the Kings of Scotland, but they are so black and ugly that I think they must be libellous. I have since heard that they were painted by contract – long and short, dark and fair – 30/- per head, which really seems quite probable, as anything more hideous in the way of portraits I have never seen.*

* In 1684, Charles II commissioned Jacob de Wet the Younger to produce portraits of 110 real and imaginary kings of Scotland. The intention was to show that Scotland was one of the oldest countries in Europe, and that it had been ruled by an unbroken line of monarchs since time immemorial.

* David Rizzio
(1533–66) was an
Italian courtier who
acted as private
secretary to Mary,
Queen of Scots from
1564. Lord Darnley,
Mary's husband,
became jealous of
their friendship and
joined a conspiracy
of Scottish nobles,
who had political and
religious differences
with the queen, to
murder the Italian.
He was stabbed to
death in Mary's private
chamber, then flung
down the stairs of the
palace and buried
within two hours.
† The custodians of
the palace state that
the chamber floor
has been replaced
a number of times.
Visitors are just as
insistent that they can
see a blood stain.

Lord Darnley's and Queen Mary's rooms are the only other places on view. They contain much old furniture – including the Queen's bed – all of which is much the worse for wear, cords being tied across the chairs to prevent visitors sitting down on them. Last, but – to many people – most interesting of all, is the identical stain caused by the blood which flowed from Rizzio when he was killed there.* The mark is by no means clear, and we joked with one of the attendants saying he might easily make the spot darker by a little extra blood. I have been informed that at least three new floorings have been put down since the tragedy occurred, but this I hardly believe and am inclined to place credence in the generally accepted theory, as the event only happened about 300 years ago, and certainly took place in this room.† The chapel or abbey dates from 1128 and is much older than the palace, but it is quite a ruin, as merely the walls and two rows of pillars are now standing. Always on the lookout for old tombstones, we here thought we had at last discovered one as ancient as 1274, but this date proved to relate to some historical event, and the earliest recognisable memorial was 1455.

It being now 1.30 p.m. the time was drawing nigh when we should be compelled to bid farewell to Scottish scenes. So, first

Queen Mary's bedchamber, Holyrood Palace.

procuring our luggage, we made for the railway station, and on our way met the two brothers whom we had last seen near Stronachlacher, and found that they, like ourselves, were going by the afternoon boat. When at the booking office taking tickets for Granton, I saw a gentleman who much resembled Mr Marshall of Salem Chapel, but as he looked at and did not recognise me I thought it as well not to introduce myself, and so avoid the possibility of a contretemps, especially as there was but little time for conversation.*

Having seated ourselves in the train, after the usual delay, it started off with a tremendous jerk which caused most of the passengers to make motions as if they wished to visit the opposite end of the carriage. One elderly female near us gave such an agonised clutch in the air that had a gentleman been facing her she would undoubtedly have embraced him. Such not being the case, she merely looked very ridiculous, but her action quite upset our gravity. The frequent stoppages and slow rate of travelling were themes for much joking among the passengers, one suggesting it was to enable us to view the scenery, which consisted mainly of dirty houses; while another said that when the company had sufficient money they would use horses instead of the present engine, and so be able to proceed at a reasonable speed.

We arrived at Granton with plenty of time to spare, and here we found our old friend 'The Libra' commanded by Captain Wilson waiting to receive us, so immediately went on board and secured our berths. Then, having watched the loading of the cargo by means of cranes, which was rather an interesting process, all was at length ready, and at 3.15 p.m. we bade farewell to the shores of Scotia, where I think we had enjoyed ourselves as much as possible during the last ten days. Almost immediately after we had started, the gentleman whom I had seen at the booking office asked me if I did not rejoice in the name of Freeman. I pleaded guilty to the indictment, and then ascertained if I was correct in my first surmise as to his identity. He

* There were a number of buildings called Salem Chapel, all Baptist places of worship. Given the Freeman brothers' religion and places of living and work, the most likely Salem Chapel was the one behind numbers 8 and 10 Meard Street in Soho. This was built in 1824 for the Rev. John Stevens and a congregation of Particular Baptists. The congregation met here until 1878.

had experienced a very bad passage to Scotland last week, nearly everyone on board being ill, even one of the mates, so once more we felt extra thankful for our pleasant voyage.

4 p.m. Dinner was announced and duly appeared, but only about 20 sat down thereto, shortly after which we passed the celebrated Bass Rock. This remarkable object rises – far away from the shore – almost perpendicular to a height of about 300 feet from the water; it is uninhabited save by myriads of sea fowl, which may be seen perched on every projecting point. As we passed, the captain ordered the steam whistle to be blown, and as its piercing scream rent the air, up flew thousands of birds hovering around and making a great noise. I hardly think the members of the winged tribe approved of being so rudely disturbed during their evening meditations.

When off St Abb's Head, Captain Wilson came round to inspect our tickets, and soon afterwards one of the passengers was assisted downstairs in a state of helpless intoxication. He came to Granton in our carriage and began to smoke, but desisted at my request; he then seemed rather queer. As he was now being taken in the direction of the sleeping compartments, all who saw him thought and many said: 'I hope he is not going to be my companion for the night'! As he appeared to be making for our part of the vessel, we anxiously followed until he was safely lodged in the next division to us.

7.30 p.m. Had a very good tea, after which we did not go on deck again as it had begun to rain and the general lookout was very cold and cheerless. We preferred the warmth of the saloon, where we read, played at dominoes among ourselves, and chatted with some of the passengers until it was time to turn into our berths, shortly after which the under-steward came round and locked the window saying 'Rough night tonight, gentlemen', which of course was very consoling.

THURSDAY 31 AUGUST

During the night, I dreamt that we reached home about 2 o'clock in the morning, but just as we were being welcomed by our relatives – though I scarcely think they would have cared to see us so early in the day – I awoke and found I was occupying a berth on board 'The Libra'. Considering our novel position, we slept very fairly, though the captain said for three hours the wind had been exceedingly high. About 6 a.m. Charley tumbled up on deck to see Scarborough and a little later I followed his example. The man who was so intoxicated last night now made an attempt to perform his toilettes, and to my great astonishment endeavoured to shave; what with the motion of the vessel, and the equally unsteady movements of his hand, it is a puzzle to me how he accomplished this feat without cutting his face, but I believe the operation was at last brought to a termination without an accident.

An Enigma

On reaching the deck, I found the wind so cold that all who had overcoats were glad to don them and march to and fro like pedestrians training for a race. When near Flamborough Head we met 'The Virgo' – a steamer belonging to the same company as our own – and mutual courtesies were exchanged. We appeared to be travelling at a pretty fair speed, and overtook several other vessels about this time. At 9 o'clock breakfast – consisting of steaks, chops, sausages, eggs and fish – was attacked with much success, the bracing air having apparently given everyone excellent appetites.

Our company did not number more than 50 altogether, amongst whom were a few young men – especially one with a shark-like mouth – who, when they discovered what an argumentative man our captain was, tried to raise discussions with him. Mainly with this view, I believe, they expressed opinions of an infidel character, and were certainly very successful in 'drawing out' the skipper, who however was quite equal to the occasion, so that it was quite amusing to see the group of disputants – for

Captain Wilson could not stand still – walking up and down the deck and arguing the whole time.

After dinner, the weather did not improve; in the rear were heavy black clouds whence we could plainly see the rain falling in torrents, and when off Yarmouth forked lightning was very vivid. However, we were only visited by an occasional shower, though it afterwards appeared we barely escaped by two or three hours a fearful storm which took place in the North Sea when vessels were wrecked and life lost amongst the smaller craft. So we had good reason to lift up our voices in thankfulness to our Heavenly Father for His preserving mercies in not only keeping us from danger, but even giving us a comparatively calm voyage.

After tea the inebriate before alluded to was assisted to his berth in a fearful state of intoxication. He had been spending the whole day either there or sitting over the engine room, but always in company with a whisky bottle, and the consequence was he was now quite helpless. Those who occupied the other berths in his compartment declared at first he should not enter, but they afterwards changed quarters instead, leaving him to himself.

The night was fine, both moon and stars shining brightly, and we appeared to be making a good passage, the various craft which we met gliding past like the 'Flying Dutchman' of phantom notoriety. About a dozen of the passengers belonging to the sterner sex assembled together near the helmsman and passed away the time by singing songs, some of which were very well given. Charley joined this party, but as it was rather chilly I marched to and fro in company with Mr Marshall until it was time to retire to rest.

FRIDAY 1 SEPTEMBER

During the night, the inebriated passenger turned out of his berth and, wrapping himself in a sheet which he imagined was his night dress, made fruitless endeavours to find the arm holes. In this classical attire he paid a visit to the steward, and afterwards awoke me by continually counting aloud all the odd numbers as far as nine, when he would recommence and have a fresh trial. As this pastime seemed to afford him endless amusement, I rose, shut our door and was not again troubled by his vagaries.

About 6 a.m. we reached Gravesend. The steam whistle was blown as a signal that a pilot was required to come from the shore and take us on to London. This noise did not bring the necessary assistance, but effectually aroused me, and more sleep – owing to the incessant movement overhead – being unattainable, we rose, dressed and went aloft with the view of gaining some information if not satisfaction regarding the state of things in that quarter.

Here we found that the pilot – after a delay of an hour – had at last come on board, but during that interval the stream had turned 'The Libra' completely round, and in trying to put her head once more in the right direction the strain had snapped in two the connecting rod – solid steel nearly four inches in diameter – which worked the rudder. A makeshift apparatus consisting of ropes had been hastily constructed which required six men to work it, but all in vain: every effort to turn the steamer Londonwards proved abortive. At each trial it appeared to non-nautical eyes as if she were going round capitally but, just as she reached the turning point, back she would swing to her original position. This was repeated several times with precisely the same result, and we were so close to the shore that it seemed as if we might run aground any minute. After many attempts – mainly owing to an eddy, without which Captain Wilson said we should have been obliged to wait until the tide changed – the desired-for object was at last accomplished, and at 7.40 a.m. we were once more on our voyage.

On nearing our destination, the intoxicated passenger once more appeared on deck and declared he had lost his watch, which was rather unpleasant for ourselves as we had slept so

* The brothers William and John Marshall Trotter were in business as Trotter Brothers, hosiers, at 20 Newgate Street, according to court records of 1875 and 1876. The letters E.C. stand for East Central, the early 'postcode' for this district of London.

near to him, though of course no one could tell but that he had thrown it overboard during the night. After enquiries in various quarters, it was ascertained he had given it – whether to keep, or only to take care of, did not transpire – to one of the firemen, and he brought his holiday to a fitting termination by confessing he had not enough money to pay his bill, which came to about 13 shillings. He promised to forward it to the steward, but it would have been a just retribution had this latter individual lost the money, as he ought not have supplied the man with additional stimulants – as he had most undoubtedly done – when he was in such a state of intoxication. The name of this drunkard deserves to be recorded, and should the reader ever come in contact with Mr Trotter, hosier, of 20 Newgate Street, E.C. he will do well to avoid his company.*

About 9.20 a.m. the Tower of London came in view, at which spectacle everyone secured his or her luggage and after much careful piloting we were once more alongside the wharf whence we started. Captain Wilson then gave a hearty goodbye to each passenger which was as heartily reciprocated, as all felt he had done his very best to render our trip cheerful and pleasant. Stepping from 'The Libra', we were once again in the gigantic metropolis, our holiday was ended and we were doomed to pass another year amidst scenery as different from that of Scotland as are the . . .

Fashions of 1820 and 1876.

THE WYE VALLEY   1877   SOUTH WALES

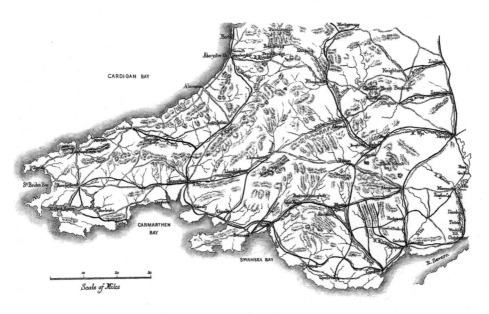

CARDIGAN BAY

CARMARTHEN
BAY

SWANSEA BAY

Scale of Miles

PROLOGUE

Five years have now elapsed since first I went
With Charles my brother for a walking tour,
Which trip we thought a pleasant week well spent,
Its recollections ever will endure.

And since that time, when holidays came round,
Sometimes with friends, at other times alone,
We two together have each summer found
How joyous 'tis midst hill and vale to roam.

This year however Charley thought it best
To spend his time at Worthing by the sea,
Thinking in fact he ought to have more rest,
He therefore took his pleasure quietly.

And thus it happened that I had the task
Of finding someone who his place would fill,
But there were few I really cared to ask
And those few could not, though they had the will.

I wanted someone who would like to walk
A distance – say – of 20 miles per day,
One who could also take a joke and talk,
But then he must not have too much to say.

A friend who would not grumble and complain
If any little troubles should arise:
For heavy clouds must come, and storms, and rain,
As well as pleasant azure summer skies.

And neither should I care to have, I fear,
A friend who liked and often smoked a pipe,
Nor one who could indulge in wines or beer,
For to these things I have a great dislike.

I thought and searched and searched and thought again
In hopes that I might a companion find,
But all enquiries seemed to be in vain,
I could not hear of one to suit my mind.

'When things get to the worst', 'tis said, 'they mend',
Which – often true – now proved to be the case,
For when I quite despaired to find a friend,
My brother George stepped in and filled the place.

A record of our travels here appears,
The which I trust may not be quite in vain,
For by its aid I hope in future years
To see – in fancy – each bright spot again.

SATURDAY 4 AUGUST

Suddenly awakening, I was startled at seeing that the small hand of my watch pointed to 7 o'clock. In vain I looked at it again and again; there was no mistake about it. By thus oversleeping ourselves not only have we missed the early train by which we had intended to start, but also the second one, so that we could not reach our journey's end until the evening, thus losing nearly a day, compelling us to spend the Sunday at Chepstow and putting out all our preconceived arrangements. To say that I lost my temper would be mild language; I was in a perfect rage which only abated when I opened my eyes, found I was lying on my back, daylight had not yet appeared, and it was all a dream.

4 a.m. Down came our alarum with a seemingly terrific noise, at the first sound of which my bedfellow and myself started up with an agility only to be obtained by those who are going out for a holiday. If the reader be of a meditative turn of mind, he will perhaps answer the following question: 'How is it we can rise so very early on such an occasion and not feel the least sleepy, while on Sunday mornings some three or four hours later we are exceedingly disinclined to turn out of bed, and often actually indulge in another snooze?' 4.40 a.m. Of course at such an early hour no one had the courage to rise and see us off, so having partaken of a substantial breakfast we bade adieu to 134 Regent Street, and then started off for our holiday.

On the road we rejected the proffered services of a cabman, noted a policeman doing his best to awaken an early riser, and finally arrived at Paddington Station in about half an hour with plenty of time to spare.* Having had the forethought to obtain our tickets previously, we at once secured good seats in the train, whilst those who were not so provided waited and grumbled in front of the booking office, hoping the ticket clerk might soon

* Paddington Station was operated by the Great Western Railway Company and opened in 1838.

appear. At such a time of the day, one might be excused for thinking that the railway platform would be a scene of perfect tranquillity; but such was by no means the case: a van load of newspapers was being sorted into lots in order to leave at the various stations on our route, and as the carriages filled up rapidly, persons darted to and fro in a very excited state of mind. One lady having after much exertion managed to seat herself and her et ceteras in our compartment, was informed by her husband they were too early and could not go by that train so with much evident annoyance, and hardly convinced they could have made a mistake, she was again landed on the platform.

5.35 a.m. The signal is given and at last we are off; yesterday having been a very wet day, we were afraid this morning might be so likewise, but as we sped along, there seemed indications of fine weather. At Swindon we changed into another train and then, having waited a short time, resumed our journey. Near Stroud is a long tunnel, and the country is very pretty, presenting a charming succession of wooded hills with a river meandering though the valley. Farther on, we passed through the city

Chepstow Castle.

BRADSHAW ON CHEPSTOW

Chepstow is a market town, in the county of Monmouth, situated near the mouth of the River Wye. The town is large and has within the last few years been much improved. It was formerly surrounded by walls and defended by a castle. Population 3,364. Distance from station: ¼ mile.

A TELEGRAPH STATION. HOTEL: THE BEAUFORT ARMS.

of Gloucester, where the cathedral is a conspicuous object of admiration. Here, being rather hungry, we indulged in refreshments, and on nearing our destination (or 'destiny' as one of our fellow passengers informed a little girl) a river appeared on the left hand side which we were told was the Wye, but the banks were so flat and muddy that we really could not see the beauty for which that stream is so famed. On referring to our map, we ascertained it was the Severn, and rejoiced to find such was the case, for there would have been little pleasure in walking near so uninteresting a river.

10.10 a.m. Chepstow. This was the termination of our railway journey, which was performed with great celerity as we only stopped at seven stations while the following train stops at 23, and is two hours longer on the road. Our first care was to send our wardrobe on to Monmouth then, having posted a card to inform those at home of our safe arrival, we immediately proceeded to inspect the town. The streets are steep and irregular, but it possesses a clean market where a butcher was arguing with a gentleman upon the utter impossibility of providing him with a sirloin of beef, whenever he might require it. We did not stay to hear the result of the discussion, but repaired to the bridge which crosses the Wye. The river here is of considerable width, but the banks at low water are exceedingly muddy; according to the guide book it often rises 50 and has been known to rise 70 feet. This I think must be an exaggeration, for if it were true

Windcliff Hill, near Tintern.

the bridge would be completely covered and the town swamped. The main centre of interest is the castle, which – to my mind – is not a very interesting-looking ruin, and as we had but little time to spare on this day, we postponed the inspection thereof until our return to Chepstow. The church has a fine door and a beautifully shaded avenue of trees, but one of the chapels – Ebenezer – was so very dirty and in such a general state of dilapidation that it would be an act of charity if the deacons at Soho would present the congregation with their old lamp.

11.15 a.m. Having seen all the marvels of Chepstow, we began our tour of the Wye, and had just started when two lads

BRADSHAW ON THE WYNDCLIFF

The Wyndcliff rises in the background of the view from the road out of Chepstow to Monmouth. Having ascended the crag, the eye ranges over portions of nine counties, yet there seems to be no confusion in the prospect; the proportions of the landscape, which unfolds itself in regular, yet not in monotonous, succession; there is nothing to offend the most exact critic in picturesque scenery.

BRADSHAW ON THE RIVER WYE

👉 *The River Wye, which runs through the county of Monmouth, is celebrated for its picturesque scenery. The peculiar characteristics of this beautiful river are its sinuous course, the uniformity of its breadth and the variegated scenery on its banks. The views it exhibits are of the most beautiful kind of perspective.*

requested us to 'scramble a ha'penny between them', upon which I expostulated with them upon the inexpediency of thus wasting the coin of the realm, and finally invited them to show me how it was done, but as they declared they 'hadn't nary one' we continued our journey and left them to their reflections.* The road at first seemed glaring and dusty, but on arriving at St Arvans we turned across some fields to reach Windcliff Hill, but soon came to a standstill where two paths met, not knowing which to take.† Before long the Tintern coach appeared, and as it is usual for passengers to dismount here and ascend the hill, we were no longer in doubt as to the correct route and were soon on the summit.

From this elevated position (800 feet) a really splendid view is seen, the course of the Wye to its mouth being plainly visible, and its various windings appearing like streaks of silver threading the foliage on its banks, which – especially at the foot of the hill – is extremely luxuriant. Having rested here and thoroughly enjoyed the prospect for some time, we then descended by a very steep and stony path to a small house called Moss Cottage where 'Sixpence each please, Sirs' met our astonished ears. It is nothing new to be asked for money when entering a place, but it certainly did seem strange to have such a demand made on our departure. I suppose we could have gone back again, but this we did not relish, so paid the fee and passed on. Just here we met four pedestrians clothed in flannels and walking as if for a wager. So fast were they going, that one who asked me 'How

Tintern Abbey.

far is it to Moss Cottage?' could hardly stay for a reply. As I have before observed: 'There really is no accounting for the way in which some people enjoy themselves.'

Our route now lay near, though some distance above the River Wye, every bend of which brought fresh views and by 1.45 p.m. Tintern was reached. This spot is very prettily situated amongst the surrounding hills and is celebrated mainly for its abbey where, having rung the bell, we were at once admitted to view the ruins, first paying a shilling for the privilege. The

---

BRADSHAW ON TINTERN ABBEY

This is one of the most rare and magnificent structures in the whole range of ecclesiastical architecture. As you descend the road from Chepstow, the building suddenly bursts upon you, like a gigantic stone skeleton, its huge gables standing out against the sky with a mournful air of dilapidation.

The castle is a noble and massive relic of feudalism; the boldness of its site, on a rock overhanging the river, the vastness of its proportions, render it a peculiarly impressive ruin. The chapel is one of the most elegant structures ever built within a house of defence.

BRADSHAW ON MONMOUTH

☞ *Monmouth, the capital of Monmouthshire, is on a delight-ful part of the Wye, at the junction of the Monnow, a parliamentary borough, with an agricultural population of 5,710, which is rather on the decrease, but this will no doubt be augmented by the recent opening of the railway from Pontypool. Monmouth was once famous for its woollen caps.*

TELEGRAPH STATION AT PONTYPOOL ROAD, 18 MILES. HOTELS: THE BEAUFORT ARMS HOTEL, THE KING'S HEAD HOTEL.

* The Devil's Pulpit stands close to Offa's Dyke on the east bank of the River Wye. Here, the Wye forms the border between Wales and England, so Tintern Abbey is in Wales, and the Devil's Pulpit is in England.

pillars have mostly fallen down, but the walls and one of the windows especially are very perfect, and altogether it is well worth a visit. A narrow and very much worn stone staircase leads to the top of the walls, which we mounted and had a capital view therefrom, but almost expected someone to appear and say: 'Three pence please, Sir, to come here?' Near at hand is a rock named after his Satanic majesty, from whence during the middle ages – according to tradition – he used to preach dreadful things to the monks who lived in the abbey, and at last grew so bold that he occupied the roof-loft of the building the better to deliver his orations.* The inhabitants – preferring his room to his company – sprinkled his lordship with holy water, which scorched him so severely that he fled in great haste to Llandogo. The marks of his talons can still be seen upon the stone, so therefore it must, of necessity, be true. What a pity he was not killed!

On leaving the abbey we felt rather hungry, so rested for half an hour, lunched, and started off again at 3.15 p.m. At Llandogo it was necessary to cross the railway; the gates were shut and the individual in charge said he could not possibly open them until the next train had passed. As it was not even in sight, we climbed over and thus at once settled the difficulty. Here the road crosses to the other side of the river and, of course, a toll is demanded. I wonder how much is collected during the day? Evidently there is never any great crush of people, as there is not

* The term 'wife corrector' was applied to a bullying husband who attempted, through mental and physical means, to change his wife's beliefs or behaviours. John seems to suggest that those from Lancashire were the most extreme.

even a turnstile. The scenery during the remainder of our walk was very pleasing, the Wye running between high hills covered with short trees interspersed at regular intervals with taller ones. Houses were scarce, and inhabitants few and far between; this was also the case with the milestones or else we must have missed them. Monmouth was soon reached by 6.20 p.m. and our first day's travel thus brought to an end. The distance by road from here to Chepstow is 15 miles and a half without counting the ascent to Windcliff Hill, and was really rather too far for the first day, especially after a long railway journey, but there was no suitable intermediate place where we could have passed the Sunday. This town was certainly the most eligible spot, nor did we afterwards have reason to regret our decision.

Having, after some little trouble, secured apartments in Mary Street, we procured our bag and then proceeded to discuss a very good tea, being equally willing and able to do so. Our landlady's little daughter then brought in a nosegay of flowers, and invited us to come to her chapel on the morrow saying they had a very good minister. On questioning her, we found she went to Sunday School and declared her teacher was the best in the school; altogether it was very evident that her attendance there was not merely a matter of duty but of love. Our appetites being appeased, we strolled out to see in what sort of a place we were located.

Monmouth is situated at the junction of the rivers Monnow and Wye. It contains about 6,000 inhabitants, many good houses and a variety of shops; hats are to be obtained for the trifling sum of one shilling and trousers are given away in exchange for five times that amount. Ladies can also gratify their taste for false hair, and boots are sold of a thickness that would satisfy the most confirmed Lancashire 'wife corrector'.* It boasts of a town hall, a large stone building ornamented (!) with a statue of King Henry the Fifth, and a gun captured during the Crimean War. There are also some remains of the old wall, in the shape of a miniature Temple Bar in Monnow Street, and an extensive range of almshouses and a grammar school which were founded by a certain

Mr Jones under the following circumstances. Leaving Newland a poor lad, he gradually amassed a large fortune and then returned to his native town disguised as a mendicant and soliciting relief. The inhabitants – not recognising him – behaved so inhospitably that he resolved to try some other spot, and being much better received in Monmouth he built and endowed these charities for the poor of the town as a reward for the kindness shown him by the inhabitants thereof.* It being by this time quite dark, we returned indoors and soon after retired to rest.

SUNDAY 5 AUGUST

7 a.m. After a good night's rest we arose to find the sun shining in all his glory, and half an hour later walked past the church and as far as the Union, from which elevated position a good view of the town and adjoining country is obtained, the church spire standing in bold relief, but the morning mists had not cleared away sufficiently to enable us to see it at its best.† The inhabitants were evidently aware the 'day of rest' had arrived, as hardly any of them were to be seen in the streets, we therefore returned and improved the occasion by making a good breakfast. Variety is said to be charming, and if so the furniture of our sitting room must be admitted to have been perfection itself. Firstly there was an armchair large enough to seat the 'unhappy nobleman' now confined in Dartmoor, and a number of smaller chairs with velvet cushions which made the occupants thereof very warm.‡ Then, though not a large room no fewer than 22 pictures hung upon the walls, including paintings both in oil and watercolours, photographs, coloured prints from the 'Illustrated London News' and ordinary woodcuts. Added to these were a variety of china ornaments representing dogs, lambs, angels and other figures, two clocks both of which had struck work and consequently did not strike the hours, a stuffed hawk and an owl. Finally, beneath our feet on the floor lay five rugs each made of

* William Jones, a leading merchant in Monmouth in the 17th century, did give money to fund 'a preacher, a free-school and alms-houses' in the town. The school continues, as the Monmouth School, and celebrated its 400th anniversary in 2014. There appears to be less truth in the second part of the tale, which is also perpetuated in Bradshaw.

† The 'Union' was the Monmouth Poor Law Union, which was founded in 1836. When John visited, its workhouse stood in Hereford Road.

‡ The 'unhappy nobleman' was Arthur Orton, who had claimed to be the long-lost Roger Tichborne, heir to the Tichborne baronetcy. Having failed to convince the courts he was Tichborne, he was found guilty of perjury and sentenced to 14 years' imprisonment.

* The Independent Chapel, in Glendower Street, was established in 1832.

some hundreds of pieces of coloured cloth, so we could not well complain of the lifeless monotony of our surroundings.

Breakfast being finished, a certain Mr Lindsay – who resided in the same house as ourselves – invited us to go to the Independent Chapel where he, as well as our landlady and her family, were in the habit of attending.* To this we acceded but first of all took a walk with him to the Chippenham Meadow. This is a large field by the side of the River Monnow, but it is public property and much used by the inhabitants as a promenade, especially on Sundays. In the winter it is almost converted into a lake as the river often rises and overflows the low lying lands, which must be the reverse of pleasant to the population. It now being near service time we entered the above named chapel – a tolerably large, clean, light, well ventilated edifice – and seated ourselves in Mr Lindsay's pew. The first hymn having been announced, the customary pause was made in order that the organist might give the congregation some idea of the tune to which it was to be sung. Upon this, the instrument sent forth a growl and then immediately stopped, which proceeding was repeated three or four times with sundry pauses. Those present, evidently thinking it a very curious melody, turned round and gazed aloft, but as the organ was certainly out of sorts, the hymn was read and sustained by the choir, and it really seemed to go quite as well as those which were afterwards sung with the assistance of a harmonium brought up from the school room.

The pastor, Mr Nimmo, preached a very good sermon from Isaiah, chapter 26, verse 3: 'Thou will keep him in perfect peace, whose mind is stayed on Thee', pointing out that Christ alone is able to give perfect peace from all our troubles. His manner was quiet, but he seemed to gain the attention of the congregation which however was not very large. After service, we strolled down Monnow Street and, as we intended to visit the Baptist Chapel in the evening, peeped in to see what sort of a place it was. We were not at all surprised to find it down a court, but in other respects it was not very inviting, cleanliness – especially by the pew-opener – being evidently not thought to be next to godliness. As it was a small building and the preacher reported to be a 'regular roarer' we decided to think again of the matter before the hour for evening service.

Returning to Mary Street, we sat down to dinner and then, having rested, went out at 2.30 p.m. for a walk with Mr Lindsay. The day being very fine and hot, George suggested puggarees would be suitable for the occasion; we therefore adopted that head dress. Crossing the Wye, we began to ascend the hill known as the Kymin by a very rough, steep, and stony path, which we found to be much hotter than Sunday School work. Perhaps the flies mistook me for Charles; at any rate they mustered round my head in the most provoking manner and I was not sorry when we reached the top. Here is a bower erected in commemoration of the victories of various British admirals – though I must confess I had never before even heard of some of the names inscribed thereon – but it is sadly in want of repair. The view from this point might and probably would be very good, if it were not for the fact that it is much obscured by trees which are allowed to grow on the summit.

After a short rest we descended the other side of the hill, and then came in contact with five men of Monmouth; as they knew Mr Lindsay and were going in the same direction as ourselves, we all mounted a still higher hill to see what is called the Buckstone. This is an ancient Druidical rocking-stone: it stands just beneath the brow of the hill, is 12 feet in height, measures 54 in circumference near the top, but only three at the bottom. Though such an enormous mass of stone is so very nicely balanced that it can be made to sway to and fro, not so much as my imagination had pictured, for on first pushing it the motion was scarcely perceptible. Afterwards it certainly did move about two inches, which could be both seen and felt by those who were on it. I suppose if it were to rock much more it might topple over, in which case it would roll right down the hill. By the aid of small crevices in the stone most of us clambered on to the top, from which a magnificent view is seen all over the surrounding coun-try. The guide book says for a circumference of 300 miles, but this I think must be 'taken with a grain of salt'; nevertheless it certainly was very fine, the Wye valley near at hand with high mountains in the distance – and the sun shining brightly over the whole – looking extremely beautiful.

Descending from the Buckstone is rather more difficult than ascending, as it is impossible to see exactly where it is neces-sary to tread. We eventually reached terra firma, and then left the men of Monmouth in the rear, Mr Lindsay agreeing with us that they were not very desirable companions. Returning by a different and rather dusty road we reached Monmouth at 5.25 p.m. having walked about seven miles, and were quite ready for our tea, which happily was equally so for us. After duly considering the attractions of the Independent and Baptist Chapels, we decided to visit the former once more, but this time sat in the gallery with the choir. Whether it was supposed that persons who sit upstairs do not need such good accommodation as those who remain below, or – as is more likely – sufficient funds were not obtained to complete the re-pewing of the whole chapel I cannot tell, but the seats in these upper regions were of the straight old uncomfortable type and consequently were occupied by very few persons.

Musically speaking, we profited by the change as we obtained the loan of a tune book (the 'Bristol'), but otherwise it was not advantageous as our attention was much distracted by three boys in the pew before us who were as inattentive as they could pos-sibly be, first turning around and staring at us, then poking their fingers through large knot holes in the back of the pew, so I was obliged to expostulate with them on their conduct. During the sermon they seemed so unnaturally quiet that I peered over and found one was engaged in the interesting operation of making a doll with his pocket handkerchief while the other two were most eagerly watching him. As words seemed of no avail, I tapped the chief culprit sharply on the head, which greatly surprised him and they all at once retired to their respective places and behaved better during the rest of the service. Afterwards George went for a walk with Mr Lindsay while I wrote a letter to those at home, and we then retired to make a closer acquaintance with Mr Morpheus.

MONDAY 6 AUGUST

After a very uncomfortable night's rest which was disturbed by a cat, cock and donkey – doubtless they were anticipating the enjoyment of the coming bank holiday – we rose, packed up our extensive wardrobes, and went out for a short walk. On account of the before mentioned festive occasion (today being the first Monday in August), the majority of the shops were closed, and that mark of civilisation, a public barometer, not being visible, we were rather anxious regarding the weather, as the wind had veered to the south and the sky looked very cloudy. Before long it began to rain a little so we returned indoors, breakfasted, settled our 'William' and then prepared to start.

9.30 a.m. Though it still rained slightly we did not see much utility in waiting, so went down to the railway station and booked our bag for Ross, where a regatta was to be held. Quite a crowd of people were going, causing the little platform to wear an aspect of unwonted activity. Instead of taking the high road, we kept close to the right hand side of the Wye, imagining that the best scenery must be near the river. At first an ugly black fence hid the prospect to a great extent, but this soon disappeared, and then the view became exceedingly pretty. On each side rose a steep verdant hill between which ran the Wye. About this time the slight drizzle which had been falling – though hardly sufficient to lay the dust – ceased, and soon after the sun broke through the clouds, so the scenery was greatly brightened and thereby rendered doubly enjoyable.

The road hereabouts consisted of loose stones, which being

* A drag, sometimes
called a drag cart
shoe, is a device
that is placed on
the back wheels of
horse-drawn carts,
and acts either to lock
the wheels in place
or to allow only slow
forward movement,
for example when
the horse and cart is
descending a steep
slope and the weight
of the cart could push
the horse over.

exceedingly uncomfortable for the pedestrian exercise, we
adjourned to the railway line which ran parallel to the road, and
walked on the sleepers, the scarcity of trains rendering such a
proceeding perfectly safe. About mid-day after a very pleasant
walk – during which we only met two persons – we arrived at
Symonds Yat. Here the river makes a most extraordinary pear-
like curve, which while only 400 yards in width at the neck is no
less than four miles in circumference. At the narrow part is a
steep elevation of 600 feet, this we at once began to ascend and
on the road were met by various itinerant provision merchants
who, taking advantage of the momentary weakness of any tourist who might chance to pause for breath, endeavoured to make
a sale of their wares, and as by this time the sun was exceedingly
hot they ought to have done a good stroke of business. On reaching the summit, the toilsome ascent was amply rewarded, and
the view all around exceedingly fine. Monmouthwards lay the
well-wooded hills we had just passed, while in the direction of
Ross the country was much more level and the many windings
of the Wye were very noticeable. A tunnel for the railway is cut
through the hill on which we were standing, and we had the
pleasure of hearing a train enter on one side and emerge from
the other with a tremendous noise.

After staying here half an hour, we directed our footsteps to
the other end of the curve before alluded to, and on the road met
a cart behind which came a lad laden with a very large stone.
This I suppose was to place under the wheel when the horse
required a rest; perhaps drags are not known in these districts
but I wonder the boy did not put the stone in the cart; I think I
should have done.* Dinner time was now near at hand, but an
inn or indeed any accommodation for travellers was totally out
of the question. We had provided for such a contingency, and
on nearing a farm resolved to enquire if milk was obtainable.
Having first convinced a large dog that we were quite harmless,
we were then told by the farmer's wife she feared all the milk was
sour, but our wants were eventually supplied and sitting under

some trees we rested and enjoyed our mid-day meal as only hungry pedestrians can.

1.30 p.m. Resuming our journey, we soon came to Huntsham Ferry, where it was necessary to cross the Wye. This fact was quite patent; the only question was 'How?'. There certainly was a ferry, propelled by chains and evidently used for conveying horses and carts, but as no one was in sight we did not think it advisable to try and manage it by ourselves. Before long, a boat containing a man appeared and, in reply to our request, 'Please row us across!' he said the ferry house was a little lower down. This having been discovered, the next thing was to make our wants known. It was on the other side of the river and not a soul was to be seen, so George called again and again, then I tried to make myself heard, after which we both shouted together, but the only response was the echo, 'Hi ferryman!', 'Hi ferryman!' At last, a woman appeared, brought a boat across and took us over; whether she came in reply to our summons we could not tell, as she was so deaf that it was difficult to make her understand even when close to her.

Once more on terra firma we made at once for the high road, and soon came to the village of Goodrich, with its church and school. In this latter building, the juvenile Goodrichites were trying to acquire the rudiments of knowledge, but I fear our appearance rather disturbed their studies as they evidently regarded us with great curiosity. Enquiring of an old man as to the 'lions' of the place – whether he was that wonderful celebrity

The oldest Inhabitant.

* Goodrich Castle is a ruined Norman castle dating from the middle of the 12th century, described as one of the most complete medieval strongholds in the United Kingdom, and with striking views of the surrounding countryside.

'the oldest inhabitant' I cannot tell – he strongly advised us to pay a visit to the castle, as from its summit could be seen the finest view in England.* Though not fully trusting his information – especially as his sister had the 'privilege of showing visitors over the castle' – we thought we might as well inspect the ruin, and were soon within its walls. The castle is situated on the top of a hill close to the Wye, surrounded by a moat and some fine trees. Over the entrance are large holes, whence the defenders in times of war were accustomed to drop molten lead and sand on the heads of their assailants, which really must have made it rather hot for them.

The walls in many places are overgrown with ivy and of considerable strength – that of the keep being nine feet thick – whilst from the summit a very good view is certainly obtained, but nothing extraordinary. The woman in charge seemed rather surprised we did not display more enthusiasm concerning it, but probably she had lived there all her life and therefore thought it the prettiest spot in existence. After spending some time here, we descended to the river and walked along its banks, passing Goodrich Court, a castellated mansion, on our left. For some

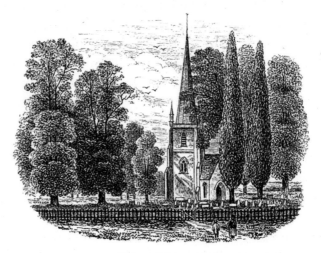

Ross Church.

BRADSHAW ON ROSS

Ross has a population of 3,715; it is situated on a rocky elevation on the east bank of the Wye. In the church are several monuments of the Rudhall family, one of whom opposed Cromwell in his siege of Hereford. There is also one of Mr J. Kyrle, the celebrated 'Man of Ross', who was interred there. Ross has great attractions during the summer months.

TELEGRAPH STATION AT HEREFORD, 12¼ MILES. HOTELS: THE ROYAL HOTEL, THE KING'S HEAD HOTEL.

time the sky had been rather gloomy, and it now began to rain; not very much but just enough to make it unpleasant, so we hastened our steps and soon came in sight of Ross, which is situated on elevated ground, the church spire rising very conspicuously from its midst.

6.30 p.m. Entered Ross, which was *en fête* on account of the previously mentioned regatta. Our first care was to visit the railway station – which is quite a credit to the town – procure our luggage and then inspect the timetable for tomorrow's journey. Two splendid sheep with thick yellowish curly wool were here waiting to be taken away, and attracted the attention of everyone, so much so that I felt sure they would have won the first prize in their class at any agricultural show. Unfortunately it now began to rain very fast, so we were glad to find a refuge near at hand called The New Inn, where the festivities had evidently brought extra business, a large room on the first floor having been converted into a dining room for visitors who had apparently been rather numerous. Here a young lady was trying to sing to a pianoforte accompaniment; at first it was endurable but afterwards she attempted something much beyond her capacity and was evidently 'feeling for the notes'. I suppose my face indicated the agony I endured, as the question was asked: 'Do you object to the music, Sir?' As I could not well say, 'Yes, very much indeed!' I replied that it was rather difficult to write at the same

View from Prospect Walk, Ross.

time, which I was trying to do. Upon this being conveyed to the performers, the pianist played a few more bars, ended up with a loud bang and then sailed out of the room in a manner peculiar to certain ladies when they are offended. On the piano was a large variety of music, comprising among other items 'Hymns Ancient and Modern', Sankey's 'Sacred Songs and Solos', 'Five Fingers Exercises' and 'The Three Little Pigs', so that if possible every one might be pleased.

By the time we had made a good tea, the rain had ceased, so we sallied forth to see what was to be seen. The streets of Ross are steep and irregular, and there is a town hall in the last stage of consumption, but the place is chiefly noted for having been the residence of John Kyrle, the 'Man of Ross', who, being wealthy, spent his money for the benefit of his fellow townsmen.* The house where he formerly lived is ornamented by a suitable inscription, and his portrait is displayed in many of the shop windows. The church is situated on an elevated spot and surrounded by some very fine trees. The edifice at the time of our visit was undergoing repairs, so we were not able to inspect the interior. Adjoining the churchyard is a pretty cemetery and a fine lawn-like piece of ground, the gift of the famous 'Man of

Ross', called Prospect Walk from the fact that it entirely over-looks the surrounding scenery.

Just beneath, on the other side of the Wye, were the head-quarters of the regatta, which was now being brought to a termination by the pastime known as 'the tug of war' to the accompaniment of a brass band, the trombone player being conspicuous for his energy. A large number of the people were present and – as the bridge is much lower down – all had to be punted across the river. This was done by taking as many as 25 in one load and, though several boats were employed, I should think the owners thereof made a pretty good harvest. By this time it was getting dusk, so we returned to The New Inn and fin-ished writing our letters, after which we retired to rest.

TUESDAY 7 AUGUST

As the country between Ross and Hereford is very flat and not worth exploring on foot, we had determined to depart by the first morning train to the latter place, and then walk to Hay if found advisable. To do this, it was necessary to have breakfast in good time and whilst waiting for that most important meal our attention was drawn to a print which hung on the parlour wall. The engraving itself was not at all remarkable, being only the portrait of one Thomas Holt of Petworth, but beneath was recorded the fact that he was president of a temperance society and had never tasted spirits or fermented liquors during his life. Notwithstanding this – to some people – apparent disadvantage, he was in the habit of walking to London, a distance of 50 miles, in 13 hours, resting there one day and returning on the next in the same manner. The last time he performed this feat he was 85 years of age, and then felt quite equal to making the journey again. The singular thing was that such a testimony to the value of temperance should be exhibited at a place where, if it were only largely imitated, the proprietor would soon be compelled to

* The Star Brewery, in Maylord Street, was founded in 1540 and was brewing until 1900.

retire from business. We did not mention this fact to him, or he might have taken down the picture and consigned it to oblivion.

Whilst at breakfast, rain began to descend heavily, and our day's prospects looked very gloomy. As, under such circumstances, it was quite evident we should be at least as well off in Hereford as in Ross, we repaired to the railway station and there waited for the train. Whilst gazing on the advertisements with which the walls were ornamented, my attention was arrested by the words 'Nicholas Heins, pianoforte warehouse, Hereford', and it at once struck me that this must be the identical gentleman who was formerly organist to the now defunct Tonic Sol-fa Choral Society of which I was a staunch member, so we determined to renew his acquaintance.

Arrived at Hereford by 9.15 a.m. and at once repaired to the Star Brewery, not for libations but for a certain Mr Tredaway (I wonder if he had ever performed on the 'endless wheel') who was recommended by a London friend as likely to give us suitable information regarding the country etc.* He seemed exceedingly foggy on the subject, which perhaps could only be expected from one who lived in an atmosphere of beer. The city of Hereford contains about 20,000 inhabitants, several very old churches and the cathedral, of which more presently. The streets are wide and clean, and the whole place looks very good

---

BRADSHAW ON HEREFORD

Hereford, as its old Saxon name explains it to be, stands at a military ford on the Wye, which King Harold protected by a castle, the site of which at Castle Green is now occupied by the Nelson Column. Parts of the town are low and old fashioned, and some remains of the old town walls are still visible. The internal trade is chiefly in agricultural produce, good cider and perry, wool, hops and prime cattle.

A TELEGRAPH STATION. HOTELS: THE CITY ARMS HOTEL, THE GREEN DRAGON.

---

and decorous, as is only proper in a cathedral city. Having made these few observations, Jupiter Pluvius – who had been quiet for some time – began to send down copious showers, and we were so glad to find ourselves in front of a music shop bearing the name N. HEINS that we opened the door and at once walked in.*

Standing near was Mrs Heins, who gazed in astonished surprise as I greeted her in my most affable manner, George at the same time looking as virtuous as possible. She had never been very intimate with me, nor had we seen each other for seven years, but the magic name of Freeman soon set matters straight and she immediately invited us to make ourselves at home, saying that her husband was unfortunately away on business, but if we would stay to dinner, he certainly would return by that time. Whilst waiting, two sisters of mercy came in and wished to buy a £25 harmonium for about a fifth of its value, but – as might be expected – did not succeed. We also had the pleasure of seeing 25 old fogies belonging to the Archaeological Society walk in procession to hear a lecture by Sir Gilbert Scott.† They were all dressed in black and preceded by a functionary clothed in a scarlet gown and carrying a silver staff; as it was raining very hard umbrellas were the order of the day, and very miserable they all looked, but perhaps that was only in accordance with their learned pretentions.

Thinking we might as well make the best use of our time – I was about to say 'make hay while the sun shone', but that would be obviously inappropriate – we sallied forth to inspect the cathedral, which fortunately was close at hand. This fine old ecclesiastical pile dates from 1074; a portion of it fell down in 1786, and was afterwards restored by one Wyatt who – to quote the words underneath a picture hanging on the walls – 'tinkered it to the extent of £20,000 and succeeded in completely spoiling it'. The roof is richly ornamented, and the principal objects of interest we noted were a representation in inlaid marble of 'Ouda King of Mercia beheading Ethelbert in 793', a splendid white, black and coloured marble tomb, the reredos, some finely

* Nicholas Heins (1839–1910) moved from London to Hereford in 1871, and opened the London Pianoforte and Music Warehouse, selling instruments and both publishing and selling sheet music. He was a successful composer of church music and a former tenor soloist for Queen Victoria at Her Majesty's Chapel Royal.

† Sir Gilbert Scott (full name Sir Giles Gilbert Scott) was the leading Gothic Revival architect of the Victorian age. His works include St Pancras Railway Station and Hotel, London (1865), and the University of Glasgow (1870).

* The Shire Hall was built in 1818 to replace the old town hall, and included court rooms.

† Since 1719, the cities of Hereford, Gloucester and Worcester have taken turns to host an annual music festival, which became known as the Triennial Festivals, since each town hosted one every three years. It is the oldest surviving non-competitive music festival in the world. Lady Clive would appear to be Lady Kathleen Elizabeth Mary Julia Clive (née Feilding), daughter of the 7th Earl of Denbigh, wife of Charles Meysey Bolton Clive, and mother of Sir Robert Henry Clive.

carved oaken stalls, and a monumental brass in memory of the officers of the 36th Regiment who fell during the French wars overshadowed by the remnants of the flags under which they had so bravely fought. The following quaint inscription is copied from the walls:

Goode Christeyn people of youre Charity,
That here abide in thys Transitorye lyfe,
For the Soules of Richard Dinas pray ye,
And also for Annie hys dere beloved wyfe.

Having watched the choristers rehearse in processional order their portion of the afternoon service, we had 'done' the cathedral and were thinking over the generosity of the authorities in not making any charge for admittance, when a clean shaven dignitary politely requested us to sign our names in a book and with a graceful wave of his hand pointed to a receptacle over which was written: 'Visitors if so disposed are requested to deposit a sum of not less than sixpence in this box.' This brought our meditations to a close, and at the same time lightened our purses.

Wending our way to the Shire Hall amidst a deluge of rain, we asked for a certain Mr Winter, and, having introduced ourselves as friends of Mr Heins, he volunteered to show us over the building.* In the large hall – which is used for secular concerts at the Triennial Festivals – one of the neighbouring ladies (Lady Clive) had offered to paint at one end a series of water views, and at the other figures of Religion, Mercy, Justice, Music and Agriculture, all at her own expense, and she was engaged on them at the time of our visit.† Some of the inhabitants did not look upon her gift with much favour, thinking it was more likely to originate from pride than generosity, as she was exceedingly near, not to say mean, in all her business transactions, and also regarding the subjects chosen as rather incongruous, though I must say they did not seem so to me.

After visiting the courts of justice and other minor rooms, we thanked Mr Winter for his courtesy and then made for the Castle Green, which marks the spot where the castle once stood, overlooks the Wye, and is said to be well worth seeing. We certainly did see it, but that was all, for the rain was descending in such a persistent and drenching way that we hastily beat a retreat to the house of our hospitable hostess. Here we changed our boots, and made ourselves generally comfortable. Soon after, dinner appeared, to which we did justice in company with Mrs Heins, her sister, and her two daughters, and just as we had finished Mr Heins came in, recognising me immediately, and was very glad to see us.

During the previous week Mr Townsend Smith, the cathedral organist, had died, and as Mr Heins intended as a last mark of respect to follow the corpse to the grave, we went at once with him and his wife to the cathedral, where a full choral service was to take place at 2 o'clock. After some time, the coffin, a splendid oaken one covered with flowers, appeared at the door borne by six men who had as much as they could do to carry it, and was met by the choristers who, forming in procession, walked slowly to the top of the cathedral chanting at the same time portions of the funeral service; the remainder was then read by the Bishop of Hereford, but owing to the loftiness of the roof and great echo the words were very indistinct. Spohr's 'Blessed for ever' was then most exquisitely sung, and the organist played 'The Dead March' as the coffin was being carried out.* There were a large number of people present, but many seemed to regard it more as a spectacle than a solemn service.

Quitting the cathedral, we visited the Free Library, where the people of Hereford can go and read any of the books, daily papers or monthly serials quite gratuitously, which must be a great boon. Then, after looking in at a collection of pictures on sale in the Corn Exchange, we procured our bag etc. and departed with Mrs Heins for the railway station to catch the 3.40 p.m. train. However, on the road our hostess persuaded us to return and spend the remainder of the day with them, to

* 'Blessed for ever' is taken from the oratorio *The Last Judgement* (1826) by the German composer Louis Spohr (1784–1831); 'The Dead March' is taken from the oratorio *Saul* (1738) by the German-born composer George Frederick Handel (1685–1759).

* There are no records of a board game called bogium. John may be pulling our leg here, with a mythical pastime with a name reminiscent of 'bogus'.

† Hereford town council, following the Hereford Improvement Act of 1854, built its waterworks on Broomy Hill in 1856. They are now the site of the Hereford Waterworks Museum.

which we easily agreed as it was still raining and it was hardly likely we should be able to employ the time profitably on our arrival in Hay. Returning, Mr Heins soon after came in, and we entered into conversation on old times and musical subjects.

On the eve of our departure from London, my brother Charles had said: 'Suppose I make you a bogium board; the weather may be wet, and then you will find it very useful.'* Carrying out this idea, he had manufactured a portable affair with card which we could easily put in our knapsack. This now proved very useful for, tea having appeared and disappeared in the most approved manner, our conversational powers began to show signs of exhaustion, when – at my companion's suggestion – the bogium board was brought forth, and we were soon deep in its mysteries and excitement. Our friends were so pleased with it they resolved to make one for themselves, and if any reader wishes to acquire a knowledge of the game, either of my brothers will I am sure do his best to instruct, and then beat him or her on any given occasion, time and place being quite a secondary consideration.

7 p.m. As the rain had at last ceased, Mrs and Miss Heins offered to take us for a short walk, to which we gladly acceded and off we at once went to the waterworks; this is really a reservoir of water pumped from the Wye which, after being filtered, supplies Hereford with its daily consumption of *aqua pura*.† The grounds are planted with trees so as to form a public promenade and, being in an elevated position, command a good view of the surrounding country. By this time blue sky had appeared and the sun was shining brightly, so we quite enjoyed our walk, but as the hour for our departure was rapidly drawing near, we

---

BRADSHAW ON HAY

 Hay is an old Norman town; part of the castle remains, which was destroyed by Owen Glyndwr. It is exactly on the borders of three counties. Here the Upper Wye scenery ends.

---

hastened back and most heartily thanked the Heins family for their very cordial welcome.

Heins frère saw us safely to the railway station, and at 8.05 p.m. we departed for Hay and arrived there by 9 o'clock. It had been described to us as a 'dead and alive place' but it seemed rather more of the former than the latter. We soon procured accommodation and then went to the post office to see if there were any letters waiting for us, which we found not to be the case. On our return we lost our way, as there was no gas in the streets and we had forgotten to notice the name of our inn. This was rather confusing, but we eventually found it and were before long trying to go to sleep in a room so small that – speaking figuratively – there was hardly room to swing a cat round in it (a large one of course). As we did not have a cat to swing, that did not very much matter.

WEDNESDAY 8 AUGUST

During the night we were awakened by a most persistent barking, and there seemed to be a republic of dogs near at hand; the juniors yelped and the seniors growled, to a cranking of chains accompaniment which was anything but delightful at that hour of the night. After an animated concert, a woman could be heard pacifying the animals, and then all was again quiet; they broke out a second time before morning, and we almost began to wonder whether it had been 'raining cats and dogs', as people at times assert. With these exceptions, we slept very well, but did not venture out before breakfast, and whilst partaking of that meal we were favoured by a series of showers till near 10 o'clock, during which time we took refuge in bogium. As it then appeared little brighter, we walked to the railway station, sent our bag on to Aberystwyth, and then started for Builth, with many fears and misgivings as to the wisdom of such a proceeding, as the weather looked very doubtful.

Imaginary portrait of a Hay dog.

The appearance of Hay by daylight did not impress us very favourably. It consists mainly of one long straggling street of mean-looking houses, without a single building worthy of mention; to live in such a place during the winter would seem like being buried alive, but I suppose one could get accustomed to anything, as the old lady said of the eels which she was skinning. For the first hour we were favoured with alternate showers and sunshine, but at the end of that time the latter prevailed, blue sky and flies appeared, so there seemed every probability of a change in the weather, and our spirits rose in proportion. The country around was very flat, not calling for any particular notice, but on reaching Glasbury rain began to fall once more and we were compelled to take shelter. As there did not seem any prospect of much improvement, we decided to go a part of our journey by rail, so crossed the Wye and between the showers managed to reach Boughrood just as it began to rain very heavily. Here we took tickets to Aberedw, whence – being only four miles to Builth – we wished to walk, all the more so as the scenery thereabouts is very pretty.

On arriving at Aberedw it was still raining fast, but as it was only 2.30 p.m. we alighted thinking it would certainly clear off sufficiently to enable us to walk the remaining distance; meanwhile we took refuge in the station. Station did I say? Will the reader please imagine a wooden hut about 12 feet long, and half as wide, divided by a partition into booking room and waiting room, and he will have a very good idea of Aberedw Railway

Station. If then it be further taken into consideration that the falling rain was of the thickest and most penetrating kind and that there was no train till 6.20 p.m., some idea may I think be had of our situation. The prospect of passing four hours in this solitary spot was by no means inviting, and the village being some distance away we were precluded by the state of the weather from visiting it, even had we wished to do so. This being the position of affairs, there we sat endeavouring to look as happy as possible, and holding a council of war regarding the steps to be taken supposing the present dampness of the atmosphere should continue.

Every now and then, one of us would go to the door and peer out to see if there were any signs of a cessation, but "twas all in vain'; the hills around were half hidden by the rain which swept up the valley literally in clouds, so our expectations of a change grew fainter and fainter. Under these circumstances, I think it was to our credit that we remained tolerably cheerful, though in saying this I hope I shall not be accused of 'blowing my own trumpet', if I were in the habit of practising on such an instrument. I think the inhabitants of 134 Regent Street would rise in open rebellion, for what with the violins, 'cello and pianoforte, it would doubtless be 'the last feather which breaks the camel's back'. This of course is speaking figuratively, as I do not wish to compare any member of our family to that very useful but somewhat ungainly-looking quadruped.

As there seemed no chance of resuming our journey on foot, the bogium board was brought into requisition, and several games played thereon. At last we tired even of this, so visited the stationmaster, inspector, clerk, ticket collector and porter, all of which offices were combined in one person, and invited him to play with us. This he declined, pleading ignorance.

Hanging on the walls was a portrait of Caradog, the leader of the South Wales Choir which sang at the Crystal Palace Competitions in 1873.* Underneath was the sentence: 'He led them on to victory.' Welshmen appear to be under the delusion that

* More than 12,000 people crowded into the Crystal Palace in July 1873 for the National Music Meeting to hear Caradoc and his Welsh choir compete for the Challenge Prize (1,000 guineas) against the London Tonic Sol-fa Choir, led by Joseph Proudman (and including one John George Freeman). The Welsh, with 500 voices against the home team's 300, were victorious, as they had been in 1872.

they were then singing against a choir selected from all musical London, while the truth is it was composed solely of Tonic Sol-fa-ists, by no means the pick of them, and not much more than half as numerous as their own.

The stationmaster had lately been sent from Brecon and said he found it very dull: only three passenger trains passed in each direction during the day, and his chief occupation seemed to be reading a newspaper, smoking a pipe and talking to his dog. Towards 5 o'clock, he said if the luggage train – then due – did not arrive soon he could not wait any longer but should go to his tea. After a short period it appeared, and he then locked up the booking office and departed, leaving it to take care of itself.

Having pretty well exhausted our patience, conversational powers and means of amusement, and having inspected and remarked upon every object within the four walls of Aberedw railway station, our unwilling imprisonment at last came to a termination at 6.30 p.m. The long hoped for train at last arrived and we, joyfully seating ourselves therein, were conveyed through some exceedingly pretty wooded scenery – which we only regretted not having seen under more favourable circumstances – reaching Builth in a quarter of an hour. Here rain was descending so heavily that we were afraid to quit the railway station, as it was necessary to cross a bridge in order to enter the town and we should certainly have been drenched had we attempted to do so.

After some time, a slight cessation occurred, and we then sallied forth, but had not proceeded as far as the aforesaid bridge when down came the rain once more with renewed violence and we were compelled to take refuge in the nearest house, which

---

BRADSHAW ON BUILTH

 Builth, in a fine part of the river, has remains of a castle, and a long bridge. Trout and salmon fishing; fine scenery.

---

fortunately proved to be The Llanelwedd Arms. Here we found good accommodation, and were glad to change our boots for warm slippers; tea also was not long in making its appearance, and we soon began to feel quite ourselves again. After this we wrote home. Our windows commanded a good view of the Wye which, augmented by the continual rains, had become much swollen, and rushed along foaming and frothing in quite a remarkable manner. Some idea may be formed of the dampness of the atmosphere from the fact that we saw a man wring the tail of his coat just as a laundress would a blanket and with the same result, at which he did not seem at all surprised.

Retired to bed in the blissful anticipation that the clearing showers had at last arrived, and trusting it would be fine on the morrow, as it hardly seemed likely we should have three wet days in succession.

THURSDAY 9 AUGUST

After a good night's rest in a very comfortable bedroom, we opened our eyes, immediately looked out of the window to see if the weather had improved and ascertained it had ceased raining but was still gloomy, so our prospect did not seem very encouraging. We rose and walked across the bridge – through the arches of which the Wye was rushing and whirling with great velocity – to Builth. This seems a cheerful prosperous little place, having some very fair shops with several modern houses, a chapel and a public hall in the course of construction. These we inspected and then, walking through the churchyard, returned to The Llanelwedd Arms, fortified ourselves with a good breakfast and without further delay at once set out on our journey. In the first place we visited the post office, which has a glass portico in front where persons can write telegrams or take shelter from a passing shower, of which latter privilege we availed ourselves, rain having commenced once more to fall. Here we also posted our letters, and had expected to find one awaiting our arrival but such was not the case. Then, visiting the railway station, we noted the stations and times of the trains on our route, in expectation that stress of weather might possibly compel us to take advantage thereof. It being by this time 10 o'clock and rain having ceased, we at last bade adieu to Builth and started off in earnest.

Our road lay along a gentle ascent by the side of the Wye, which was rushing down with great velocity, the view being very fine. The rain was determined to bear us company and before long it descended in torrents; luckily we obtained shelter under some trees, and as there was little or no wind did not get wet. On its cessation we once more advanced, but after a short interval the clouds again discharged their contents, and this time no better refuge was at hand than a hedge. As this sort of thing seemed very likely to continue, we began seriously to debate whether it would not be wiser to go by train direct to Aberystwyth in the hope that it might be finer by the seaside than amongst the hills. As the clouds appeared to be rising and breaking a little, we determined to press on if possible, nor did we have cause to regret our resolution, for the weather continued to improve till we reached the River Ithon (12.30 p.m.), when as the sun was shining forth in all his splendour, we rested, drank his health and engaged in conversation with a native who gave us the joyful intelligence that the barometer was rising. Yesterday, the bed of the Ithon was plainly visible, but now owing to the incessant rains it was a turbid torrent three feet deep by eighty wide rushing past with great swiftness. When watching it from the bridge, it seemed exactly as if we were moving and the water standing perfectly still.

On reaching Newbridge the special constable of that favoured locality accosted us and wished to know if we had met a gentleman on the road. Perhaps he wished to arrest him for some crime, probably he did not, anyhow though we had seen several persons of the male persuasion none of them answered to that designation, so therefore we could not help him. The scenery hereabouts is well worthy of mention: high hills rising on each side of the Wye, covered with fine trees, tall, verdant and of great variety. Arriving at Doldowlod by 2 o'clock, we rested by the side of a sparkling torrent and lunched, the sun shining brilliantly, rendering our al fresco repast doubly enjoyable. Continuing our journey through a splendid road much resembling the 'Hobby' at Clovelly, save that there was the rapidly running stream with a hill on the opposite side instead of the sea, we came to a wooden foot-bridge whence there was a very fine view of the river in both directions, and soon after reached the junction of the Elan with the Wye. Proceeding onwards, the hills assumed a more rocky appearance, like the Pass of Llanberis but on a much smaller scale, and we eventually arrived at Rhayader after a thoroughly enjoyable walk – showers excepted – of 14 miles, the scenery being very varied and – according to the guide book, which opinion I heartily endorse – 'such as to fully establish the reputation of the Wye for beauty'.

It was now only 4.15 p.m. so, having visited the post office and procured three letters which were awaiting our arrival, we made enquiries respecting The Red Lion, intending to take up our abode there for the night, but that animal was so voracious that we left him to his own devices and took refuge with one of his relations, viz: The Lion and Castle, where a good tea was soon provided, and the merits thereof – demerits there were none – discussed to our entire satisfaction. We then took our walks abroad to view Rhayader, or Rhayadrgwy as the Welsh prefer to call it, but the reader will please be careful in pronouncing the latter name.* This signifies 'the cataract of the Wye', though a great portion of the rock which formerly obstructed the course of the water was removed when the present bridge was built. There is still a small cascade which has a very pleasing aspect. Some of the houses are erected on the solid rock, the doorsteps being cut out of the stone, and the *tout ensemble* as seen from the river is altogether rather picturesque.

* The present Welsh spelling is Rhaeadr Gwy.

Repairing to the railway station, we watched a luggage train to which was attached some of the most disreputable-looking carriages I have ever had the pleasure – or pain – of seeing. The passengers thereof seemed rather in a hurry, but that did not affect either the engine driver or stoker, who both dismounted and calmly perused some advertisements which happened to be near at hand. We joked with the porter regarding these facts, remarking at the same time that the railway clock had disappeared; the latter he retorted had gone to the pawnbroker's, while as to the former the carriages were old ones and put on for the convenience of visitors during the holiday season. Of the village of Rhayader little can be said. Of antiquated type, it might not form a bad field for the sale of those extremely ancient flowery waistcoat patterns, of which a certain relation of mine has an unsaleable stock.

Ever since our arrival in Rhayader a slight drizzle had been falling, and as the surrounding hills had now a very misty appearance, and seemed to indicate the approach of more rain, we retired to the Castle, and spent the remainder of the evening writing and jotting down notes for our diaries. Our sitting room was a very comfortable one, containing a number of pictures and, best of all, a barometer, which we were excessively glad to see had a decidedly upward tendency.

Eventually we retired to rest in a bedroom large enough to have slept eight people – this of course does not refer to the bed – some idea of its size may be formed when I mention it contained 11 chairs, two tables, two double wash stands, two chests of drawers, besides minor articles; and there was plenty of spare room. On the wall was a framed certificate relating that Miss Mary Jane Jones had successfully passed the examination for the elementary requirements in the Tonic Sol-fa Notation, as testified by the signature of Mr Evan Evans, so we did not appear to be in such an uncivilised place after all, and began to feel quite at home. Consequently, we were soon fast asleep.

FRIDAY 10 AUGUST

Rose just before 7 o'clock, strolled down to the river, visited the churchyard and then made enquiries regarding the best route to the Devil's Bridge. The old road is shorter and more direct than the new one, but is not so well made, and is open to the great objection that there are no villages on the way where the tourist can halt if the weather should prove rainy, and he is also compelled to sleep at the Devil's Bridge Hotel, which is rather an expensive proceeding. This being the case, we decided to travel via Llangurig as far as Pont Erwyd – distant 24 miles – and prepared ourselves for a good walk. 8 a.m. Sat down to breakfast, to which we did ample justice, then having settled our little account with the proprietor of The Lion and Castle, we shouldered the knapsack, and started off by 9 o'clock. Our road still lay close to the River Wye, which by this time was only a narrow stream, with hills rising on each side clothed with abundance of rich vegetation. On reaching the third milestone, the railway – near which we had travelled ever since leaving Chepstow – branched off to the right so that now we had only the 'marrowbone stage' to depend upon to reach Aberystwyth. The inhabitants seemed few and far between, but we met a very diminutive boy gathering wild raspberries, which he impaled upon a straw. This did not look as if he expected a very successful harvest, but we afterwards saw that his sister was near at hand with a basket to carry the proceeds of the straw when heavily laden.

The scenery now grew wilder, the hills being bare and rocky with numerous cascades and torrents, all hurrying to join the Wye as if they had not a second to lose. At the sixth milestone (11 a.m.) we rested, but not for long, as the morning was rather cloudy and we thought it better to push on. Unfortunately, I had two blisters on one of my feet, so did not feel quite so comfortable as I could have wished, nevertheless an hour later we arrived at Llangurig, a picturesque village of about 20 houses, the inhabitants of which manage to support a church, two chapels and three

public houses, but where the congregation for the one and the customers for the other come from I am quite at a loss to know, as the surrounding population is exceedingly scanty.

The whole of the Llangurig constabulary force – one man, whom we carefully counted – came out to welcome us, and seemed so delighted at meeting someone with whom he could converse that he walked with us for more than half a mile. Our informant said he had – professionally speaking – little or nothing to do, and left us with the consoling remark that it was a good thing we had come here on a fine day, as the road for the next ten miles was very indifferent, and had the weather been bad we should not have wished to repeat the experiment.

Sometime after this we met an old man, and being rather undecided as to our route, asked his advice and were directed to take a road to the left and cross a wooden bridge which was little better than two poles. Following these directions, we came to a road composed of loose stones and rough to the last degree, but then 'Robert' had said it was bad, so we pressed on hoping for better prospects. However, as things seemed to go from bad to worse, we at last halted and waited for some natives who were coming across the fields; from them we ascertained that we ought not to have quitted the high road, so with many thanks we returned – having wasted more than half an hour – and once again resumed our journey wondering whether we could possibly have reached Pont Erwyd today if the whole of the road had been as bad as that we had just quitted.

Crossing the River Bidno, we ascended a hill to a good height, and then rested and lunched. Before today we had not really been in Wales, for though Radnorshire formerly belonged to the principality it is now reckoned as an English county. Llangurig seemed to form a line of demarcation, and whilst hitherto we had not heard a word of Welsh, we now came across persons who were but very imperfectly acquainted with our native language.

2 p.m. Resumed our travels, which now lay through the mountainous district near Plinlimmon. Up to this time we had

been favoured with fine weather, our old friend Sol trying every now and then to acquaint us with the fact that he was still alive, but here the hills began to look very cloudy, and the farther we advanced the more gloomy seemed our prospects; there was no alternative but to advance with the not very cheering knowledge that there was no habitation for at least six miles. 2.35 p.m. Pont-rhyd-galed – 16 miles from Rhayader – is a little bridge crossing the River Wye, near the banks of which we had travelled from Chepstow almost to its source, a distance of 107 miles. Its many beauties and picturesque views had been duly admired and chronicled, and we now bade it adieu, as to an old friend with whom we were at last obliged, but still very sorry, to part.

Just here a slight drizzle commenced to descend, which soon turned to a heavy driving mountain rain. Most fortunately – or, rather, providentially – a deserted stone cottage stood just by the roadside and in this we at once took refuge. Part of the roof was gone, and the ground in places was very muddy, but not-withstanding these trifling drawbacks we managed to find good shelter from the inclemency of the weather. Most anxiously we gazed on every side, hoping it might only be a passing shower, but all the surrounding hills were covered with misty clouds which discharged their contents in torrents.

Things now began to look serious, and the question arose: 'If the rain continues what shall we do?' To remain in our present shelter all night would be very unpleasant, not to say danger-ous, on account of the heavy mountain dews, whilst to proceed through the rain would entail the certainty of being drenched to the skin. Happily, we were not compelled to solve this diffi-cult problem for, after an hour, the storm ceased and we once more resumed our walk, the road being wet, but not so bad as might have been expected. Though at times inclined to grumble when a misadventure occurs, we were now very thankful that we had been misdirected near Llangurig, for had this not been the case we should have been at least a mile past the deserted cottage when the rain commenced and consequently must have

* Driffell Castell is now known as Dyffryn Castell.

been completely soaked as no possible kind of shelter was visible between that spot and Steddfa Gurig, where we arrived at 4.30 p.m. Here is a small collection of mean-looking houses, among which is an inn used as a halting place for tourists who make the ascent of Plinlimmon, but this we had no intention of doing, as reports say it is seldom worth the trouble, for the very good reason that there is no very prominent peak, like Snowdon, from which a splendid view is obtainable; and on this particular occasion the whole range of hills was covered with clouds. Disreputable-looking fellows – guides I presume – were lounging about the place, and altogether we felt glad we were not obliged to pass the night at Steddfa Gurig.

Meeting a man accompanied by his wife and daughter, we accosted them but found they were not well acquainted with the English language, for the first referred us to his better half and when the conversation grew too deep for her wisdom she took counsel with her daughter, who could comprehend us very fairly. We were seeking information as to the method of gathering the flocks of sheep together by means of dogs, which operation was being most intelligently carried out at the time on the adjoining hillside, under the direction of a native who shouted out his orders to his four footed assistants, and was immediately obeyed. It sounded to us precisely as if he were using bad language, but we charitably concluded he was only speaking Welsh.

Since leaving the Wye, the scenery had been very wild; nothing but bare rugged hills were to be seen in all directions, and when presently the sun gleamed forth, the beautiful effects produced by the ever varying shadow and sunshine were well worth seeing. Passing Driffell Castell which possesses an inn rather better than that of Steddfa Gurig, we came to a deserted tin mine – the works of which were still in motion to keep it clear of water – and then began to look out rather anxiously for Pont Erwyd.* I suppose it is as well to make a full confession, and I must say I was very tired; 24 miles over a hard, stony, though well made road is ordinarily a good day's walk, but as before stated one of my feet was not in good condition, which did not tend to improve either my speed or comfort. My companion was all right, and seemed, comparatively speaking, quite fresh.

The last two miles of a day's journey always appear to be very lengthy, and so it was on this occasion, but we eventually arrived at Pont Erwyd by 6.30 p.m. though of course the hotel was at the farther end, and on the top of a hill. It rejoiced in the rather astounding name of The Goggerddan Arms, which sounds like the cognomen of a giant in some fairy tale. The proprietor thereof, instead of making a meal of us, provided a tea excellent in every respect, which was fully appreciated and felt to have been fairly earned.

After a good rest we strolled outside, and found we were located in an exceedingly romantic spot. Immediately beneath the entrance to the hotel is a chasm about 80 feet deep, at each end of which is a fine waterfall which rushes over black-looking rocks, seething and foaming in the depths below before continuing its rapid course to the sea. The charge to descend and view all this is three pence, tickets to be obtained at the hotel. In the distance lies Pont Erwyd village, and all around lofty hills, almost high enough to be called mountains, rise, bare, rugged, and majestic. As if to add still more to the beauty of the scene on this particular evening, the whole of one side was bright and glowing with the last rays of the fast setting sun, while in the opposite direction the shades of night were rapidly advancing and everything was wrapped in gloom, the whole landscape being a fitting tableau to our day's pleasure.

Even in this out-of-the-way spot the advertiser follows his certainly not ornamental, but I suppose useful, calling, and one gentleman, under the title of 'The living skeleton', by this means indignantly denied the report that he was dead (doubtless he must have known) and 'only pitied those who were obliged to exhibit consumptive subjects in order to compete with the one, true, and only genuine living skeleton'.* Then followed a list of testimonials from members of the medical profession as to the

* The 'living skeleton' was a popular sideshow attraction in Victorian fairs and exhibitions.

truth of his assertions, all of which were without doubt exceedingly valuable.

Returning to The Goggerddan Arms we soon retired to our bedroom which, with its snowy white furniture, was a model of perfection, and were before long fast asleep.

SATURDAY I I AUGUST

Rose at 7 o'clock, before which we had heard the proprietor of the hotel arousing his servants in a rather lusty manner, so evidently laziness had found its way even to this remote corner of the world. Descending, we perceived it had been raining during the night; indeed, the above named individual said they had not had a thoroughly fine day here for five weeks, all the more reason, thought we, that there should soon be a change. A few words as to our hostelry. I have endeavoured to describe its surroundings, and now wish to speak in praise of its internal arrangements. The rooms are well furnished and exceedingly clean, though why there should be one set aside especially for commercial travellers I cannot understand. Surely it must be a joke; persons never can come here on business. Everything provided is of the best quality and well served, and lastly, but by no means least, the charges are not exorbitant, especially when its solitary position is taken into consideration, the nearest town being Aberystwyth with which there is no railway communication. Altogether we were well satisfied with our visit, and can confidently recommend The Goggerddan Arms to anyone who happens to be taking a walk in that direction.

9.30 a.m. Having put to a severe test the breakfast providing capabilities of the hotel, we started away from Pont Erwyd with every prospect of a fine day. Rugged hills, numerous streams and cataracts formed our constant companions until Ysbyty Church was reached, when we turned to the right, walked across some fields and then descended a steep and rocky gorge, at the bottom of which is the Parson's Bridge. This is merely two small planks and a handrail which derives its name from the supposed fact that the parson used to cross this way when going to church. The view all around is very fine; beneath, closely hemmed in by the rocky hills, rushes the impetuous Rheidol, foaming and boiling up as if in anger at the numerous gigantic boulders which impede its progress. Up the valley, all is bare and stony, which the brightly shining sun makes still more white and glaring, causing the onlooker to turn with relief in the opposite direction where the beautiful green of ten thousands of trees covers the hillside. At this scene we stood and gazed in admiration until warned that time was advancing, when we retraced our steps once more to the high road.

After a further walk of two miles, we arrived at The Devil's Bridge. The charming scenery, I should think, equals any in the kingdom for beauty, and however imperfect my description may

The Devil's Bridge, near Aberystwith.

be, the reader will I hope be a little wiser after perusing the following lines. Far in the distance below runs the River Rheidol,
two waterfalls being clearly visible, while all round rise hundreds of thousands of trees, but the great charm of the scene
seemed to be the fact that the valley is so open that it can nearly
all be seen from one position. The bridge, which gives its name
to the whole estate, crosses a dangerous-looking chasm, and is
so called from the belief of former superstitious inhabitants that
no one but His Satanic Majesty could have built it in so difficult
a place. It is about 800 years old, but when the present road was
made (1753) another and larger arch was erected some distance
above the original one, which may be easily seen by leaning over
the balustrades.

Wishing to view the waterfalls, we first bought tickets – one
shilling each – at the hotel, where we left our knapsack, and a
guide then accompanied us across the bridge and down a flight
of steps 114 feet below to what is known as The Devil's Punch
Bowl. Here, the River Mynach rushes over huge rocks with a
tremendous noise, and at the bottom has scooped out a smooth
cavity which gives rise to the extraordinary name given above.

The Devils Bridge Hotel, from the river Rheidol.

Of course we did not drink of any of the liquor, but stayed for some time admiring the grandeur of the sight. Ascending, the guide admitted us on the other side of the bridge and, after giving us due directions, took his departure to await the arrival of a few coach loads of visitors whom it was his special business and delight to accompany. Descending a precipitous flight of steps known as Jacob's Ladder (I will leave it to the reader to imagine who were the angels at the time of our visit) we came in view of the River Mynach which, after quitting the Punch Bowl rushes underneath the Devil's Bridge and precipitates itself beneath in four distinct falls. The first and third are about 24, and the second 56 feet in depth; then, after struggling among various huge rocks, the stream descends in one unbroken torrent of 110 feet, and as at the time of our visit the sun was shining brilliantly, the spray sparkled in his rays, and every leaf on the surrounding luxuriant foliage showed to the best advantage.

Having seen the falls from various standpoints, we ascended and found several brakes had arrived with visitors. According to the guide book, there is a nearer and much prettier road along the other side of the Rheidol valley via Capel Bangor to Aberystwyth and this – after consulting the guide and obtaining directions – we decided to take so, first procuring the knapsack, we kept along by the side of a fence for some distance and descended to the bed of the river. Here we ought to have found some stepping stones by which we could have crossed to the opposite side, but no such convenience was visible, and though the stream was only narrow, there was so great a torrent of water that it was quite impossible to reach the other bank. After a long and fruitless search we ascended to the Devil's Bridge, whence the wished-for path was so plainly seen that, meeting the guide once more, we obtained fresh directions and then proceeded to try again. However amongst the numerous paths we were soon in a perfect maze, and quite unsuccessful in finding any spot by which the river could be crossed – indeed I now think it very probable that the stones were covered with water – so at last we were obliged to mount up once again, confess ourselves defeated and acknowledge it was almost as bad as 'rounding the flagstaff' when at Ilfracombe.

We now bade adieu to the Devil's Bridge and turned our faces in the direction of Aberystwyth. Soon after this we had an al fresco dinner by the side of a running stream, to the great astonishment of three small boys who stared at us in amazement, and then – 3.30 p.m. – resumed our journey with the knowledge that there was still a walk of 11 miles before us. The road for some time consisted of a continual ascent, until we must have been quite 1,000 feet above the river beneath; however, there was a splendid breeze without which we should have been very hot, for the sun was pouring down his rays from an almost cloudless sky, and shelter was quite unattainable.

The view, as may be imagined, was well worth seeing. Far in the distance below lay the Rheidol valley with its silvery winding river, by the side of which rose numerous hills, the nearer ones being peaks, causing us to wonder whether the gigantic Cader Idris was among them, the whole forming a beautiful and most picturesque landscape. Before long, we came in sight of the sea, after which nothing particular happened until within three miles of our destination, when Aberystwyth suddenly burst upon our view, and we eventually arrived there by 6.20 p.m. Immediately we began to search for private apartments, and after some little trouble found very comfortable quarters in Bridge Street. This, though not the best thoroughfare in the town, has several new houses of a better class, and in one of these we were located, sharing the sitting room of a Welsh clergyman.

Repairing to the post office, we found three letters awaiting our arrival, after which we procured our bag from the railway station, and on the return journey seeing a crane fastened to the front of a building resembling a chapel, we enquired of a wandering native if it were used to draw in the congregation on Sunday, but he only grinned and did not seem willing to give any information on the subject. Returning to Bridge Street, we sat down to tea, and soon found that our appetites retained all their pristine vigour, after which – as may be imagined – we did not feel equal to much more exertion this week, so strolled on to the parade and perused our London letters. Here we sat and gazed at a beautiful seascape. Above, the stars were beginning to twinkle from a clear blue sky which gradually shaded to dark masses of clouds hanging over the horizon, whilst at our feet rippled the waves and everything seemed to preface a fine morrow.

Having listened to the town band for some time, and it being now quite dark we essayed to return, but stopping to inspect a shop window happened to see an advertisement in Welsh regarding some pills or ointment; it must have been something of that description because at the end was the ominous '1/1½ per box'. Whilst looking on in wonder, a many-consonant word met our view, which so tickled my brother's risible faculties that he commenced to laugh; this he did with such vigour and persistency that the shopkeeper came out to see what was the matter. No doubt a box of the pills would soon have put a stop to all merriment, but the offender was at last quieted without resorting to so rough a remedy.

On arriving at our apartments we introduced ourselves to the before mentioned Welsh clergyman. Our dissenters are so exceedingly numerous in Wales that we took it for granted that he belonged to that body, but found he was a churchman.* Still, we were none the less friendly and there were so many topics for conversation that we did not retire till 10.30 p.m., which is of course a very unseemly hour for holiday folk and for which due apologies are herewith offered.

* The 'churchman' was a member of the Church in Wales, as it styles itself.

SUNDAY 12 AUGUST

On descending at 8 o'clock, we found our Welsh clergyman just starting off to the scene of his day's ministrations, but as this was only about two miles distant we concluded he must hold a

The Queens Hotel, Aberystwith.

* The Welsh
University Committee
bought the incomplete
Castle Hotel in
Aberystwyth in 1867,
and welcomed its first
intake of students in
1872.

very early or very lengthy service. After giving us permission to read any book in his library, we bade each other 'Good morning' and went our separate ways. Strolling on to the parade, which we had nearly all to ourselves, we basked in the glorious sunshine; a gentle sea breeze was blowing, and really everything seemed so quiet and different to other days that, had I not been acquainted with the fact, I should have known at once that it was the first day of the week.

Aberystwyth is built on a small semi-circular bay, the whole frontage being formed into a parade. At one end is a fine hotel (The Queen's) and Constitution Hill, which is a favourite resort for visitors, and at the other the University of Wales which, though at present in an unfinished state, promises to be a fine building.* The beach is a mixture of shingle and sand, and 50 bathing machines stand ready to tempt the bather into the sea, but today these were of course untenanted. The town boasts a town hall, market hall and clock tower, but the streets are irregular and possess few really good houses. The post office is an exception and here we found a postcard from our brother Joseph written in his own particular clear and lucid style (N.B. this is ironical). Its mysteries we proceeded to fathom but, not

meeting with complete success, thought it would be an infrac-
tion of the fourth commandment to puzzle ourselves therewith
any more, so put it aside to wait a personal explanation on our
arrival in London.*

After breakfast, we proceeded to inspect the various places
of worship, which are sufficiently numerous to satisfy the most
exacting individual. At some, an early service in Welsh was being
held, and the volume of sound which came forth when the congregation sang should have furnished a lesson to every passer-by
worthy of imitation. Entering the English Baptist Chapel, we
asked a gentleman if he could accommodate us with a tune book;
this he did in the form of a Sol-fa 'Bristol', and seated us near the
harmonium on which a lady played from the Messiah: 'Comfort
ye', and then 'I know that my Redeemer liveth', which she did
with much expression.† The tunes sung during the service were
Syria, York June and St Budes, also a chant. Notwithstanding
there were a large number of the fair sex amongst the congregation, the singing was not at all hearty, many present not uttering
sound or even taking the trouble to stand. Surely, all should join
in the praise of God; many who can render a solo very fairly
almost think it beneath them to sing a hymn, but this is a great
mistake, and I go so far to say that it is the duty of everyone – if
possible – to acquire a fair knowledge of music, and those who
have this are doing wrong if they do not habitually sing from the
particular tune book used at their church or chapel, for only in
this way can they fully obey the exhortation to 'sing with understanding' (Psalm 47, verse 7).

The pastor – a tall, thin excitable young man – preached
from Revelation, chapter 21, verses 1 to 4 respecting 'The new
heaven and earth'. The description of the New Jerusalem he
treated in a literal sense, and his ideas were dreamy, dwelling
too much on the symbols of Paradise and too little upon the only
way of entrance thereto; we determined to visit another chapel
in the evening. The place of worship in which we were seated
was erected seven years since, for the very moderate sum of

* The fourth
commandment
prohibits any form of
work on the Sabbath:
'Remember the
Sabbath day, to keep
it holy; Six days shalt
thou labour, and do
all thy work; but the
seventh day is the
Sabbath of the Lord
thy God: in it, thou
shalt not do any work.'
Exodus, chapter 20,
verses 8–10.
† Both pieces are
from the oratorio
Messiah (1741) by
the German-born
composer George
Frederick Handel.

* 'How beautiful are
the feet (of them that
preach the gospel)'
and 'And the glory
(of the Lord shall be
revealed)' were both
composed by George
Frederick Handel.

† '134 style', after
134 Regent Street,
John's home in
London.

‡ 'The confusion of
tongues' is described
in Genesis, chapter
11, verses 1–9.

£2,500 by the Welsh Baptists – who have a chapel of their own on the opposite side of the road – for the accommodation of their English speaking brethren and, though well filled during the season, is the very reverse in the winter. It is a clean, neat, model modern building, with comfortable seats which cause the occupants thereof to wonder why our forefathers made their pews so high, straight and generally uncomfortable. Today being the anniversary of the opening of the chapel, a special pew-to-pew collection was made to assist in defraying the debt, during which time the lady at the harmonium played 'How beautiful are the feet', and afterwards 'And the glory' as the congregation were departing.*

Wending our way to the parade, we found most of the visitors had done likewise, and were gently walking to and fro in costumes greatly differing from those of yesterday, the ladies wearing silks and muslins, and for the most part bonnets, and the gentlemen black coats and the tall regulation hat. Foreigners coming to this country for the first time may possibly think this last named article is worn as a species of penance for sins committed during the week and if it were so I do not think the custom could be more rigidly observed. The day was simply delightful, not a single boat was on the sea, and everything seemed to answer to my *beau ideal* of a pleasant Sunday at the seaside.

1.15 p.m. Sat down to dinner, which really was quite up to '134' style; the company, though not numerous, being very select and thoroughly enjoying themselves.† After a rest we took a short inland walk, passing a spacious chapel called Shiloh, where we heard a tremendous din, and on cautiously peeping therein found a Sunday School was being held, all the teaching being in Welsh. Further comment is needless; double consonants were flying about in a most alarming manner, and we were able to form a capital idea of the sensation created by 'The confusion of tongues'.‡ Llanbardarn is distant one mile and a half from Aberystwyth, and we arrived there in time to see the congregation emerge from both chapel and church. The latter being open,

Llanbardarn Church.

we walked in and found it was under the restorer's hands, certainly not before it was needed, the old high backed pews being
in many cases quite rotten and falling to pieces. The cost of the
restoration (£5,000) seemed to me a great waste of money, as
the surrounding population for the most part go to chapel.

As a christening – with doubtless a most unmusical accompaniment – was about to take place, we beat a hasty retreat, and
made our way back to Aberystwyth, seeing on the road several
antiquated ladies with the national head dress. Some people
imagine that all Welsh women wear tall black hats, but it is quite
the exception and not at all the rule. They are seldom to be met
with and then only on the heads of old people who still cling to
the traditions of their youth; the younger folk follow the fashion
as ardently as any London lady, and are resplendent in feathers,
flowers and ribbons of the very latest style.

After tea we repaired to the Congregational Chapel, and were
soon seated with the choir. The building – though handsome
– was not more than half filled, and the whole service seemed
to lack heartiness and fervour. The preacher chose for his text
Psalm 72, verse 6: 'Songs of the night', and during his sermon
adverted to the Crystal Palace Choral Competition in 1873,

saying the Welsh choir was composed of unlearned persons who knew little about music whilst their opponents were the pick of musical London, many being professionals, notwithstanding which all knew the result was favourable to their countrymen. As one of their antagonists, I felt very much inclined to rise and give a denial to this perversion of facts, for while I give the Welshmen full praise for their splendid singing it is only the truth – as I have before stated – that this was by no means the case.

The hymn book used contained 1,300 hymns, and the tune book – 'The Bristol' – over 700 tunes and chants, so no one could complain of lack of variety. After the service, the choir stayed to sing over some hymns for the chapel anniversary, which was to take place on the following Sunday. The tunes and words were Welsh but we surmounted the difficulties of the language by each vocalising our own part, which answered equally well. The precentor expressed a wish to see us all again on the occasion of the anniversary, but that of course was quite out of the question as we then expected to be once more in London.

After a short stroll on the parade, we returned to our apartments, chatted with the Welsh clergyman for some time and finally retired to rest at 10 o'clock.

MONDAY 13 AUGUST

7 a.m. Strolled to the seashore, where are the walls of an old castle of little interest, which is fully proved by the fact that no charge is made for permission to view them. The wind seemed undecided as to whether it should take a N.W. or S.W. direction, and the morning was rather dull, but as a smooth sea and sandy shore seemed to offer special attractions, we were soon enjoying a capital bath, after which we took a sharp walk to the post office, where a card was waiting to explain the mysteries of, and relieve our minds concerning, the epistle mentioned yesterday. Early

this morning the Welsh clergyman had departed for London, where – we afterwards heard – he was to be married. Perhaps he was impressed with the thought of his impending doom, and therefore glad to have our company; at any rate he made us very welcome, and we were so comfortable that though we had intended to depart today, we now decided to stay till tomorrow.

9.30 a.m. Breakfast being finished, we visited the parade with the determination to spend a quiet day. Here of course bathing machines were in great request, both sexes disporting themselves in the sea at a respectful distance from each other, but the bathing attendants were a great improvement on the usual specimens seen at seaside resorts. Equally of course we were accosted by boatmen with 'Splendid morning, Captain! Just the thing for a sail or row, Sir!', but as to German musicians, the Indian Fire King, the British nigger, and the numerous coarse but not at all intellectual amusements which prevail at many watering places, they are not to be seen at Aberystwyth.*

Ascending Constitution Hill – where the cliff is being cut away to make room for a further extension of the parade – we sat down and enjoyed a capital bird's eye view of the town, pier, boats and river, every minor detail being plainly visible. Pursuing our rambles by a path close to the edge of the cliff, we came to a small river called the Clarach which gives its name to a pretty fertile valley, up which we strolled till a village was reached. When not seeing much utility in going any farther, we tried to sketch a church, made notes, rested and generally helped each other to do nothing for as I previously observed we did not intend to exert ourselves today.

A hilly road, prettily shaded by overhanging trees, soon brought us into the main road, and before long we were once again within view of Aberystwyth. During the last mile we had constantly overtaken numerous Welsh women of all ages from 20 to 70, all wearing brown straw saucer-like hats, and carrying baskets or some other kind of burden, toiling along in the most persevering manner under the almost perpendicular rays

* The listed attractions were features of the promenades and piers of more popular resorts. The 'British nigger' (the word was not as offensive then) was probably a white English or Welsh man 'blacked up' to perform in a minstrel revue, as perfected in American music halls and fairs.

of a summer's sun. Wondering as to the cause of this invasion, we continued to advance, but matters grew from bad to worse for, on reaching Aberystwyth, the town was swarming with Welsh country folk, all talking in their own peculiar manner. On enquiry, we found as it was market day excursion trains ran from many places, and people came from all quarters bringing eggs, butter, cheese etc. for sale, others also came to make purchases, some walking a distance of 12 miles in each direction. The streets had quite a lively appearance, and the single policeman, who generally only carries a small switch, had armed himself with a stout staff and called in the aid of some of his brother constables from the suburbs to assist him in keeping order.

The chief scene of action was the Corn Market, and there bacon, eggs, butter, cheese, nuts, sweets, strings of onions, china, earthenware, glass and articles of wearing apparel were to be bought. Even the very pavement outside was converted into a stall, and one energetic salesman – so as not to miss any chance customers – offered his wares first in Welsh and then in English. Another rattled a pair of scales, and earnestly entreated the onlookers to 'come and buy before everything was gone', while the general public sans permission 'tasted' the butter and cheese with a coolness which was quite refreshing to witness. No less than 40 women were standing in the road with articles for sale and, last but not least, an organ grinder was exerting himself to make the confusion more deafening.

Returning to Bridge Street, we dined and then, after taking another peep at 'Babel', repaired to the parade, where the boats and yachts were having quite a gala day. The occupants of the former certainly never rowed in the Oxford and Cambridge Boat Race, as the only style of feathering they understood was feathering the spray over their companions; and I need hardly say 'crabs' were numerous.* As for the yachts, they only held about a dozen persons and their owners seemed to think it the wisest policy to go for short trips of half an hour at sixpence per head, which they said was 'quite long enough for many of them'. There being nothing particular to do, we went for a sail as far as the Clarach. On returning, the yacht could not well run into shore, so the sterner sex were carried out on the sailors' backs. One stout old gentleman, fearing he might be suddenly precipitated into the water, clung to the bowsprit as long as he possibly could, to the amusement of the spectators, who would probably have only been too pleased if such a catastrophe had happened.

After tea we went to the railway station to ascertain the times of the trains for tomorrow's journey, and then repaired to the parade, where we found the town band actively engaged in their nightly performance. The musicians were all on a raised platform, enclosed at the back and mounted on wheels, which improved the sound, and enabled it to be moved to any part of the parade. The instrumental music was very fair, and was interspersed with vocal songs, the favourites seeming to be 'Nancy Lee' and 'The Lion and the Bear', the latter being apropos of the Russo-Turkish war then raging. In front of the platform were a number of chairs, for which of course a small charge was made, but the audience generally preferred to promenade except when a song was given, they then all congregated around and advantage was taken of this to make the usual 'half-quarterly' collection, which I should think was profitable. Returning indoors, we were soon in bed and before long once again in the arms of our friend Morpheus.

TUESDAY 14 AUGUST

Having partaken of an early breakfast, we made for the railway station, booked for Neath and started away by the 8.30 a.m. train. The morning was cloudy and seemed to betoken rain, but it improved as we advanced, which we did at such a leisurely rate that there was no difficulty inspecting the adjacent scenery. At first our route lay by the side of the Ystwyth, which had an extremely wide bed containing very little water, afterwards there were some good hills, but as a rule the country was rather uninteresting. Our fellow passengers were nearly all natives, and talked in the jargon peculiar to the country. One of them afforded us much amusement as he resembled Mr Field of Keppel Street, and to every observation of his companion replied 'Yah! Yah!' (Yes! Yes!) which he did so many times that we could scarcely refrain from laughing aloud. A small child dressed in a yellow frock and scarlet hood sat opposite this gentleman, and when he smiled and endeavoured to amuse her it was very comical, reminding us of an ogre and his victim in some fairy tale. Still there is no doubt he meant well, which is more than can be said of many who are much handsomer in appearance.

At Carmarthen, we stayed for some time, and witnessed an affecting parting between two natives, who after apparently exhausting the Welsh language in the farewell, finished by saying 'Goodbye' in English, which seemed to us rather peculiar. Throughout Carmarthenshire, as well as in many other parts of South Wales, the custom of what is termed 'Biddings at Weddings' is observed. When two young people are about to be married, they issue invitations to their numerous friends, soliciting help towards furnishing their new abode, promising at the same time to give them a like assistance when asked for under similar circumstances. This may be a very brilliant idea, but it seems to me rather akin to begging, and of course those who remain unmarried do not make much profit out of such a bargain. The following is the form of invitation sent, of which some hundred are commonly issued for a single marriage.

As we intend to enter the MATRIMONIAL STATE on Friday the 1st of April next, we are encouraged by our friends to make a BIDDING on the occasion the same day. The young man at Cwmcelly-fawr, in the parish of Mynyddislwyn and the young woman at her mother's house called Troedyrhiw, in the parish of Llanfihangel Rhos Y Corn, at either of which places the favour of your good and most agreeable company is respectfully solicited, and whatever donation you may be so kind as to confer on us then, will be thankfully received and cheerfully repaid whenever called for on a similar occasion.

By your most obedient Servants

John Jones

Mary Ap Griffiths

Leaving Carmarthen, we skirted the River Towy, passing the estuary, which is very wide, and as the tide had receded a great distance a number of women were engaged in the interesting occupation of winkle or crab catching. Reaching Landore, we entered the coal and iron district, where a smoky mist was hanging all over the town, which being of a whitish colour had a very curious appearance. The surrounding country is little better than a succession of coal heaps, and altogether the prospect is not very inviting. 2.50 p.m. Came to the end of our railway journey, Neath. Having been 6 hours and 20 minutes travelling 93 miles, I need hardly say that we were very glad to be at liberty once again. However, we did not intend to stay here as the town has few attractions, so sent our bag on to Glyn Neath and then set out thither on foot.

The Vale of Neath is very pretty, with well wooded hills rising on each side, between which runs a river and canal, but its beauty is somewhat marred by smelting and other works, which though useful are certainly not picturesque. Walking past Abergarwedd, a small village all the houses of which are built on precisely the same model, and was probably erected by the proprietor of some adjacent works for his employees, we reached Aberpergwm where is a stone seat with the following inscription: 'A resting place for a pure Welshman, let him thank God and proceed.' However, if no one stays there but those who are really pure in mind as well as descent, I rather think it cannot be often occupied.

6.15 p.m. Arrived at Glyn Neath, but found we had passed the railway station. This was unfortunate as we had wished to

* Charles Haddon
Spurgeon (1834–92)
was an influential
preacher and writer
in the Particular
Baptist tradition. He
was the pastor of
the congregation of
the New Park Street
Chapel in London for
38 years, and also
founded Spurgeon's
College, which trained
pastors.

BRADSHAW ON NEATH

 Neath is a coal and mining port, with an ancient castle and some abbey ruins. Here the fine Vale of Neath may be ascended to the beautiful waterfalls at its summit. Population 6,810.

A TELEGRAPH STATION. HOTEL: THE CASTLE HOTEL.

ascertain the times for tomorrow's trains. Still, we did not care to retrace our steps, so enquired of several natives, but their ideas on the subject were very vague, no two being alike. Glyn Neath consists of one long straggling street some two miles in length, and at the time of our visit the pitmen were just coming from their work, many being laden with a sack of coals which they are allowed to bring away for their own use without payment. To say they were grimy would hardly be correct, for their faces and hands were nearly black, and we had some difficulty to refrain from laughing as they passed us.

Pontneathvaughan was eventually reached by 7.30 p.m. Referring to our guide book, we found The Angel Inn was well recommended. We did not much like its appearance, but it seemed to be 'Hobson's choice', so in I went and soon came out again with the information that there was no sleeping accommodation for tourists – perhaps our aspect was not sufficiently angelic – but that doubtless The White Horse over the way would 'take us in'. The outside view of this hostelry was not more inviting than that of its rival, but we found its internal arrangements to be of a very comfortable and satisfactory description, the sitting room rejoicing in a capital display of silver plate, china and pictures, among the latter being a portrait in oil of Mr Spurgeon in his younger days.*

A good substantial tea soon appeared and then vanished with remarkable celerity, after which we felt more contented with ourselves and the world at large. It was by this time dark so after writing a little we retired to bed, but just as we were turning in, rain began to descend very heavily, making a great rustling amongst the surrounding trees, and causing us to be anxious for the morrow. However, this did not mend matters, so we turned over and went to sleep hoping for the best.

* John appears to mean the falls at Cil Hepste, a favourite subject for Victorian illustrators and photographers.

WEDNESDAY 15 AUGUST

The pitmen who work near Pontneathvaughan seemed to be very early risers, and rather disturbed our slumbers; nevertheless we turned out at 6.30 a.m. and sallied forth half an hour later. Our intention had been to visit the Cilpheste Falls, which are very fine, but on ascertaining that they were quite three miles distant, and that the road lay amongst long grass and was very rough, we abandoned the idea as it had been raining heavily during the night.* The clouds still had an ominous appearance, but we determined not to be idle so, crossing a small bridge, we kept by the side of a rushing, rippling stream shaded by thick foliage. The path – consisting mainly of wet grass and muddy puddles – soon became so very bad that we at last decided to try the bed of the river, which was not more than half full of water. Here, by carefully walking on the stones, we at last came to the object of our search, The Lady's Fall. This is a pretty cataract of water 30 feet in depth which shoots over with such a curve that a man can stand beneath without inconvenience.

Returning to The White Horse, we sat down to a capital breakfast with appetites to match, then having paid our debts, started away about 10 a.m. As I observed yesterday, precise information regarding the trains was unattainable, so we resolved to leave a large margin to the earliest mentioned time; notwithstanding which, on arriving at Glyn Neath station, we found all our informants were wrong, and we still had an hour to spare. The traffic here consists more of coals than passengers, who are 'requested to provide their own change'. Having so much time on hand, we made a thorough investigation of the timetables,

"The Lady's Fall", Pontneathvaughan.

* The Gadlys Colliery closed in 1939, but the pumps continued in use until the 1960s. which are very puzzling, examined the station in every direction and saw a porter lunching off a raw onion and a piece of bread. We then took tickets, the train arrived and we were at last on our way to Aberdare which, after a pleasant ride, was reached by 1 o'clock.

Our object in coming here was solely to descend a coal mine, as such an opportunity might never occur during our lives. We therefore at once made enquiries and were recommended to try the Gadlys pit, so immediately proceeded in search thereof.* Aberdare is a moderately large town with good streets and shops, and numerous dissenting chapels. Some idea of the prevalence of nonconformity in Wales may be formed from the fact that at Merthyr Tydfil there are 36 chapels, and only four churches, and in other districts a like proportion occurs.

With little difficulty we found the mouth of the Gadlys coal pit, and only wondered there was so little to see. From the shaft ran two tramways on which a few very grimy men and women were pushing trucks laden with coal as they arrived from below.

BRADSHAW ON ABERDARE

 The scenery of the Vale of Cynon here is charming. Population 32,299.

A TELEGRAPH STATION. HOTELS: THE BOOT HOTEL, THE RAILWAY HOTEL.

* John seems to be using the word 'Englishman' to mean the more inclusive 'British man'.

These, a few sheds and a chimney or two were all the visible signs of the immense amount of labour which constantly takes place beneath. We had previously endeavoured to ascertain the best way to proceed in seeking permission to view a mine, and had been advised not to ask the manager, as he might be busy or tell us to call again, but to enquire for the 'gaffer', or foreman, who is generally near at hand. This we accordingly did, and found he was at dinner in his house close by. It is generally considered dangerous to disturb an Englishman when he is dining, but as our time was limited we resolved to make the attempt.* Just as we arrived at the door, it occurred to us that we did not know the foreman's name. The reader will perhaps observe 'Why, Jones of course.' This, though highly probable, did not prove to be the case, as it was Thomas, and I may here remark that the former name is not nearly so numerous in South as in North Wales.

On enquiring for Mr Thomas, that individual came out, and in answer to our request wished to know our residence and profession and, the replies proving satisfactory, he consented, if we called again at 2 o'clock, to take us down into the depths below, for which we cordially thanked him. He was an agreeable man, and seemed in a good position in life, having a nice house, at the back of which was a large orchard where six of his children were playing. Calling to mind a former description of a mine respecting the Black Country, it may seem strange that fruit trees could flourish by the side of a coal mine, but Aberdare is as different from that district as can be imagined, which arises from the fact that all the coal is smokeless, and therefore notwithstanding that the country is literally honeycombed with pits, the surrounding vegetation is beautifully green, and as it was a very fine day we saw everything to the best advantage.

Punctually at the time appointed, we once again presented ourselves before Mr Thomas, who had previously advised us to change our attire if possible. Being on a walking tour, this was of course out of the question, so he lent us each an ancient jacket and cap which had certainly seen better days. I fear we had rather a disreputable appearance, but we were much amused at the change, and consoled ourselves with the reflection that people do not usually put on evening dress when about to descend a coal mine.

All being now ready, we walked across some fields and soon reached the main entrance to the Gadlys pit; a double lift works up and down the shaft, one side of which comes up laden with coal, while at the same time the other descends with an empty truck. Placing ourselves in a standing position on the lift, Mr Thomas said: 'Now, do as I tell you and close your eyes. Hold on to this bar at the side and don't move till I give you permission.' To this we readily assented, especially the last two items, and immediately began to descend. In what seemed only a few seconds, our mentor said: 'You can now open your eyes.' This we did, but as far as seeing was concerned no change was apparent, everything being pitchy black, but in 30 seconds we had reached the bottom and were 600 feet beneath the earth's surface, so we carefully stepped out as directed and sat down in a side room to accustom our eyes to the darkness, while Mr Thomas examined the safety lamps with which we were each provided.

The temperature down here was 62 degrees and beautifully cool compared with the atmosphere we had just quitted. After reaching a certain depth the heat gradually increases, until it is calculated that at 4,000 feet it would be 120 degrees, but it is considered doubtful whether men could work at a greater pressure than this. I should think not, indeed, to say nothing of the difficulty in supplying them with pure air. Being now both ready and willing to begin our explorations, our guide led the way. The mine is worked by means of numerous parallel cuttings about eight feet in width and six in height, a wall of coal being left at each side for support. Sometimes it is not so lofty, as may be judged from the fact that my head came in contact with the roof on more than one occasion. Smaller cuttings connect the longer ones together, and the air is properly circulated and prevented from rushing down with too much force by means of huge wooden, or sometimes canvas, doors which it is quite a task to move so great is the pressure. In order to ensure a good supply of pure air, a huge furnace is kept up, constantly burning two tons of coal. On reaching this spot we made a halt; the heat was very great, and close at hand were two men whose sole duly was to cut coal and attend to the furnace, also a donkey that had not seen daylight for nearly four years.

After inspecting the various points of interest, Mr Thomas said to us: 'Now as you are down here, you must cut a piece of coal and take it away as a memento of your visit.' To this we assented and, pick in hand, I made an attack against the nearest wall. It was much harder work than I had anticipated, for dust and splinters were very plentiful, and it was not till about the tenth strike that I succeeded in bringing down a fair sized piece of the precious black diamond. George then followed suit, and we each brought away a trophy of our visit which can be seen on application at 134 Regent Street.

When first cut, the mineral is laden in trucks which hold one cwt.* Each horse then draws these to the main cuttings, where they are formed into trains of about 20, and then conveyed to the pit's mouth by means of a stationary engine and an immense coil of steel wire one inch in thickness. This is coiled round two circular drums and is upwards of three miles long. A conductor, who holds telegraphic communication with the people at the engine, accompanies each train, and by this means it can be stopped at any moment which is often required. In the 'good old days' the coal trucks were pushed by women and lads with their heads, and it was not at all a rare occurrence to see young people

* 'Cwt' is short for hundredweight. There are eight stone in a hundredweight, and 20 hundredweight in one imperial ton (1,016 kilograms).

* The Mines and
Collieries Act 1842.

nearly bald from this exercise. An Act of Parliament was passed
by Lord Shaftesbury which prohibits the employment of women
in the interior of the pit, and lads altogether beneath a certain
age.* Horses were afterwards used, and many of these animals
almost spend their lives down below, some being even born
there, but steam power is now employed as much as possible, to
the great saving of both capital and labour.

The Gadlys pit extends for a distance of two miles, and 1,600
men are sometimes at work therein, but at the time of our visit
trade was very bad so that not more than half that number were
then employed. The wages are one shilling and sixpence per ton,
and as to cut three tons of coal is a good day's work, the miners
cannot I think be overpaid, considering the nature and risks of
their calling. Their wages are exceedingly grim and the coal dust
seems to penetrate right through their skins, giving them the
appearance of demons rather than men. Mr Thomas seemed to
know them all, and had a word of greeting for every one he met.

Immediately beneath the shaft is a well of 48 feet deep, into
which drains the moisture from the mine; the water here collected we found was being emptied by means of a huge bucket
which descended into the well with a tremendous noise and was
then drawn up again, the water at the same time falling down
on every side. The well when not being emptied is covered with
a lid, and a few weeks previous to our visit a tourist came down
– like ourselves – in the lift, but was in such a hurry to reach the
bottom that he jumped out before he was bidden. Unfortunately
he made his exit from the wrong side, alighted on the covering of
the well – which could not have been firmly secured – knocked it
aside, was precipitated into the water and no assistance being at
hand was drowned. Since this sad calamity, further security has
been taken so that there is little fear of such an accident happening again. Having been in the bowels of the earth over an hour, we
ascended to the top and once more found ourselves in God's own
pure and beauteous sunlight, well pleased with that which we had
seen, and thankful that we had been preserved from any dangers.

Close to the pit's mouth were some brickworks, where the whole of the labour was performed by girls. The clay, being mixed by machinery, was raked together by one of the hands who presided like a queen over the revels; to this spot came a number of other workers each having a handkerchief tied round her head. These snatched up two huge lumps of clay, deposited one on their head, hugged the other to their breast and then rushed away with the burden to the moulders who, having shaped the brick, passed it on again to another set of carriers. We were informed each moulder can turn out 3,000 bricks per day of ten hours; for this they are paid the liberal sum of two shillings and sixpence, but the carriers only receive about half that amount. The damp clay of course dries upon the girls' hands and faces, and certainly does not improve their personal appearance. Nevertheless, Mr Thomas said they are as a rule well conducted, and make very good wives; there is no doubt but they are amazingly quick and have little or no opportunity to exercise their unruly members during working hours, but notwithstanding all these recommendations I cannot say I felt inclined to choose a partner from amongst them, nor should I think many cases of love at first sight occur at the Gadlys brickworks.*

By this time, as may be imagined, we had a very grimy aspect, and what with the smuttiness of our faces, and the exceedingly curious garments we were wearing, I think our London friends – could they by chance have seen us – would have imagined we had suddenly come down in the world. A visit to Mr Thomas's office and a good ablution soon made matters wear another aspect, and we felt once more like civilised beings. Though rather in doubt as to the wisdom of such a proceeding, I offered our mentor a gratuity, but he quietly refused all remuneration, and in such a way that I could not press the matter, so we bade him adieu, not forgetting once again to thank him for all the trouble he had taken, and courtesy he had shown us.

As we now began to feel rather hungry we spent half an hour in a refreshment room, and then repaired to the railway station.

* The phrase 'unruly members' refers to the women's tongues.

Crumlin Viaduct.

* Crumlin Viaduct
was built to carry the
Taff Vale extension
of the Newport,
Abergavenny and
Hereford Railway
across the River Ebbw.
It was completed in
1857, and was the
third-highest railway
viaduct in the world.
It remained in place
until 1967.

On the train arriving, we took places therein, and were soon travelling through a succession of beautifully wooded hills and vales until Crumlin was reached; here the Ebbw valley is crossed by a viaduct well worthy of mention.* It is supported by ten piers, each of which is 150 feet apart, and the highest is 204 feet from the ground; it is an elegant structure and is supposed to be the most economical of its kind ever built, not having cost more than £40,000. As Crumlin railway station is only a short distance from the viaduct, we had a capital view thereof whilst the train was stationary, after which we crossed the valley, enjoying a magnificent prospect in both directions.

Hitherto the day had been very fine, but clouds now began to gather and a sharp shower fell, after which a rainbow appeared and all was bright again. After this, we travelled so slowly that it was 6.45 p.m. ere Newport was reached, which was just a quarter of an hour too late for the Chepstow train, and there was no other till 9.30 p.m. It was all in vain that we made enquiries of the railway officials, and examined the timetables; there was no alternative but to stay at Newport for nearly three hours. This would not have been of much consequence had there been anything of interest to see, but such was not the case. On asking a policeman this question he replied: 'Well, there's the docks (!) you know, two miles distant, and – and – well, I don't think there's anything else.'

Newport is a prosperous town with a large shipping trade, principally in the products of the mining districts, but like all seaports it is not remarkable for cleanliness. Near the bridge are the remains of an old castle, but it now forms part of a brewery and is probably the origin of quite as many evil deeds as in former days. The main street runs right down to the docks but the only thing we saw which calls for remark was the fact that 'Hot fagots are sold every evening' (the reader can form his own opinion of this information), and it may be as well to know that the rail conveys coals etc. straight to the docks, crossing on its way the public streets level with the road.* Sometimes gates are provided, so that foot passengers may not meet an untimely end, but often no barrier is seen, nor is there even a notice warning 'pedestrians to beware of the engine', or vice versa, which

* Fagots, or faggots, are traditionally made from offal, minced and seasoned, rolled into balls and wrapped in caul (the membrane that surrounds animal intestines). They are baked in an oven and served with mashed potatoes, mushy peas and gravy.

BRADSHAW ON NEWPORT

This is a seaport town of some importance, having a population of 23,249. It has a constant steam packet communication with Bristol and various parts of South Wales; and by means of its ready access by railway with the many iron districts in the neighbourhood, its traffic in that mineral, as well as coal, of late years has greatly increased. With the exception of the church, which presents various styles of architecture, the town itself has no prepossessing attractions.

A TELEGRAPH STATION. HOTELS: THE KING'S HEAD HOTEL, THE WEST GATE HOTEL.

* Freeman is once again quoting from the poem 'Excelsior' (1841) by Henry Wadsworth Longfellow.

seemed to us rather dangerous, but I suppose the Newportonians ought to be the best judges.

On nearing the docks, the 'Shades of night were falling fast', so we returned to the railway station, waited patiently for a train, and were eventually conveyed safely to Chepstow by 10 p.m.* Here everything was very different compared to our former visit; then, it was broad daylight and all was life and activity, now, darkness reigned supreme with scarcely a lamp to dispute its monopoly, and most of the Chepstownians were in bed and snoring. Applying at The White Hart, we found that interesting animal could not entertain us, but we met with better fortune at The Old Bell. As may be imagined, we were somewhat fatigued and quite ready for bed which, being soon made, we retired thereto and were soon asleep.

There being no necessity to record our journey to London on the following day, thus ended the adventures which are now duly noted in black and white of our holiday through the...

ACKNOWLEDGEMENTS

I would like to take this opportunity to heartily thank a host of individuals who have been instrumental in keeping this journey on track and producing a first-class book. I hope John George Freeman would have been proud of it.

I am indebted to: Harry Scoble and the Random House Books team for taking on this project and transforming John's written journals into this wonderful book; my agent, Gordon Wise at Curtis Brown, for again being such a pillar of wisdom and support; Ronnie Scott, the genius editor, who has yet again done such a grand job in editing the journals and adding the inserts and explanations to enhance the reader's enjoyment of John's Victorian adventures; Barnardo's, Richard and Michael Hale, and Ann and Rachel Bond for trusting in me and allowing John's work to be published; Linda Coxall for her initial support and advice; and lastly Joan Bower, my amazing partner, who unselfishly gives me the freedom to start and finish these literary adventures.

I have been very fortunate to be the conduit of John George Freeman. He has given me the greatest of times and knowing that his daily jottings will now give such enjoyment to many more people gives me great pleasure.

Hurrah for John George Freeman and long live the puggaree!

Shaun Sewell, Northumberland, 2015

INDEX

Psalms xiii, xiv, 21, 193, 252, 255,
321, 323
Revelation 255, 321
Romans 56, 113
Bible Christian Church 56
'Biddings at Weddings' 328–9
Bideford, Devon 97, 106, 110
Bidno River 310
billycock hats 82
Binney, Thomas 140
Birmingham, England 134
Birnam, Perth and Kinross 248, 249,
253–6, *254*
biscuits 185
Black, Adam 199
Black, Charles 199
Black Country, England 134, 333
Black Draught 147
Black Watch 253
Black's Guide to Jersey 9, 11, 15, 26, 27,
34, 36, 40, 41, 48, 49, 58, 64
Black's Picturesque Tourist of Scotland
199
blackberries 53
Blackpool, Lancashire xii
Blairgowrie, Perth and Kinross 257
Blaizemoor (tune) 113
'Blessed for ever' (Spohr) 299
Blind Bale 84–5
Bliss, Philip 182
Bloomsbury, London 246
Bloomsbury Chapel, London 204
Blue Pills 147
Boat Road, Dunkeld 250
'bogium' 300, 301, 303
bogs 228
Bomb Battery, Edinburgh Castle 209,
212
Bonne-Nuit Bay, Jersey 15, 29
Bont Newydd, Gwynedd 190
Bothwell, earl of (James Hepburn) 216
Boughrood, Powys 302
Bouley Bay, Jersey 24, 40–1, 52, 54
Bournemouth, England xii
Bow Street Magistrates Court,

Westminster xiv
bowler hats 82
Bowler, William and Thomas 82
bowling hoops 21
Box Tunnel, Somerset 126
Boylston (tune) 140
Braan Falls, Perth and Kinross 248
Braan River 259
Bracklinn Falls, Callander 238
Bradshaw, George xi
*Bradshaw's Descriptive Railway Hand-
book* xi, 71, 131, 197
on Aber 157
on Aberdare 333
on Balloch 229
on Bangor 158
on Barnstaple 111
on Bideford 110
on Bridge of Allan 219
on Bristol 74
on Builth 304
on Callander 224
on Carnarvon 159
on Chepstow 279
on Conway 156
on Doune 222
on Dunblane 220
on Dunkeld 248
on Edinburgh 208
on Granton 207
on Hay-on-Wye 300
on Hereford 296
on Ilfracombe 93, 99
on Llanberis 162
on Llangollen 136, 138
on Llanrwst 152
on Loch Lomond 231
on Lynton and Lynmouth 77
on Monmouth 285
on Mount Snowdon 164
on Neath 330
on Newport 339
on Ruabon 142
on Ross-on-Wye 293
on Stirling 215

public houses 31, 113, 137, 152–3, 310
puggarees 97, 98, 186, 213, 220, 240,
    257, 287
Pullar, James 219
Pullar, John 219
Pullar, Robert 219
Punch xiii–xiv, 52
purgatives 5, 147, 219
Puritanism x, 37
Pwllheli, Gwynedd 161, 168

'Quarrel of Oberon and Titania, The'
    (Paton) 264
quartz 187
Queens Hotel, Aberystwyth *320*
Queensberry House, Edinburgh 213

rabbits 86, 257
Radnorshire, Wales 310
'Ragged Jack' 93
Railway Regulation Act (1844) xi, 73
railways xi, 5–7, 18, 23–4, 25, 50, 73–4,
    110–11, 116, 126–7, 133, 138, 143,
    151–2, 154, 161, 174–8, 192–4, 213–14,
    217, 227, 228, 240, 247, 302, 306, 308,
    327, 337–8, 260–2, 267
  accidents 5, 6
  competition xi
  concertina players 18
  luggage allowance xi
  postal carriages 6–7
  Railway Regulation Act (1844) x–xi,
    73
  second-class carriages 5, 6, 74
  smoking 133
  third-class carriages x–xi, 6, 73, 74
Rampling's Waterloo Hotel, Edinburgh
    209
rams 54, 95
raspberries 81, 92, 102, 309
Reading, Berkshire 133
'Reconciliation of Oberon and Titania,
    The' (Paton) 264
Red Funnel line 7
Red Lion, Clovelly 105, 107

Red Lion, Rhayader 307
Rednoch Castle, Stirling 226
Reformation 213
regatta 289, 293, 295
Regent Street, Mayfair ix–x, xiv, 73,
    127, 202, 277, 303, 322, 335
Reinagle, Ramsay Richard 264
Resting Place, Llanberis Pass 169
Rhaiadr Mawr, Gwynedd 157
Rhayader, Powys 307–9
Rhayader Castle 308
Rheidol River 315, 316, 317, 318
Rhine River 123, 131, 138, 181
Rhondda Cynon Taf, Wales 332
Rhyl, Denbighshire 154
Richards, Henry Brinley 119
Riddell, W.K. 88
River Braan 259
Rizzio, David 209, 266
Robert II, king of Scots 253
Robert Spittal's House, Stirling 217
Rochead, John Thomas 218
Roman Catholic Church 79, 204, 206,
    255
Roman Empire 18, 36, 74, 159
Roman road 74
Romantic movement 234, 260
Rome, Italy 118, 255
Romeo and Juliet (Shakespeare) 63
Root, George Frederick 184
Ross Church, Herefordshire *292*, 294
Ross-on-Wye, Herefordshire 289, 290,
    292, 293–5
Rossini, Gioacchino 102
Rouge Bouillon, Jersey 15
Rousseau, Jean Jacques 205
Rowardennan, Loch Lomond 232
rowing 326
Royal Academy of Music, London 180
Royal Alfred Aged Merchant Seamen's
    Institution, Belvedere 201
Royal Blue Car 15–19, 24, 31, 39–44
Royal Commission on the Ancient and
    Historical Monuments of Scotland
    226

hrough the legacies of John Freeman's descendants part of his estate now resides with
rnardo's. Thomas Barnardo himself was born a year before John, in 1845, and began
s charitable work in London in 1866. To celebrate the 150th anniversary of Barnardo's
e thought it appropriate to highlight their continued support for the most vulnerable
ildren within our society, much of it funded by donations from the public. We think
hn would have approved.

Believe in
children

Barnardo's

No child should feel they
have nobody to turn to.
Not now. Not ever.

Leave a vulnerable
child **someone to turn to.**
Leave a gift in your **Will
to Barnardo's**

www.barnardos.org.uk/giftsinwills
020 8498 7880